Answers To Objections Source Book

4
Heidi Heiks

TEACH Services, Inc.
PUBLISHING
www.TEACHServices.com • (800) 367-1844

World rights reserved. This book or any portion thereof may not be copied or reproduced in any form or manner whatever without the written permission of the publisher, except as provided by law or except by a reviewer who may quote brief passages in a review.

The author assumes full responsibility for the accuracy of all facts and quotations as cited in this book. The opinions expressed in this book are the author's personal views and interpretations, and do not necessarily reflect those of the publisher.

This book is provided with the understanding that the publisher is not engaged in giving spiritual, legal, medical, or other professional advice. If authoritative advice is needed, the reader should seek the counsel of a competent professional.

Copyright © 2015 Heidi Heiks

Copyright © 2015 TEACH Services, Inc.

ISBN-13: 978-1-4796-0597-2 (Paperback)

ISBN-13: 978-1-4796-0598-9 (ePub)

ISBN-13: 978-1-4796-0599-6 (Mobi)

Library of Congress Control Number: 2015917756

Published by

www.TEACHServices.com • (800) 367-1844

**Dedicated To
Those Who Demand
Nothing But The Truth**

CONTENTS

Preface vii
Acknowledgments xv
Introduction xvii

Chapter 1: A Reply to the Allegations 1
Chapter 2: Clarifying the Issues 91

Appendix I 111
Appendix II 159
Appendix III 208

PREFACE

This fourth volume of my series on the prophetic periods described in the books of Daniel and Revelation stems primarily from my dialogue with an excellent historian who perceived errors in my research and conclusions. Readers will notice that on a few occasions, I made a point to remind him that our only source of trustworthy understanding is the Scriptures. We interpret history based solely on the specifications given to us in God's Word, and in no other way.

Jesuits introduced the futurist and preterist interpretations of the prophecies to counter the Reformation; the Evangelical world of today follows in their train. The Evangelicals have abandoned the historicist method of interpretation of the Scriptures. They no longer acknowledge the biblical hermeneutics that render pre-cross prophecies to be literal/local, and post-cross prophecies to be spiritual/world-wide, as witnessed and explained in my books. Rather, these interpreters tend to focus the mind solely on horizontal matters (earthly), rather than the vertical (heavenly) or central issue of the prophecies and of Christ's mission, which has ever been to vindicate the government of God and to fulfill the law of God (Isaiah 9:6). Faithful to His appointed task, Christ is able to save humanity to the uttermost.

Futurists and preterists steer the mind into side issues; their private interpretations turn the truth into a lie, away from the primary issues—issues that always pertain first and foremost to the vertical issues, the government and law of God. Their efforts to deceive and draw away reveal they are actuated by the same spirit and motive that resulted in the age-old great controversy that began between Christ and Satan (Rev. 12:7-9), which resulted in open rebellion against Heaven.

The horizontal issues of the prophecies (earthly) and their repercussions now bring that same issue and choice to all of humanity. The question that is put before us is, "Will we stand on the side of Satan and his angels in open rebellion against God's government and His Law, or will we stand with Christ and His angels in perfect harmony with God's government and His Law?" That is the horizontal question the prophecies of Daniel and Revelation are asking of all humanity. Our response and attitude determines where we will spend eternity!

My four-volume set exposes these deceptions and private interpretations, so no man need be deceived as to what the mark of the Beast is and what it is not, according to Revelation 14:6-12, and who the man of sin is, as delineated in Scripture (2 Thessalonians 2:1-12). The four segments that follow define the issue, identify the man of sin, and show us the earthly repercussions of that ongoing vertical rebellion.

We now supply the reader with the Ten Commandments by which all humanity is to be judged (James 2:10-12 KJV), as they were written in stone with the finger of the great *I Am*—none other than Christ Himself:

Ex. 20:1 "And God spake all these words, saying,

Ex. 20:2 I am the LORD thy God, which have brought thee out of the land of Egypt, out of the house of bondage.

(1). Ex. 20:3 Thou shalt have no other gods before me.

(2). Ex. 20:4 Thou shalt not make unto thee any graven image, or any likeness of any thing that is in Heaven above, or that is in the earth beneath, or that is in the water under the earth:

Ex. 20:5 Thou shalt not bow down thyself to them, nor serve them: for I the LORD thy God am a jealous God, visiting the iniquity of the fathers upon the children unto the third and fourth generation of them that hate me;

Ex. 20:6 And shewing mercy unto thousands of them that love me, and keep my commandments.

(3). **Ex 20:7** Thou shalt not take the name of the LORD thy God in vain; for the LORD will not hold him guiltless that taketh his name in vain.

(4). **Ex. 20:8** Remember the sabbath day, to keep it holy.

Ex. 20:9 Six days shalt thou labour, and do all thy work:

Ex. 20:10 But the seventh day is the sabbath of the LORD thy God: in it thou shalt not do any work, thou, nor thy son, nor thy daughter, thy manservant, nor thy maidservant, nor thy cattle, nor thy stranger that is within thy gates:

Ex. 20:11 For in six days the LORD made Heaven and earth, the sea, and all that in them is, and rested the seventh day: wherefore the LORD blessed the sabbath day, and hallowed it.

(5). **Ex. 20:12** Honour thy father and thy mother: that thy days may be long upon the land which the LORD thy God giveth thee.

(6). **Ex. 20:13** Thou shalt not kill.

(7). **Ex. 20:14** Thou shalt not commit adultery.

(8). **Ex. 20:15** Thou shalt not steal.

(9). **Ex. 20:16** Thou shalt not bear false witness against thy neighbour.

(10). Ex. 20:17 Thou shalt not covet thy neighbour's house, thou shalt not covet thy neighbour's wife, nor his manservant, nor his maidservant, nor his ox, nor his ass, nor any thing that is thy neighbour's." KJV

Below are the Ten Commandments as changed by the entity in prophecy:

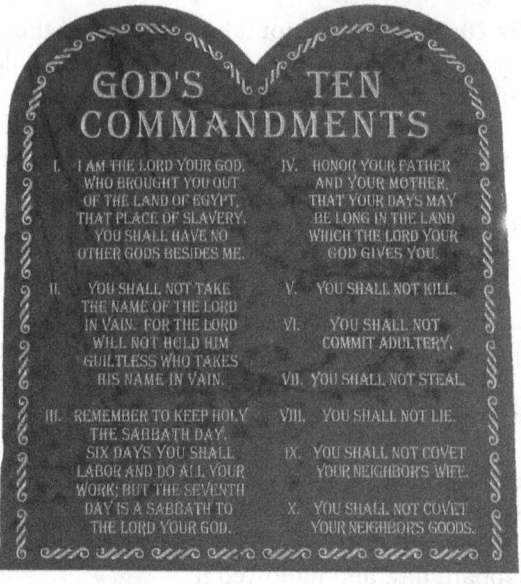

Picture of Catholicism's Ten Commandments Monument Written in Stone at St. Luke's Catholic Church in Danville, Ohio, USA.

The following Roman Catholic quotations are a sampling of claims of authority to make changes in God's law, as pictured above:

> "The observance of Sunday by the Protestants is an homage they pay in spite of themselves to the authority of the Catholic Church." *Plain Talk for Protestants*, 213. ~~~"Ques.—How prove you that the church hath power to command feasts and holy days? "Ans.— By the very act of changing the Sabbath into Sunday, which Protestants allow of, and therefore they fondly contradict themselves by keeping Sunday strictly, and

breaking most other Feasts commanded by the same church. "Ques.—How prove you that? "Ans.—Because by keeping Sunday they acknowledge the Church's power to ordain feasts, and to command them under sin." *Douay Catechism*, 59. ~~~ "If the Bible is the only guide for the Christian, then the Seventh-day Adventist is right, in observing the Saturday with the Jew.... Is it not strange, that those who make the Bible their only teacher, should inconsistently follow in this matter the tradition of the Catholic Church?" *Question Box*, Ed. 1915, 179. ~~~ "The Catholic Church for over one thousand years before the existence of a Protestant, by virtue of her divine mission, changed the day from Saturday to Sunday." *Catholic Mirror*, September 1893. ~~~ "...People who think that the Scriptures should be the sole authority, should logically become 7th Day Adventists, and keep Saturday holy." *Saint Catherine Catholic Church Sentinel*, May 21, 1995. ~~~ "Of course the Catholic Church claims that the change was her act.... And the act is a **MARK** of her ecclesiastical authority in religious things." (H. F. Thomas, Chancellor of Cardinal Gibbons)

The following Scriptures testify to the fact that the great *I Am* never changes:

"My covenant will I not break, nor alter the thing that is gone out of my lips." Ps. 89:34. (See Ex. 20:1, emphasis mine)

"For I am the LORD, I change not...." Mal. 3:6

"Jesus Christ the same yesterday, and to day, and for ever." Heb. 13:8

The consequences that will befall those who, in the final events of earth's history, choose to follow after the beast and his image, rather than a "thus saith the Lord," are delineated in Scripture:

"The beast with two horns 'causeth [commands] all, both small and great, rich and poor, free and bond, to receive a mark in their right hand, or in their foreheads: and that no man might buy or sell, save he that had the mark, or the name of the beast, or the number of his name.' Revelation 13:16, 17. The third angel's warning is: 'If any man worship the beast and his image, and receive his mark in his forehead, or in his hand, the same shall drink of the wine of the wrath of God.'

"'The beast' mentioned in this message, whose worship is enforced by the two-horned beast, is the first, or leopardlike beast of Revelation 13—the papacy. The 'image to the beast' represents that form of apostate Protestantism which will be developed when the Protestant churches shall seek the aid of the civil power for the enforcement of their dogmas. The 'mark of the beast' still remains to be defined.

"After the warning against the worship of the beast and his image, the prophecy declares: 'Here are they that keep the commandments of God, and the faith of Jesus' [Rev. 14:12]. Since those who keep God's commandments are thus placed in contrast with those that worship the beast and his image and receive his mark, it follows that the keeping of God's law, on the one hand, and its violation, on the other, will make the distinction between the worshipers of God and the worshipers of the beast.

"The special characteristic of the beast, and therefore of his image, is the breaking of God's commandments. Says Daniel of the little horn, the papacy: 'He shall think to change times and the law.' Daniel 7:25, R.V. And Paul styled the same power the 'man of sin,' who was to exalt himself above God. One prophecy is a complement of the other. Only by changing God's law could the papacy exalt itself above God; whoever should understandingly keep the law as thus changed would be giving supreme honor to that power by which the change was made. Such an act of obedience to papal laws would be a mark of allegiance to the pope, in the place of God.

"The papacy has attempted to change the law of God. The second commandment, forbidding image worship, has been dropped from the law, and the fourth commandment has been so changed as to authorize the observance of the first instead of the seventh day as the Sabbath. But papists urge, as a reason for omitting the second commandment, that it is unnecessary, being included in the first, and that they are giving the law exactly as God designed it to be understood. This cannot be the change foretold by the prophet. An intentional, deliberate change is presented: 'He shall think to change the times and the law.' The change in the fourth commandment exactly fulfills the prophecy. For this the only authority claimed is that of the church. Here the papal power openly sets itself above God.

"While the worshipers of God will be especially distinguished by their regard for the fourth commandment,—since this is the sign of His creative power and the witness to His claim upon man's reverence and homage,—the worshipers of the beast will be distinguished by their efforts to tear down the Creator's memorial, to exalt the institution of Rome."[1]

---

[1] Ellen White, *The Great Controversy* (Nampa, Idaho: Pacific Press, 1911), 445-6.

ACKNOWLEDGMENTS

Once again I wish to thank Jean Handwerk as an excellent copyeditor whose input has brought this volume to fruition, and again express my deepest gratitude to my wife Robin, who has faithfully stood by my side in another endeavor to build a wall of fortification for those who love and cherish the truth!

INTRODUCTION

I first want to speak to the readers who have stood by me through the years and for the encouraging words for a monumental task now brought to completion. Thank you! And thank you for allowing me to serve you again.

The purpose of this fourth volume in my series dedicated to the prophetic periods of Daniel and Revelation is to clarify my documentation and to resolve all the best arguments brought against what I consider to be, and have presented as, correct interpretation. Everyone writes for different reasons and motives. I write to resolve issues, and if I cannot do that, there is no need for me to write. By resolving issues, I fortify myself with truth for the coming holocaust. I also share that research and understanding among those who not only earnestly desire to know the truth, but who also want to prepare themselves as much as humanly possible for what is to break upon the world as an overwhelming surprise. The Bible-believing Christian understands we are about to experience the last act in the drama of the Christian church. No words can describe what is about to be unleashed upon the world in the closing scenes of earth's history. I will not speculate, for this is not where we gather our strength. The Christian does not prepare as the world prepares, with firearms, ordnances and artillery. To do so would guarantee shipwreck of faith. Rather, his path is by faith alone. His principles come solely from "it is written," and his march follows in the blood-stained footsteps of Christ, "holy, harmless and undefiled." He does not lean on the arm of flesh.

In Chapter 1 the reader will find twenty **(20)** objections brought forth by a very versed and honest historian that I have come to respect. When referring to my friend the historian, I have chosen to use only his initials NL. You will find all of his objections addressed. In fact, all objections that I have ever received since I wrote my

Preliminary book back in 2005 have been only for the years and events connected to AD 508 and AD 538, and they have all come from NL. In Chapter 1 the reader will be reading exactly what he sent to me, as well as exactly what I sent back to NL in September of 2014. I have received no further comments from him, and at this point, I do not expect any.

In Chapter 2 the reader will find a short list of other issues that demand clarification. They are alphabetically labeled for easy reference. To the best of my understanding, all known and perceived objections or issues have now been brought forth and have been met with a reply. Therefore, I hope this volume will be a confirmation and witness to the truth that we have presented all along—truth as it is written in the Scriptures.

Appendices I–III contain my *Source Books* bibliographies for the simple reason that it took years to learn of these many primary and secondary sources, since I literally was starting from scratch. They will prove to be a valuable aid for any scholar, historian or layperson hoping to do any additional research in those eras.

For all my books and more, see my website at www.thesourcehh.org.

1

A Reply to the Allegations Concerning the AD 508 and AD 538 Source Books

Heidi Heiks
August 2014

Greetings, NL.

In this rebuttal, I first want to thank you for what I perceive to be an honest assessment of my works in your line of reasoning, and for your congenial and professional spirit. Also, in your handling of the primary and secondary sources, which I know well, I find you to be honest. That has been a rare commodity, in my experience. For those reasons, I will gladly answer your questions, with your promise that you would also answer mine. In our dialogue I trust we may continue to speak in a forthright manner, with no offense taken and none intended.

I will largely retain your submitted format for continuity. My critique of what you submitted will begin with the quotations taken from my books in a reduced marginal format numbered in bold font **(01)**–**(20)** in the order they were submitted to me. This, in turn, will be followed by your comments that I will put in parentheses. My response will follow in brackets. The twenty quotations taken from my books in the reduced marginal format and the footnotes will be numbered according to the page numbering of my books, not from the PDF that you are using.

HH

Note to readers: So that the reader can quickly identify from which of my books NL was quoting, I have coded my three successive *AD Source Books* as 1, 2, and 3 (508, 538, 1798-1843). A reference reading "2:21" means the second volume (*AD 538 Source Book*), page 21. Also, I am fully familiar with NL's references, which he cited in brief as one researcher to another. Full references were not necessary in our correspondence with one another.

HH

(01).

"In an extremely significant letter, Pope Hormisdas writes to Justinian in February of 519. Amazing as it seems, the papacy singles herself out as the pope identifies the Catholic Church as the true source in rooting out her enemies, working from behind the scenes, fulfilling Scripture.

(A portion of the pope's letter to Justinian reads:)

"'The way to unity of the church is clear, the prescriptions for it are known; the priests who love the Catholic peace must not reject the Catholic confession. For it is necessary that the falsehood not be just partly improved but torn out by the root.... Therefore go forth as you have begun.... Your sentiments as they appear in your writings to us are of the kind such that not much exhortation is required for the execution of your good intentions.'

"With the church ultimately doing the rooting out, commissioning Justinian to 'go forth as you have begun' with 'the execution of your good intentions,' this excerpt requires no commentary. We will shortly view those so-called good intentions of Justinian in his *Corpus Juris Civilis* which was backed by the church when he became the emperor in 527." 2:40-41.

(I think the excerpt does require some commentary since Hormisdas' 519AD letter was specifically addressing negotiations meant to end the 35-year Acacian Schism. Heidi Heiks mentions this religious quarrel on several occasions in his *A.D. 538 Source Book* (pages 63, 127, 169), so he should be familiar with it. The "falsehood" needing to be "torn out by the root" was the Eastern Church's continued support for the deceased Patriarch Acacius, among other things. Yes, Hormisdas did indeed lay out the prescriptions for clearing the "way to unity of the church" in resolving the schism; he required Acacius' condemnation, rejection of the Henoticon,[2] and universal acceptance of Hormisdas' Formula along with Leo's Tome.[3] About a month later, Emperor Justin (who Justinian represented in his letter to Hormisdas) made good on those intentions; he, along with the Patriarch of Constantinople and several hundred chief bishops, condemned Acacius, signed the Formula of Hormisdas, and issued an imperial decree declaring that the true faith was only found in union with the Roman church.[4]

(So all Hormisdas' letter really tells us is that the prescriptions for ending the Acacian schism were known, the pope was not going to be satisfied until all of his conditions were met, and he encouraged the emperor and Justinian to continue actively facilitating the schism's resolution. I think Heiks' explanation goes well beyond what was actually said, taking Hormisdas' admonition concerning a specific issue (reconciliation within the church), and wrongly turning it into a papal commission about sending forth the emperor's nephew to root out the church's enemies – a topic the letter simply does not address.) NL

[Among my peers it is rightly understood that one of the specifications designating the character and attributes of the papacy in the books of Daniel and Revelation is that she is *intolerant*. This I have repeatedly shown and so stated in my books. She "persecutes and destroys the saints," according to chapters 7, 8, and 11 of Daniel. In Revelation chapter 13 there are fifteen specifications that identify the sea beast; all of those specifications find their fulfillment in

---

[2] Joseph F. Kelly, *The Ecumenical Councils of the Catholic Church*, 50.
[3] Volker L. Menze, *Justinian and the Making of the Syrian Orthodox Church*, 75.
[4] Ibid.

the papacy, and the papacy alone. Chapter 17 of Revelation outlines ten specifications of this same resurrected intolerant entity. Again, all specifications find their primary fulfillment in the papacy (the "Mother of Harlots"), and no other. "Wine" denotes doctrines or teachings. Intoxicating wine denotes false doctrines. This is confirmed in the context of Scripture and also acknowledged by Inspiration.[5] Revelation 17:2 and explicitly 14:8 declare she is yet to make *"all nations drink of <u>the wine</u> of the wrath of her fornication."* "Fornication," in a religious sense, means illicit union: union with the civil power, union with the world, or union with false worship. It is unfaithfulness to Christ. The Lord likens himself to the husband of the church, and if the church is unfaithful to him and seeks the favor of others, that is classed as spiritual adultery or fornication. The fornication of Revelation 14:8 and 17:2 is the union of church and state. But what is meant by "the <u>wrath</u> of her fornication"? When men assimilate the wine or doctrines of spiritual Babylon, they become wrathful and *intolerant*. They become *intolerant* of truth and *intolerant* of people who hold to the truth. As Revelation 12:17 declares, "The dragon was <u>wroth</u> with the woman [the church] and went to make war with the remnant of her seed, which keep the commandments of God and have the testimony of Jesus Christ."

[The irony of it all is that Pope Hormisdas' letter uses the very language found in Daniel 7:8 to "root" out all that she is not in harmony with. Along with that, if nothing else, the letter plainly reveals motive and intent. It was this crystal-clear intent of the papacy, consistent throughout all her reign, which I was trying to get across, but I admit my wording did not convey that properly. Further, you are right that I should be familiar with Pope Hormisdas' letter. In fact, not only have I read the entire letter, but I translated the entire letter, as well. And you are right concerning the contents of that letter. I stand to be corrected. If I am wrong, I will be forthright and tell you so, as I expect the same in return. I will also state that there has been no intent in my books to deceive.] HH

---

[5] "The fallen denominational churches are Babylon. Babylon has been fostering poisonous doctrines, the wine of error. This wine of error is made up of false doctrines...." Ellen White, *Testimonies to Ministers and Gospel Workers* (Nampa, ID: Pacific Press, 1962), 61.

(02).

> "Simply put, the uprooting of a race is when the nationality of those peoples no longer exists. The uprooting of a kingdom occurs when its legislative branch no longer functions and its means of civil enforcement ceases to exist. *The Billings Gazette* fully illustrates this universally accepted and understood principle. By setting up Catholic legislation as supreme in a previously held Arian territorial jurisdiction, that kingdom was 'plucked up by the roots.'" 2:75-76.

(I tend to agree with the first part of Heiks' statement; if a kingdom's legislative branch no longer functions and if its means of civil enforcement ceases to exist, then for all intents and purposes that kingdom has been uprooted. On page 76 of his *A.D. 538 Source Book*, Heiks refers to the fall of Poland in 1939 as an example of such an uprooting; the note from Ambassador Molotov mentioned in *The Billings Gazette* stated that "(t)he Polish-German War has revealed the internal bankruptcy of the Polish State. During the course of ten days› hostilities Poland has lost all her industrial areas and cultural centers. Warsaw, as the capital of Poland, no longer exists. The Polish Government has disintegrated, and no longer shows any sign of life. This means that the Polish State and its Government have, in point of fact, ceased to exist."[6] I'm fine with using that as an example of uprooting. However, I completely disagree with Heiks' further assertion that setting up Catholic legislation in something as loosely defined as "previously held Arian territorial jurisdiction" is somehow synonymous with plucking up a kingdom by its roots; after all, a kingdom can lose some of its territorial jurisdiction to a foreign power while retaining a functioning legislative branch as well as its means of civil enforcement.

(Regarding the Visigoths, Heiks believes they were the first of three horns to be plucked up by the roots when Clovis defeated the Visigoths at the Battle of Vouille in 507AD. (He also claimed the latest academic scholarship

---

[6] David G. Williamson, *Poland Betrayed*, 118.

supported the 508 AD date;[7] however, since his book was published, more recent scholarship has upheld 507 AD[8]– scholarship that actually comes to us from one of Heiks' highly touted sources.[9]) According to him, the Visigoths were uprooted when nearly all of Gaul came under the jurisdiction of Clovis.[10] So was the Visigothic kingdom really uprooted as a result of Vouille?

(We can answer that question by viewing the Visigoths in light of Heiks' Molotov example; the ambassador concluded that the Polish state ceased to exist when the country lost "all her industrial areas and cultural centers." The capital city of Warsaw "ceased to exist," and the Polish government disintegrated without showing any "sign of life." How does this situation compare to the Visigothic kingdom following the Battle of Vouille? Well, did the Visigoths lose all of their "industrial" (i.e., economic) areas and cultural centers as a result of the battle? The answer is no; Roger Collins tells us that a substantial number of Visigoths settled in Spain during the 490s, which in his opinion may have contributed to their vulnerability in Gaul over a decade later.[11] Economic/cultural centers like Barcelona, Cordoba, Toledo, Tarragona, etc. remained in Visigothic hands following the conflict. So the Frankish takeover of a large portion of Gallic territory resulted in the loss of some–but certainly not all–of the Visigoths' economic/cultural centers.

(Did the Visigoths lose their capital? Yes; the Visigothic capital of Toulouse was taken by the Franks. However, unlike the Poles, the Visigoths reestablished a new capital in the city of Narbonne soon afterward.[12]

(Did the Visigothic government disintegrate without showing any signs of life? The answer of course is no. The Visigothic nobles immediately replaced Alaric with King Gesalic. Gesalic was later overthrown by King Theodoric,

---

[7] Heidi Heiks, *AD 508 Source Book*, 40.
[8] Ralph W. Mathisen & Danuta Shanzer, *The Battle of Vouillé, 507 CE: Where France Began*.
[9] Heiks, *AD 508 Source Book*, xvii-xviii.
[10] Heidi Heiks, *AD 538 Source Book*, 71-73.
[11] Roger Collins, *Early Medieval Spain*, 34-35.
[12] Ibid., 33.

who acted as regent,[13] and he was followed by Alaric's son, King Amalaric, who was then replaced by Theudis the Ostrogoth, and so on and so forth. The fact of the matter is, a Gothic monarchy ruled the Iberian peninsula for two centuries after the Battle of Vouille; its Western, Spanish provinces–including some Gallic territory–remained under Visigothic control after the battle. Losing most of Aquitania proper to the Franks was definitely a major setback for the kingdom, but the Visigothic state and monarchy did not cease to exist as a result. When judged by the Molotov litmus test, the kingdom of the Visigoths was not plucked up by the roots by 508 AD. We'd have to wait another 200 years for the Umayyad invasion to perform that task.

(Now, of course, Heiks' primary focus is on the religious ramifications of Clovis' war, so let's look at those. In Heiks' search for an uprooted horn,[14] he zeroed in on Gaul, describing it as "the last territory of Christendom in Western Rome,"[15] a statement that would have come as a complete surprise to the Ibero-Roman Church in Spain, I'd imagine. Heiks used Procopius to show how the Visigoths "took possession of all of Gaul as far as the Alps;"[16] he said the Gothic tribes were largely in control of "all of Gaul and Italy." After the Battle of Vouille "nearly all of Gaul" was under Clovis' jurisdiction,[17] and Gaul changed hands from Arian to Catholic jurisdiction.[18] I have a feeling that uninformed readers who study chapter 5 in Heiks' book may accidentally get the impression that Gaul represented the totality of the Visigothic kingdom, since Heiks equates the Visigoths with Gaul almost half a dozen times in that chapter, but gives the Visigothic presence in Spain barely more than a passing mention on page 73. And although Procopius did acknowledge the Visigoths taking Gaul as far as the Alps around 476 AD, he first mentioned how they had previously "seized all of Spain and the portion of Gaul lying

---

[13] Herwig Wolfram, *History of the Goths*, 310.
[14] Heidi Heiks, *AD 538 Source Book*, 61-62.
[15] Ibid., 64.
[16] Ibid.
[17] Ibid., 73.
[18] Ibid.

beyond the Rhone River and made them subject and tributary to themselves."[19]

(Then on page 75, Heiks makes his point clear: "(t)he real emphasis of the Scriptures was the removal of Arian jurisdiction from the three main and distinct Arian kingdoms, as stated by Procopius, and having it replaced with Catholic jurisdiction. As long as that Arian principle of religious liberty ... was still in place and upheld judicially by those Arian powers and enforced by civil means, the Scriptures could not yet be fulfilled."

(Ok, so did the Visigothic kingdom lose its Arian jurisdiction and its ability to enforce religious liberty as a result of Vouille? Over most of Gaul? Certainly. But "most of Gaul" represented a little less than half of the entire Visigothic kingdom, the same kingdom Heiks maintained judicially upheld the "Arian principle of religious liberty." Heiks had already defined a horn as a "king or kingdom" on page 33; therefore, the loss of provinces or territories did not equal an uprooted kingdom, especially in light of the Molotov example Heiks himself provided. Was the principle of religious liberty upheld by the Visigothic horn and enforced by civil means after the Battle of Vouille? The answer is yes. Heiks recognized that the Council of Agde served as a "proclamation of tolerance for West Gothic Arianism"[20] for Roman Catholic subjects of the Visigoths, but although the Visigoths' territorial borders shrank significantly after Vouille, their kingdom remained; the Catholic Church within the Visigothic kingdom would not have been able to replace religious liberty with Catholic dogma in Spain and Southern Gaul. Also, Agilan's dispute with Gregory of Tours in 570 AD confirms that religious liberty was "still in place and upheld judicially" within the Visigothic kingdom some six decades after the Battle of Vouille[21] (with a few exceptions).

(So if the Visigothic kingdom continued to exist, and if it maintained Arian jurisdiction and protected religious liberty after 508 AD, then one of Heiks' Arian kingdoms

---

[19] Procopius, *History of the Wars*. Translated by H. B. Dewing. Bks. 1–8. In Loeb Classical Library, edited by Jeffrey Henderson (Cambridge, MA: Harvard Univ. Press, 2000–2001), Book V, Ch. XII.
[20] Heidi Heiks, *AD 538 Source Book*, 65.
[21] Richard North, Heathen Gods in Old English Literature, 151-152.

opposing "the principles or government of the Catholic Church"[22] was still rooted after the Battle of Vouille; its legislative branch continued to function, its means of civil enforcement continued to exist, and, most importantly, the kingdom remained an opposing Arian armament in Europe until the end of the 6th Century when the Visigoths converted to Catholicism following the Council of Toledo.) NL

[Brother L, as a historian I commend you on your knowledge and your honest use of the sources, but you have put a "human construction" upon them that the Scriptures do not support, and at this point in time I believe you have done so innocently. However, at the end of this dialogue, the true motive that governs both of us as to why we do what we do and why we say what we say will be readily apparent before all. Your weakness becomes obvious when you never reference, quote, or even acknowledge the Scriptures. With all due respect, some of your suppositions that you have brought forward have been based solely on a personal, private interpretation, because you have clearly walked away from the text and have failed to make the Scriptures your reference point. I will now prove my point, if you please. We shall begin by addressing one of your questions: "So was the Visigothic kingdom really uprooted as a result of Vouille? We can answer that question by viewing the Visigoths in light of Heiks' Molotov example."

[No! We can answer that question only in light of the Scriptures. In fact, in order to resolve the arguments being put forth, we need only to rehearse a few specific biblical specifications that pertain to the commencement of the little horn and the uprooting of the three horns of Bible prophecy. Then we will have a meter stick by which all can judge honestly and intelligently in this entire discourse as to just what the truth is, according to the Scriptures and history. But remember, history will always take a back seat at first to everything that is presented. It is during the confirmation phase of prophecy, and only then, that history finds a place in the Scriptures—never the other way

---

[22] Ibid., 40.

around, as in the path taken by many others. As we proceed through this treatise, I will from time to time submit additional documents in order to capitalize on specifications that I did not include or left too much to assumption in my books because I thought they were self-explanatory, but which now I see were overlooked or misunderstood. We begin in the book of Daniel, chapter 7:

> Dan. 7:8 "I considered$^{H1934\ H7920}$ the horns,^{H7162} and, behold,^{H431} there came up^{H5559} among^{H997} them another^{H317} little^{H2192} horn,^{H7162} before$^{H4481,\ H6925}$ whom there were three^{H8532} of^{H4481} the first^{H6933} horns^{H7162} plucked up by the roots:^{H6132} and, behold,^{H431} in this^{H1668} horn^{H7162} were eyes^{H5870} like the eyes^{H5870} of man,^{H606} and a mouth^{H6433} speaking^{H4449} great things."^{H7260}

"I considered the <u>horns</u>...." In 2:33 we recognized that in Bible prophecy a "horn" represents a kingdom or in the plural, kingdoms, because it's understood that the Bible is its own interpreter. "...[A]nd, behold, there came up among <u>them</u>...." Clearly the "them" is alluding to other horns or kingdoms that already had an established judiciary in place (very important) when the little horn is being recognized by Heaven as becoming a kingdom in the new world sometime after AD 476. There is no such thing in the Bible as a "horn" in the prophetic sense being recognized as a kingdom without a legislative and judiciary branch in place. Other specifications will give us the time and place of this rise. Continuing on with our next word study,

"...Another little horn, <u>before</u> whom...."$^{H4481,\ H6925}$

[We have previously discussed this Hebrew word *Min* or "before," and concluded from the Scriptures the following]: "It must be concluded, therefore, that the reference to the three horns' being plucked up <u>before</u> the little horn gives no indication as to the timing of the 1260 days, and that any discussion based on the supposition that it does, is without value."[23]

---
[23] Ibid; footnote.

A Reply to the Allegations

[See also 2:34-37, footnote 41-42. However, we will come back to the Hebrew word *qodam* in this text to a *very* important point that was completely over looked by Maxwell. Continuing on,]

"...Before whom there were three of the first^{H6933} horns...."

"6933. קַדְמָי *qadmāy*: An Aramaic adjective meaning first, former. It refers to the initial item(s) in a sequence of things but also to previous item(s) with respect to a later item mentioned (Dan. 7:4, 8, 24)."[24]

[Underlining mine. A more accurate translation reads: "...Before whom there were three of the former^{H6933} horns [kingdoms with a legislative and judiciary branch already in place]

"...Plucked up by the roots:"^{H6132}

[Who, then, were the "them" or the "former" established kingdoms that were to be plucked up by the roots in the New World sometime after AD 476? It had been demonstrated and documented to be the Visigoths, Vandals and Ostrogoths. Notice, the Scriptures are speaking about a removal of three kingdoms during the rise of the little horn "to power," not when she was "in power." The scriptural specifications also reveal the allotted time period "given" to the papacy in her rise "to power" (AD 508-538 = 30yrs.), as well as to the time period "given" (Dan. 7:25, Rev. 13:5) to her by Heaven during which she would be permitted to be "in power" (AD 538 to 1798 =1260 yrs.). We will briefly rehearse certain necessary issues pertaining to these time periods soon enough. First, we must continue to remove an enigma surrounding a much-misunderstood phrase in Scripture found in Dan. 7:8: "plucked up by the roots:"^{H6132}

6132. עֲקַר '*aqar*: An Aramaic verb referring to plucking up by the roots. It refers to tearing something

---

[24] Warren Baker and Eugene Carpenter, *The Complete Word Study Dictionary: Old Testament* (Chattanooga, TN: AMG Publishers, 2003), 979.

out, destroying it, pulling it out by the roots. It is used figuratively of tearing out men or <u>rulers</u> (Dan. 7:8)."[25]

[Underlining mine. "Plucked up by the <u>roots.</u>" What does the Bible mean when it says a horn or horns are plucked up by the roots? NL has correctly stated my position, which is the position of the Scriptures, as well:

> "Simply put, the uprooting of a race is when the nationality of those peoples no longer exists. The uprooting of a kingdom occurs when its legislative branch no longer functions and its means of civil enforcement ceases to exist." 2:75-76.

[In the prophecies of Daniel and Revelation, God has always held the accountability of a nation or kingdom to its legislative and judiciary authorities, and not the military, as the military takes orders from the legislative branch of government and acts on them; it does not give the orders. The "speaking" of a nation, is the action of its legislative and judicial authorities, never the voice of the military in Bible prophecy as the following Scriptures and previous documents of mine have confirmed:

> "And he shall <u>speak</u>[26] ... think to change times and <u>laws</u>." Daniel 7:25

> "Laws" in the plural sense are designated here: the law of God and civil law. It was legislation that ultimately "set up" the little horn in A.D. 508[27] and it was legislation that brought down the little horn in A.D. 1798,[28] and it will be legislation that sets up or resurrects *again* the beast power in the form of the image to the beast.[29] [See Rev. 13:15] In the final events of his-

---

[25] Ibid., 864-865.

[26] "The "speaking" of the nation is the action of its <u>legislative</u> and <u>judicial authorities</u>." Ellen White, *Great Controversy*, (Nampa, ID: Pacific Press, 1911), 442.

[27] See my *AD 508 Source Book*.

[28] See my *AD 1798 1843 Source Book*.

[29] "When our nation shall so abjure the principles of its government as to enact a Sunday law, Protestantism will in this act join hands with popery; it will be nothing else than giving <u>life</u> [Rev. 13:15: "And he had power to give <u>life</u>...."] to the tyranny which has long been eagerly watching its opportunity to spring again

tory, universal legislation will be the signal that brings down the little horn *again*, but this time it will be by the means of the seven last plagues."[30] [See Rev. 18] 2:39-40.

[So what role, then, does the military play in the eyes of Heaven in the uprooting of a horn or kingdom, as depicted in Daniel 7:8? None! In the eyes of humanity, the military may have been a means, and many follow that lead even to this day, but they do so without the endorsement of Scripture, thus rendering their suppositions private interpretation. *Mark this next point with care, as the ramifications here are huge.* A prophetic horn or kingdom does *not* have to be equipped with an army to be recognized by Heaven as being a kingdom. Did the "little horn" (papacy) ever have a military of its own? No! This I previously stated in my book, 2:36. Was it so considered to be a kingdom in the eyes of Heaven? Yes! So then the *definition* for the uprooting of a prophetic horn or kingdom in the eyes of Heaven is reserved *solely* to the "uprooting of that kingdom's legislative and judicial branches of government," whether there be a standing army out in the field or not. Thus saith the Scriptures! The following Scripture acknowledges and confirms the "little horn" had no military:

"And arms [Clovis] shall stand on his [papacy's] part, and they [church & state] ..." Dan. 11:31.

[The Scriptures have spoken! If any man shall add unto or take away from this meaning, it will become clear before all that he speaks from his own devising.

---

into active despotism.... If popery or its principles shall again be legislated into power, the fires of persecution will be rekindled against those who will not sacrifice conscience and the truth in deference to popular errors. This evil is on the point of realization." Ellen White, *Testimonies for the Church*, (Boise, ID: Pacific Press, 1948), 5:712.

[30] "Babylon the great is fallen, is fallen.... And I heard another voice from Heaven, saying, Come out of her, my people, that ye be not partakers of her sins, and that ye receive not of her plagues. For her sins have reached unto Heaven, and God hath remembered her iniquities." When do her sins reach unto Heaven? When the law of God is finally made void by legislation" [universally]. Ellen White, *Signs of the Times*, June 12, 1893.

[We now turn our attention back to the *rise* of the little horn "to power," for a fuller overview and more biblical specifications to what the Bible calls the "setting-up" period of the papacy that was to consist of a time span of 30 years, as we witnessed in my books. During this thirty-year time period, the Scriptures declare the papacy would be permitted to "set up" her rule, or dictatorship, in the region of what is now Western Europe. To secure this end, she would need to be in league with a civil power or powers in order to uproot the Visigoths', Vandals' and the Ostrogoths' legislative and judicial branches of government by the year AD 538. Daniel 11:31 confirmed just such a union. After the Ostrogothic legislative and judicial government was dismantled in AD 538, the Scriptures *then* move the "little horn" to a status of "in power," meaning in position to commence her reign of terror and persecution until the deadly wound was administrated to her by a civil state in 1798, 1260 years later, just as the Scriptures had declared it would be, and as my books have proven it to be.

[There is another Biblical specification that has been totally overlooked by the masses, which has resulted in a huge array of private interpretations leading to utter confusion. In fact, this specification will prove to be another vindicating and irrefutable position for the historicist method of Biblical interpretation. Where do we find this vital piece of Biblical information? Daniel 7:8. It is the Hebrew word *q°ḏām*, or the English word "before":

> Dan. 7:8 "I considered the horns, and, behold, there came up among them another little horn, before[H4481, H6925] whom there were three of the first horns plucked up by the roots: and, behold, in this horn *were* eyes like the eyes of man, and a mouth speaking great things."

[Further Biblical specifications clarified:

> "4481. מִן *min*: An Aramaic preposition meaning from, out of, among, more than. It means out of something, e.g., a threshing floor (Dan. 2:35) or from a specific area, e.g., a temple as a storage area (Dan. 5:2). It is used with *yaḏ*, hand, to give the figurative idea of

A Reply to the Allegations 15

from the power of (Dan. 3:15). It is used to express comparison meaning different from (Dan. 7:3) or more than (Dan. 2:30). It is used to express the idea of a part of something or some group, etc. (Dan. 2:33, 41; 5:13). With *we'aḏ* following it, it expresses the temporal idea of since (Dan. 2:20; Ezra 4:15; 5:16). Followed by *dî*, it functions as a conjunction expressing cause, because (Ezra 5:11). With a pronoun suffix, it means from me, from you, etc. (Dan. 2:5). It is used to express with, to point out an instrument or agent (Dan. 4:25[22]). It expresses the idea of based on or according to, e.g., the word or command of God (Ezra 6:14). The expression *min-yaṣṣib* means truly, certainly (Dan. 2:8). It is used in the idiom *min-qešōt dî* indicating in fact, surely (Dan. 2:47). Judgment is rendered idiomatically as judgment upon (from, *min*) him, her, etc. (Ezra 7:26). Something may be changed from (*min*) what it was (Dan. 4:13[10])."[31]

"6925. קֳדָם *qᵒḏām:* An Aramaic preposition meaning before, in the presence of. It refers to being in front of spatially or temporally; in time (Ezra 4:18, 23; Dan. 2:9; 7:7). It has the sense of in God's judgment, before Him (Dan. 6:22[23]). It means to be afraid of something from before one (*min* (4480) *qoḏāmôhî;* Dan. 7:8). It is used with words meaning to pray, to answer before (Dan. 2:10, 11, 27). It describes a decree going out from (before) a king (Dan. 2:6; 6:26[27])."[32]

[The following paragraphs presented in smaller font were pulled from my book (2:35, footnote 41) by Mervin C. Maxwell for a thesis. Maxwell's entire reasoning here was about time, as the last paragraph clearly confirms. His conclusion was correct:

"According to *Young's* Concordance, the Aramaic word qodam is used 31 times in the Old Testament: Three times in Ezra, and twenty seven times in Daniel. Thirty of these times it is translated 'before,' and once,

---

[31] Baker and Carpenter, *The Complete Word Study Dictionary: Old Testament*, 625-6.
[32] Ibid., 978, underlining mine.

'in the presence of.' Daniel 2:27. In every case but two there is no question but that the word means 'in the presence of.' Examples of such usage include Ezra 7:19 and Daniel 6:10, 26; 7:10, 13, where the translation is 'before God.' Obviously this cannot mean 'before God was in existence,' and so must mean 'in His presence.' In Ezra 4:18 it is 'before the people.' In most other references it describes activities taking place 'before' the king, and again there is no question but that the usage is in reference to location, and not time.

"The two cases where there might be any question are in Daniel 7. Daniel 7:7 says, 'And it [the fourth beast] was diverse from all the beasts that were before it.' Here time might be indicated instead of location, but verse 12, which says the lives of the beasts were prolonged, and Revelation 13, which shows them all living in composite form even after the fall of Rome, indicate that the first three beasts stayed 'in the presence of' one another as they appeared in turn.

"The other verse where there might be a question is, of course, verse 8, the one under discussion: 'before whom there were three of the first horns plucked up by the roots.' In this case the usage of qodam in 29 other instances should be conclusive, but there is further evidence. In this verse and in the parallel passage, verse 20, which contains the phrase 'before whom three fell,' the word qodam is coupled with the word min to form the phrase min qodam, meaning, literally, 'from the East.' This Aramaic idiom cannot, by any stretch of the imagination, be said to convey the sense of time. Other instances of the use of this idiom occur in Daniel 5:19 and 6:26, where reference is made to the people fearing 'before' God. Since, as above, this cannot be construed to mean 'before God existed,' it must mean 'in His presence.'

"It must be concluded, therefore, that the reference to the three horns' being plucked up before the little horn gives no indication as to the timing of the 1260 days, and that any discussion based on the supposition that it does, is without value."[33]

---

[33] Mervin C. Maxwell, *An Exegetical and Historical Examination of the Beginning and Ending of the 1260 days of Prophecy with special attention given to A.*

A Reply to the Allegations

[However, *qᵒdām* has another definition that had been rightly understood by Maxwell, but he never made the connection. The meaning is found: "in His presence." However, Maxwell correctly interpreted its Biblical meaning:

> "According to Young's Concordance, the Aramaic word qodam is used 31 times in the Old Testament: Three times in Ezra, and twenty seven times in Daniel. Thirty of these times it is translated 'before,' and once, 'in the presence of.' Daniel 2:27. In every case but two there is no question but that the word means 'in the presence of.' Examples of such usage include Ezra 7:19 and Daniel 6:10, 26; 7:10, 13, where the translation is 'before God.' Obviously this cannot mean 'before God was in existence,' and so must mean 'in His presence.' In Ezra 4:18 it is 'before the people.' In most other references it describes activities taking place 'before' the king, and again <u>there is no question but that the usage is in reference to location and not time.</u>"[34]

[So what is the connection? It is simply this:

[NL advocates that the Visigoths were not uprooted in AD 508, as I had advocated. NL points to Spain and claims that the Visigoths were not "plucked up" until the beginning of the eighth century—until that time still retaining a functioning government, commerce, etc., a historical fact that NL claims I recognized and so stated in my book. So, is it true that the Visigoths in Spain were not uprooted until the beginning of the eighth century? Yes. Is it true that I recognized and so stated that belief in my book, as NL claims? Yes— 2:73, to be exact. So why did and do I still reject the claims put forth by NL, and upon what grounds? Because one cannot advocate that premise and also claim to stand on the Bible, because the Bible will prove the man out of step with Scripture. How? It is all right here:

D. 538 and 1798 as Initial and Terminal Dates. A Thesis Presented to the faculty of the Seventh-day Adventist Theological Seminary Washington, D.C. August 1951. (Andrews University, Berrien Springs, MI.), 24-26. Quoted from Heidi Heiks, *AD 538 Source Book,* Vol. 2, 35 (footnote 41).

[34] Ibid., emphasis mine.

"In the presence of...." "There is no question but that the usage is in reference to "location" and not time." [Emphasis mine]

[In other words, *all* the specifications of the prophecy that were given to take place between the years 508 and 538—including, of course, the uprooting of the three horns—must and did take place *only* in the "presence" of the papacy, and thus *only* in the "location" where she was able to stretch her tentacles far enough to secure her dominion during her thirty years' crusade for power. This means that even the opposition is confined to the geographical and chronological stipulations of the Scriptures for their interpretations from this day forward. This totally negates all the accusations put forward by NL with just one text: "It is written...."

[During our deliberations about the uprooting of the Visigothic horn, NL has also objected about my reasoning of the uprooting of the Ostrogothic horn, as well. Therefore, I have decided to jump ahead to number **(11)** of his paper in order to address just those concerns about the uprooting of the Ostrogoths. NL objections are as such:

(11).

("...And as shown in the above quote, Heiks also recognized that Justinian overthrew the Vandals in 534 AD. Again, it did not matter that the tide-turning battles took place in 533 AD, or that Justinian was proclaiming Africa's reclamation in December of that year;[35] what matters is the Vandals were overthrown when the war ended in 534 AD.

(Now all Heiks has to do is apply that same reasoning to the Ostrogothic War. Did the Ostrogoths surrender in 538 AD? No. Did the war come to an end in 538 AD? No. As with the battles of Adda and Ad Decimum, did it matter that the failed siege of Rome was a tide-turning event early in the conflict? Again, no. And unlike the 7-month Vandal War, the Gothic War lasted 18 years, with the war's momentum swinging in the Goths' favor at times. But regardless, the last Ostrogothic king

---

[35] Heidi Heiks, *AD 538 Source Book*, 94-95.

perished in 553 AD and the remains of the Gothic military negotiated an end to the conflict with General Narses shortly thereafter.[36] 553 AD was the year the Ostrogoths were overthrown, not 538 AD....") NL

[The Scriptures had declared there would be three prophetic horns or kingdoms uprooted between the years AD 508-538. I will cement the accuracy of the Scriptures before the end of our presentation on this topic, as that is precisely what history will attest to. The three uprooted horns were the Visigoths in AD 508, the Vandals in AD 534 and, as we will witness, the Ostogoths in AD 538. In response to NL's comment on the uprooting of the Vandals, ironically, in their case, their legislative and judicial branches of government fell simultaneously with their military defeat. We have already established and previously stated what the Scriptures have identified as the uprooting of a prophetic horn or kingdom according to the Scriptures:

"It is the uprooting of a kingdom's legislative and judicial branches of government."

[We also understood it makes no difference to Heaven whether there is a standing army left in the field or not. Now all we have to do is apply the same specifications given to us by the Scriptures to pinpoint when the Ostrogoths were no longer recognized as a kingdom in the eyes of Heaven. This brings us to one question and one question alone. Did the Ostrogothic legislative and judicial branches of government cease to exist in the year AD 538? Yes! The very last specification of the Scriptures to be fulfilled took place during the very last year of the thirty-year crusade for power, as the prophecy had previously declared. Proof? We turn to the historian Thomas Hodgkin, in his book *The Letters of Cassiodorus*.

[Cassiodorus was the Praetorian prefect for the Ostrogothic government. Hodgkin, having meticulously reviewed the primary sources, recounts how and when the legislative and judicial branches came to their demise. I will submit short paragraphs of his essential thoughts

---

[36] Procopius, *History of the Wars*, Book VIII, Ch. XXXV.

on the subject. As always, the full document under discussion (pages 48-54 of Hodgkin's book) will be included, so the reader will have the entire context to judge for himself. This will be followed by copies of some of the last of the original letters that were sent out of the official office of Praetorian prefect of the Ostrogothic government by Cassiodorus, cited by Hodgkin and dated by him. Having gone through the entire twelve books or letters of Cassiodorus, I have also found myself in perfect harmony with historian Theodor Mommsen's work of dating[37] the letters of Cassiodorus. I have found nothing that is dated by him or myself to extend past the year AD 538.

[I now submit the key remarks of Hodgkin. Emphasis is mine:

> "It is possible that the Prefect may have continued to hold office down to the capture of Ravenna in May, 540, which made Witigis a prisoner, and seemed to bring the Ostrogothic monarchy to an end. *Upon the whole,* [51] *however, it is rather more probable that in the year 538 or 539 he finally retired from public life. The dates of his letters will show that there is nothing in them which forbids us to accept this conclusion.*" (Pages 50-51.)

[After Hodgkin surveyed the primary sources, he so stated his belief and understanding. Then on page 54, he made this declaration in a footnote following the sentence reading, "He was now sixty years of age." The footnote reads, "Fifty-eight, *if the retirement was in 538."*

> "The line of thought indicated by the 'De Animâ' led in such a country as Italy, at such a time as the Gothic War, to one inevitable end—the cloister. It can have surprised none of the friends of Cassiodorus when the veteran statesman announced his intention of spending the remainder of his days in monastic retirement. *He was now sixty years of age.*[38] (Page 54.)

[Hodgkin's remarks state his considered conclusion that the Ostrogothic legislative and judicial branches of

---

[37] Theodor Mommsen, *Cassiodori Senatoris Variae* (Berolini, 1894).
[38] Fifty-eight, if the retirement was in 538.

A Reply to the Allegations

government ultimately terminated in the year AD 538. Hodgkin then went on to show how Cassiodorus went about gathering all the documents and tidying up all the loose ends. That is proof positive that no one was filling his place of office. I myself can attest to the fact, as do Hodgkin and Mommsen, that "[t]he dates of his letters will show that there is nothing in them which forbids us to accept this conclusion." That is, the demise of the legislative and judicial branches of government of the Ostrogoths came in the year AD 538!

[Hodgkin wrote,

> "I have endeavoured as far as possible to fix the dates of these later letters. It will be seen that we have one[39] probably belonging to the year 536, five[40] to 537, and one[41] (possibly) to 538. These later letters refer chiefly to the terrible famine which followed in the train of the war, and of which Cassiodorus strenuously labored to mitigate the severity." (Page 50.)

[These letters were significant to Hodgkin, so we have included them for the benefit of the reader. What follows next is from Hodgkin's *Introduction—The Life of Cassiodorus*, pages 48 to 54 in Hodgkin's book, *The Letters of Cassiodorus*:

> [48] (Marginal Reading: "Theodahad deposed, Witigis elected, Aug. 536.").
> "...The onward march of Belisarius trampled all the combinations of diplomatists into the dust. In the early part of July, 536, he had succeeded in capturing the important city of Neapolis, and had begun to threaten Rome. The Gothic warriors, disgusted at the incapacity of their King, and probably suspecting his disloyalty to the nation, met (August, 536) under arms upon the plain [49] of Regeta,[42] deposed Theodahad, and elected a veteran named Witigis as his successor. Witigis at once ordered Theodahad to be put to death, and being himself

---

[39] Var. xii. 20.
[40] Var. xii. 22, 23, 24, 27, 28.
[41] Var. xii. 25.
[42] The situation of this plain is unknown.

of somewhat obscure lineage, endeavoured to strengthen his title to the crown by marrying Matasuentha, the sister of Athalaric and the only surviving descendant of Theodoric.

(Marginal Reading: "Letter on the elevation of Witigis.")

"Whether Cassiodorus had any hand in this revolution—which was pre-eminently a Gothic movement—we cannot tell; but certainly one of the best specimens of his letters is that written in the name of the new King,[43] in which he makes Witigis thus speak, 'Universis Gothis'—not as Theodoric had so often spoken, 'Universis Gothis et Romanis:'

"'Unde Auctori nostro Christo gratias humillimâ satisfaction referentes, indicamus parentes nostros Gothos inter procinctuales gladios, more majorum, scuto supposito, regale nobis contulisse, praestante Deo, dignitatem, ut honorem arma daren't, cujus opinionem bella pepererant. Non enim in cubilis angustis, sed in campis, late patentibus electrum me esse noveritis: nec inter blandientium delicate colloquia, sed tubis concrepantibus sum quaesitus, ut tali fremitu concitatus desiderio virtutis ingenitae regem sibi Martium Geticus populous inveniret.'

(Marginal Reading: "Letters written in name of Witigis. Share of Cassiodorus in the administration during the war.")

"We have only five letters written by Cassiodorus for Witigis (who reigned from August, 536, to May,[44] 540). One has [sic] already described. All the other four are concerned with negotiations for peace with Justinian, and may probably be referred to the early part of the new reign.

"It will be seen that the letters written by Cassiodorus for the Sovereign during the five years following the death of Athalaric are few and somewhat unsatisfactory. [50] But, on the other hand, it was just during these years that he wrote in his own name as Praetorian Praefect the

---

[43] Var. x. 31.
[44] We get this date only from Agnellus (loc. Cit. p. 522).

letters which are comprised in the Eleventh and Twelfth Books of his collection, and which are in some respects the most interesting of the whole series. There is a strong probability that he was not present at the long siege of Rome (March, 537, to March, 538), nor is it likely that he, an elderly civilian, would take much part in any of the warlike operations that followed. Upon the whole, it seems probable that during the greater part of this time Cassiodorus was, to the best of his power, keeping the civilian administration together by virtue of his own authority as Praetorian Praefect, without that constant reference to the wishes of the Sovereign which would have been necessary under Theodoric and his daughter. Perhaps, in the transitional state of things which then prevailed in Italy, with the power of the Gothic sceptre broken but the sway of the Roman Caesar not yet firmly established in its stead, men of all parties and both nationalities were willing that as much as possible of the routine of government should be carried on by a statesman who was Roman by birth and culture, but who had been the trusted counselor of Gothic Kings.

(Marginal Reading: "Dates of later letters.")
"I have endeavoured as far as possible to fix the dates of these later letters. It will be seen that we have one[45] probably belonging to the year 536, five[46] to 537, and one[47] (possibly) to 538. These later letters refer chiefly to the terrible famine which followed in the train of the war, and of which Cassiodorus strenuously labored to mitigate the severity.

(Marginal Reading: "End of Cassiodorus' official career.")
"It is possible that the Praefect may have continued to hold office down to the capture of Ravenna in May, 540, which made Witigis a prisoner, and seemed to bring the Ostrogothic monarchy to an end. Upon the whole, [51] however, it is rather more probable that in the year 538 or 539 he finally retired from public life.

---

[45] Var. xii. 20.
[46] Var. xii. 22, 23, 24, 27, 28.
[47] Var. xii. 25.

The dates of his letters will show that there is nothing in them which forbids us to accept this conclusion; and the fact, if it be a fact, that in 540, when Belisarius, with his Secretary Procopius in his train, made his triumphal entry into Ravenna, the late Praefect was no longer there, but in his native Province of Bruttii, a little lessens the difficulty of that which still remains most difficult of comprehension, the entire omission from Procopius' History of the Gothic War of all mention of the name of Cassiodorus.

(Marginal Reading: "The Variae edited.")

"The closing years of the veteran statesman's tenure of office were years of some literary activity. It was in them that he was collecting, and to some extent probably revising, the letters which appear in the following collection. His motives for publishing this monument of his official life are sufficiently set forth in the two prefaces, one prefixed to the First Book and the other to the Eleventh. Much emphasis is laid on the entreaties of his friends, the regular excuse, in the sixth century as in the nineteenth, for an author or a politician doing the very thing which most pleases his own vanity. A worthier reason probably existed in the author's natural desire to vindicate his own consistency, by showing that the influence which for more than thirty years he had wielded in the councils of the Gothic Sovereigns had been uniformly exerted on the side of law and order and just government, directed equally to the repression of Teutonic barbarism and the punishment of Roman venality.

(Marginal Reading: "What alterations were made in the letters.")

"The question how far the letters which now appear in the 'Variae' really reproduce the actual documents originally issued by Cassiodorus is one which has been a good deal discussed by scholars, but with no very definite result. It is, after all, a matter of conjecture; and every student who peruses the following letters is [52] entitled to form his own conjecture—especially as to those marvelous digressions on matters of Natural History, Moral Philosophy, and the like—whether they were veritably included in the original letters that issued from the Royal Secretum, and were carried over Italy by the Cursus Publicus. My own conjecture is, that though they may have been a little amplified and elaborated, substantially they were to be found in those original documents. The age was pedantic and half-educated, and had lost both its poetic inspiration and its faculty of humour; and I fear that these marvelous letters were read by the officials to whom they were addressed with a kind of stolid admiration, provoking neither the smile of amusement nor the shrug of impatience which are their rightful meed.

(Marginal Reading: "Illum atque Illum.")
"The reader will observe that in many, in face most of the letters which were meant to serve as credentials to ambassadors or commissions to civil servants, no names are inserted, but we have instead only the tantalizing formula, 'Illum atque Illum,' which I have generally translated, 'A and B.' This circumstance has also been much commented upon, but without our arriving at any very definite result. All that can be said is, that Cassiodorus must have formed his collection of State-papers either from rough drafts in his own possession, or from copies preserved in the public archives, and that, from whichsoever source he drew, the names in that source had not been preserved: a striking comment on the rhetorical unbusinesslike character of the Royal and Imperial Chanceries of that day, in which words were deemed of more importance than things, and the flowers of speech which were showered upon the performer of some piece of public business were preserved, while the name of the performer was forgotten.

(Marginal Reading: "Treatise 'De Animâ.'")
"As soon as he had finished the collection of the 'Variae,' the Praefect—again in obedience to the entreaties of his friends—composed a short philosophic treatise on the [53] Nature of the Soul ('De Animâ'). As he said, it seems an absurd thing to treat as a stranger and an unknown quantity the very centre of our being; to seek to understand the height of the air, the extent

of the earth, the causes of storms and earthquakes, and the nature of the wandering winds, and yet to leave the faculty, by which we grasp all this knowledge, itself uncomprehended[48]. He therefore sets himself to enquire, in twelve chapters:

1. Why the Soul is called Anima?

2. What is the definition of the Soul?

3. What is its substantial quality?

4. If it is to be believed to have any shape?

5. What moral virtues it has which contribute to its glory and its adornment?

6. What are its natural virtues [or powers], given to enable it to hold together the framework of the body?

7. Concerning the origin of the Soul.

8. What is its especial seat, since it appears to be in a certain sense diffused over the whole body?

9. Concerning the form and composition of the body itself.

10. Sufficient signs by which we may discern what properties the soul of sinners possess.

11. Similar signs by which we may distinguish the souls of righteous men, since we cannot see them with our bodily eyes.

---

[48] 'Cum jam suscepti operis fine gauderem, meque duodecim voluminibus jactatum quietis portus exciperet, ubi etsi non laudatus, certe liberates adveneram, amicorum me suave collegiums in salum rursus cogitationis expressit, postulans ut aliqua quae tam in libris sacris, quam in saecularibus abstruse compereram de animae substantiâ, vel de ejus virtutibus aperirem, cui datum est tam ingentium rerum secreta reserare: addens nimis ineptum esse si eam per quam plura cognoscimus, quasi a nobis alienam ignorare patiamur, dum ad anima sit utile nosse qua sapimus' (De Animâ, Praefatio).

12. Concerning the Soul's state after death, and how it will be affected by the general resurrection.

[54] "The treatise ends with a prayer to Christ to preserve the body in good health, that it may be in tune with the harmony of the soul; to give reason the ascendancy over the flesh; and to keep the mind in happy equipoise, neither so strong as to be puffed up with pride, nor so languid as to fail of its proper powers.

(Marginal Reading: "Cassiodorus retires to the cloister.")

"The line of thought indicated by the 'De Animâ' led in such a country as Italy, at such a time as the Gothic War, to one inevitable end—the cloister. It can have surprised none of the friends of Cassiodorus when the veteran statesman announced his intention of spending the remainder of his days in monastic retirement. He was now sixty years of age[49]; his wife, if he had ever married, was probably by this time dead; and we hear nothing of any children for whose sake he need have remained longer in the world. The Emperor would probably have received him gladly into his service, but Cassiodorus had now done with politics. The dream of his life had been to build up an independent Italian State, strong with the strength of the Goths, and wise with the wisdom of the Romans. That dream was now scattered to the winds. Providence had made it plain that not by this bridge was civilisation to pass over from the Old World to the New. Cassiodorus accepted the decision, and consecrated his old age to religious meditation and to a work even more important than any of his political labours (though one which must be lightly touched on here), the preservation by the pens of monastic copyists of the Christian Scriptures, and of the great works of classical antiquity...."[50]

[This concludes the remarks of Hodgkin. We now present the letters of Cassiodorus himself, taken from Hodgkin's work. All bracketed statements therein are

---

[49] Fifty-eight, if the retirement was in 538.
[50] Thomas Hodgkin, *The Letters of Cassiodorus* (London: Henry Frowde, 1886), 48-54.

Hodgkin's. At the conclusion of each of Cassiodorus' seven letters here documented, I have cited Hodgkin's work for clarity and reference.] HH

Cassiodori Variae.

[The Letters of Cassiodorus]
Book XII. Letter 20. AD 536.

"20. SENATOR, PRAETORIAN PRAEFECT, TO THOMAS AND PETER, VIRI CLARISSIMI AND ARCARII.

(Margin: "Sacred vessels mortgaged by Pope Agapetus to be restored to the stewards of the Papal See.")
"You will remember, most faithful Sirs, that when the holy Agapetus, Pope of the City of Rome, was sent as ambassador to the Sovereign of the East[51], he received so many pounds of gold from you for the expenses of the journey, for which he gave his bond[52] and deposited some of the Church plate as security.[53] The provident ruler thus lent him money in his necessity, and now, far more gloriously, returns as a free gift those pledges which the Pope might well have thanked him for taking.

"Therefore, in obedience to these instructions of ours, and fortified by the Royal order, do you return without any delay to the stewards[54] of the holy Apostle Peter the vessels of the saints together with the written obligation, that these things may be felt to be profitably restored and speedily granted, that the longed-for means of performing their world-famous ministrations may be replaced in the hands of the Levites. Let that be given back which was their own, since that is justly received back by way of largesse which the Priest had legally mortgaged.

---

[51] He was sent by Theodahad; entered Constantinople February 20, 536, and died there 21st April of the same year.
[52] 'Facto pictacio.'
[53] 'Vasa sanctorum.' One would think this must refer to the vessels used in celebrating mass; but I do not quite see how the meaning is to be got out of the words.
[54] 'Actoribus'

A Reply to the Allegations

"Herein is the great example of King Alaric surpassed. He, when glutted with the spoil of Rome, having received the vessels of the Apostle Peter from his men, when he [511] heard the story of their seizure, ordered them to be carried back across the sacred threshold, that so the remembrance of the cupidity of their capture might be effaced by the generosity of their restoration.

"But our King, with religious purpose, has restored the vessels which had become his own by the law of mortgage. In recompense for such deeds frequent prayer ought to ascend, and Heaven will surely gladly grant the required return for such good actions."

"[There are in this letter several extremely obscure sentences as to the generosity of Theodahad. As the Papal journey was undertaken by Theodahad's orders, it was a piece of meanness, quite in keeping with that King's character, to treat the advance of money for the journey as a loan, and to insist on a bond and the deposit of the Church plate as a security for repayment. Cassiodorus evidently feels this; and very probably the restoration of the vessels and the quittance of the debt had been insisted on by him. But the more he despises his master's shabbiness, the more he struggles through a maze of almost nonsensical sentences, to prove that he has committed some very glorious action in lending the money and then forgiving the debt.]"[55]

[513] "22. SENATOR, PRAETORIAN PRAEFECT, TO THE PROVINCIALS OF ISTRIA.

"[This letter was written Sept. 1, 537, probably in consequence of the scarcity which the operations of Belisarius were already causing at Ravenna. Apparently the whole taxes levied from a Province at an Indiction were divided into two heads: so much for the central authority, and so much for the Province. Cassiodorus in this and the following letter says in effect: 'All the State's share of the taxes we will take not in money, but in your staple products, corn, wine, and oil. The rest goes as usual to the Province; but owing to the scarcity at Ravenna

---

[55] Thomas Hodgkin, *The Letters of Cassiodorus* (London: Henry Frowde, 1886), 510-511.

we shall be glad to buy all that can be spared either by the authorities of the Province or by individuals, whether farmers or merchants.'"]

"The true way to prevent the requirements of the public revenue from becoming oppressive, is to order each Province to supply those products in which it is naturally most fertile.

(M: "Requisition from Province of Istria.") "Now I have learned by conversation with travelers that the Province of Istria is this year especially blessed in three of its crops-wine, oil, and corn. Therefore let her give of these products the equivalent of ... solidi, which are due from you in payment of tribute for this first Indiction:[56] while the remainder we leave to that loyal Province for her own regular expenses. But since we require a larger quantity of the above mentioned products, we send ... solidi from our state chest for the purchase of them, that these necessaries may be collected for us with as little delay as possible. Often when you are desirous to sell you cannot find a purchaser, and suffer loss accordingly. How much better is it to obey the requirements of [514] your Lords than to supply foreigners; and to pay your debts in the fruits of the soil, rather than to wait on the caprices of a buyer!

"We will ourselves out of our love of justice state a fact of which you might otherwise remind us, that we can afford to be liberal in price because we are not burdened by the payment of freights [on account of your nearness to the seat of government]. For what Campania is to Rome, Istria is to Ravenna – a fruitful Province abounding in corn, wine, and oil; so to speak, the cupboard of the capital. I might carry the comparison further, and say that Istria can show her own Baiae in the lagunes with which her shores are indented,[57] her own Averni in the pools abounding in oysters and fish. The palaces, strung like pearls along the shores of Istria, show how highly our ancestors appreciated its delights.[58]

---

[56] The first Indiction was from September 1, 537, to September 1, 538.

[57] Here follows this sentence: 'Haec loca garismatia plura nutriunt.' Garum seems to have been a sauce or something like anchovy-sauce. Garismatium is evidently a garum-supplying place.

[58] We have a special allusion in Martial (iv. 25) to the villas of Altinum, and he

The beautiful chain of islands with which it is begirt, shelter the sailor from danger and enrich the cultivator. The residence of the Court in this district delights the nobles and enriches the lower orders; and it may be said that all its products find their way to the Royal city. Now let the loyal Province, which has often tendered her services when they were less required, send forward her stores freely.

"To guard against any misunderstanding of our orders, we send Laurentius, a man of great experience, whose instructions are contained in the annexed letter.

"We will publish a tariff of moderate prices when we next address you and when we have ascertained what is the yield of the present crops; for we should be deciding quite at random before we have received that information.'"[59]

[515] "23. SENATOR, PRAETORIAN PRAEFECT, TO LAURENTIUS, VIR EXPERIENTISSIMUS.[60]

(M: "The same subject.")

"Anyone can discharge the duties of the Commissariat in a time of abundance. It is a mark of our high appreciation of your experience and efficiency, that we select you for this service in a time of scarcity. We therefore direct you to repair to the Province of Istria, there to collect stores of wine, oil, and corn, equivalent to ... solidi, due from the Province for land-tax,[61] and with ... solidi which you have received from our Treasurer to buy these products either from the merchants or from the peasants directly, according to the information prepared for you by the Cashiers.[62] Raise your spirits for this duty, and discharge it in a manner worthy of your past reputation. Make to us a faithful report of the yield of the

---

too compares them to those of Baiae.

[59] Thomas Hodgkin, *The Letters of Cassiodorus* (London: Henry Frowde, 1886), 513-514.

[60] Evidently 'the annexed letter' referred to in No. 22.

[61] 'Ut in tot solidos vini, olei, vel tritici species de tributario solido debeas procurare.'

[62] 'Sicut te a Numerariis instruxit porrecta Notitia.' Note this use of the word 'Notitia', as illustrating the title of the celebrated document bearing that name.

coming harvest, under these three heads,[63] that we may fix a tariff of prices which shall be neither burdensome to the Provincials nor injurious to the public service.'"[64]

"24. SENATOR, PRAETORIAN PRAEFECT, TO THE TRIBUNES OF THE MARITIME POPULATION.[65]

(M: "First historical notice of Venice.")

"We have previously given orders that Istria should send wine and oil, of which there are abundant crops [516] this year, to the Royal residence at Ravenna. Do you, who possess numerous ships on the borders of the Province, show the same devotion in forwarding the stores which they do in supplying them.

"Be therefore active in fulfilling this commission in your own neighbourhood, you who often cross boundless distances. It may be said that [in visiting Ravenna] you are going through your own guest-chambers, you who in your voyages traverse your own home.[66] This is also added to your other advantages, that to you another route is open, marked by perpetual safety and tranquility. For when by raging winds the sea is closed, a way is opened to you through the most charming river

---

[63] Corn, wine, and oil.
[64] Thomas Hodgkin, *The Letters of Cassiodorus* (London: Henry Frowde, 1886), 515.
[65] Written shortly after Sept. 1, 537. This is the celebrated letter to which Venetian historians point as evidence of the existence of their city (or at least of the group of settlements out of which their city sprang) in the Sixth Century. We may set side by side with it the words of the Anonymous Geographer of Ravenna (in the Seventh Century), 'In patria vero Venetiae sunt aliquantae insulae, quae hominibus habitantur.'

The address, *Tribunis Maritimorum*, looks as if there were something like a municipal government established in these islands. Tribunus was at this time generally, but not exclusively, a military title. Compare the Tribunus Fori Suarii and Tribunus Rerum Nitentium of the Notitia (Occidens iv. 10 and iv. 17). But there can be no doubt. From the tone of this letter, that the islanders were subjects of the Ostrogothic King.

[66] An obscure sentence: 'Per hospitia quodammodo vestra discurritis qui per patriam navigates.' The idea seems to be: 'You have to sail about from one room to another of your own house, and therefore Ravenna will seem like a neighbouring inn.'

scenery.⁶⁷ Your keels fear no rough blasts; they touch the earth with the greatest pleasure, and cannot perish however frequently they may come in contact with it. Beholders from a distance, not seeing the channel of the stream, might fancy them moving through the meadows. Cables have been used to keep them at rest: now drawn by ropes they move, and by a changed order of things men help their ships with their feet. They draw their drawers without labour, and instead of the capricious favour of sails they use the more satisfactory steps of the sailor.

"It is a pleasure to recall the situation of your dwellings as I myself have seen them, Venetia the praiseworthy,⁶⁸ formerly full of the dwellings of the nobility, [517] touches on the south Ravenna and the Po, while on the east it enjoys the delightsomeness of the Ionian shore, where the alternating tide now discovers and now conceals the face of the fields by the ebb and flow of its inundation. Here after the manner of water-fowl have you fixed your home. He who was just now on the mainland finds himself on an island, so that you might fancy yourself in the Cyclades,⁶⁹ from the sudden alterations in the appearance of the shore.

"Like them⁷⁰ there are seen amid the wide expanse of the waters your scattered homes, not the product of Nature, but cemented by the care of man into a firm foundation⁷¹. For by a twisted and knotted osier-work the earth there collected is turned into a solid mass, and you oppose without fear to the waves of the sea so fragile a bulwark, since forsooth the mass of waters is unable to sweep away the shallow shore, the deficiency in depth depriving the waves of the necessary power.

---

⁶⁷ The next four sentences describe the movement of the ships when towed along the channels of the streams (Brenta, Piave, Tagliamento, & etc.) the deposits from which have made the lagunes.

⁶⁸ 'Venetiae praedicabiles.' An allusion, no doubt, as other commentators have suggested, to the reputed derivation of Venetia from *Alveroi*, 'the laudable.'

⁶⁹ Alluding probably to the story of the floating island of Delos.

⁷⁰ 'Earum similitudine.' Does Cassiodorus mean 'like the water-fowl,' or 'like the Cyclades?'

⁷¹ The reading of Nivellius (followed by Migne), 'Domicilia videntur sparsa, quae Natura non protulit sed hominum cura fundavit,' seems to give a better sense than that of Garet, who omits the 'non'.

"The inhabitants have one notion of plenty, that of gorging themselves with fish. Poverty therefore may associate itself with wealth on equal terms. One kind of food refreshes all; the same sort of dwelling shelters all; no one can envy his neighbour's home; and living in this moderate style they escape that vice [of envy] to which all the rest of the world is liable.

"Your whole attention is concentrated on your salt-works. Instead of driving the plough or wielding the sickle, you roll your cylinders. Thence arises your whole crop, when you find in them that product which you have not manufactured.[72] There it may be said is your [518] subsistence-money coined.[73] Of this art of yours every wave is a bondservant. In the quest for gold a man may be lukewarm: but salt every one desires to find; and deservedly so, since to it every kind of meat owes its savour.

"Therefore let your ships, which you have tethered, like so many beasts of burden, to your walls, be repaired with diligent care: so that when the most experienced Laurentius attempts to bring you his instructions, you may hasten forth to greet him. Do not by any hindrance on your part delay necessary purchases which he has to make; since you, on account of the character of your winds, are able to choose the shortest sea-track.'"[74, 75]

"25. SENATOR, PRAETORIAN PRAEFECT, TO HIS DEPUTY[76] AMBROSIUS, AN ILLUSTRIS.

[This letter appears to have been written in the early autumn of 538, about a year after the three last letters, and also after Letters 27 and 28, which precede it in order of date, though they follow it in this collection. For an account of the terrible famine in Italy, the beginning

---

[72] 'Inde vobis fructus omnis enascitur, quando in ipsis, et quae non facitis possidetis.'

[73] 'Moneta illic quodammodo percutitur victualis.' Some have supposed that these words point to a currency in salt; but I think they are only a Cassiodorian way of saying 'By this craft ye have your wealth.'

[74] This is the only translation I can suggest of 'quatenus expensas necessarias nulla difficultate tardetis, qui pro qualitate aeris compendium vobis eligere potestis itineris.'

[75] Thomas Hodgkin, *The Letters of Cassiodorus*, 515-518.

[76] 'Agenti vices.' See note on xi. 4.

of which is here described, see Procopius, De Bello Gotthico ii. 20.]

(M: "Famine in Italy.")
"Since the world is not governed by chance, but by a Divine Ruler who does not chance His purposes at random, men are alarmed, and naturally alarmed, at the extraordinary signs in the Heavens, and ask with anxious hearts what events these may portend. The Sun, first of stars, seems to have lost his wonted light, and appears of a bluish colour. We marvel to see no shadows of our [519] bodies at noon, to feel the mighty vigour of his heat wasted into feebleness, and the phenomena which accompany a transitory eclipse prolonged through a whole year.

"The Moon too, even when her orb is full, is empty of her natural splendor. Strange has been the course of the year thus far. We have had a winter without storms, a spring without mildness, and a summer without heat. Whence can we look for harvest, since the months which should have been maturing the corn have been chilled by Boreas? How can the blade open if rain, the mother of all fertility, is denied to it? These two influences, prolonged frost and unseasonable drought, must be adverse to all things that grow. The seasons seem to be all jumbled up together, and the fruits, which were wont to be formed by gentle showers, cannot be looked for from the parched earth. But as last year was one that boasted of an exceptionally abundant harvest, you are to collect all of its fruits that you can, and store them up for the coming months of scarcity, for which it is well able to provide. And that you may not be too much distressed by the signs in the Heavens of which I have spoken, return to the consideration of Nature, and apprehend the reason of that which makes the vulgar gape with wonder.

"The middle air is thickened by the rigour of snow and rarefied by the beams of the Sun. This is the great Inane, roaming between the Heavens and the earth. When it happens to be pure and lighted up by the rays of the sun it opens out its true aspect;[77] but when alien elements are blended with it, it is stretched like a hide

---
[77] 'Vestros (?) veraciter pandit aspectus.'

across the sky, and suffers neither the true colours of the Heavenly bodies to appear nor their proper warmth to penetrate. This often happens in cloudy weather for a time; it is only its extraordinary prolongation which has produced these disastrous effects, [520] causing the reaper to fear a new frost in harvest, making the apples to harden when they should grow ripe, souring the old age of the grape-cluster.

"All this, however, though it would be wrong to construe it as an omen of Divine wrath, cannot but have an injurious effect on the fruits of the earth. Let it be your care to see that the scarcity of this one year does not bring ruin on us all. Even thus was it ordained by the first occupant of our present dignity,[78] that the preceding plenty should avail to mitigate the present penury.'"[79]

[521] "27. SENATOR, PRAETORIAN PRAEFECT, TO DATIUS[80], BISHOP OF MILAN.

(M: "Relief of famine-stricken citizens of Ticinum and Dertona.")

"It is most fitting that good and holy men should be made the stewards of the Royal bounty. We therefore request your Holiness, in accordance with the King's commands, to open the granaries at Ticinum,[81] and Dertona,[82] and sell millet thereat to the starving people at the rate of 20 modii per solidum.[83] We are anxious that you should do this, lest the work should fall into venal hands which would sell the King's bounty to those who are able to provide for themselves. It is the poor, not the rich, that we wish to help: we would pour our

---

[78] Joseph, Praetorian Praefect of Egypt under Pharaoh.

[79] Thomas Hodgkin, *The Letters of Cassiodorus*, 518-520.

[80] Cassiodorus, like Procopius, spells this name with a 't'. Some of the ecclesiastical writers spell it with a 'c'.

[81] Pavia.

[82] Tortona.

[83] Twelve shillings for twenty pecks, or about nineteen shillings and twopence a quarter; not a very low price, one would think, for such a grain as millet.

Datius is ordered to sell *tertiam portionem* of this millet. Probably this expression has the same meaning as the 'tertia illatio' of xi. 37.

In the similar letter, x. 27, 'tertia portio' (whether of wheat or millet is not stated) is to be sold at 25 modii per solidum.

bounty into empty vessels. Let not then your Holiness think this work of compassion unworthy of your sacred office. In order to assist you we have sent A and B, who will simply obey the orders of your Holiness, doing nothing of their own motion.

"Send us an account of the solidi received in payment for the said millet, that they may be stored up with our Treasurer[84], in order to replace the before-mentioned grain, and thus provide a reserve for future times of scarcity; like a garment taken to pieces that it may be made up again as good as new.

[522] "[It is not very easy to assign a date to this letter. The mention of the famine would incline us to assign it to 538, as that seems to have been the year when the full force of the famine was felt in Italy (see Procopius, De Bello Gotthico ii. 20, where 538 and 539 seem to be marked as the two great famine years). But very early in 538 the Bishop of Milan, the same Datius to whom this letter is addressed, visited Rome to entreat Belisarius to send a small garrison to occupy Milan, which had already revolted, or was on the verge of revolting, from the Gothic King. As soon as the siege of Rome was raised, Belisarius compiled with this request, and sent 1,000 men, under Mundilas, to escort Datius back to Milan. This expedition set forth probably in April 538, and as soon as it arrived at Milan, that city openly proclaimed its defection from Witigis and its allegiance to the Emperor. It was soon besieged by Uraias, nephew of Witigis, by whom in the following year (539) it was taken. The city, we are informed, was rased [sic] to the ground, and Bishop Datius escaped to Constantinople. Evidently we have here a continuous chain of events, which makes it impossible for us to date this letter in 538 or any subsequent year.

["We ought probably therefore to assign it to the autumn of 537, and to look upon it as an attempt (unsuccessful, as it proved) to retain Datius and the citizens of Milan on the side of the Goths. We know from the Twenty-second Letter of this book that signs of scarcity had already shown themselves in Italy by the 1st September, 537; and in an interesting passage of the

---

[84] 'Arcarius'

'Historia Miscella' (Book xvi.), famine in Liguria, the year 537, and the name of Datius are all combined. 'Praeter belli instantiam angebatur insuper Roma famis penuriâ: tanta siquidem per universum mundum eo anno [the year of the siege of Rome], *maxime apud Liguriam* fames excreverat, ut *sicut vir sanctissimus Datius Mediolanensis* [523] *antistes retulit*, pleraeque matres infelicium natorum membra comederent.' I owe this reference to Baronius."][85]

"28. AN EDICT [ADDRESSED TO THE LIGURIANS].

(M: "Relief of inhabitants of Liguria.")

"Divine Providence uses adversity as a means of testing our characters. Famine has afflicted the Provinces, but the result of it has been that they have proved more fully than before the bounty of their King. Rejoice herein, oh ye Ligurians! For when, as you will remember, on a previous occasion the savage temper of your neighbours was aroused, and Aemilia and your Liguria were shaken by an incursion of the Burgundians, who waged a sneaking campaign by reason of their nearness to your territory, suddenly the renown of the insulted Empire[86] arose like the sin in his strength. The enemy mourned the ruin which was caused by his own presumption, when he learned that that man was Ruler of the Gothic race whose rare valour he had experienced when he was still a private soldier.[87] How often did the Burgundian wish that he had never left his own frontiers to be compelled to fight with such an adversary as our Sovereign; for though he found with relief that he escaped his actual presence in the field, none the less did his rashness

---

[85] Thomas Hodgkin, *The Letters of Cassiodorus* (London: Henry Frowde, 1886), 521-523.

[86] Literally, 'of the present Empire:' 'subito praesentis Imperii tanquam solis ortus fama radiavit.' I avoid the word 'present', because of its ambiguity. Observe the use of 'Imperii' applied to the Gothic Kingdom.

[87] 'Quando illum cognovits nominatae (?) gentis esse Rectorem, quem sub militis nomine probaverat esse singularem.' This evident allusion to Witigis obliges us to place the date of this Burgundian invasion not much earlier than the summer of 536, when Witigis was raised to the throne. Apparently the Burgundians were already in Italy when they heard the news of that event.

bring him in contact with the good fortune of his arms. For when with redoubled [524] fortitude[88] the Goths turned to the prosecution of the war, with such successfully combined operations did they strike the bands of the rebels, that you would have thought those were all armed men, there were all defenceless[89]. Such was the just judgment of God, that the robber should perish in those very plains which he had presumed to desolate. Exult now, oh Province, adorned with the carcases of thine adversaries! rejoice, oh Liguria, at the heap of dead bodies! If the harvest of corn is denied thee, the harvest of dead enemies shall not be wanting. Tribute thou mayest not be able to offer to thy King, but the triumphs which are won in thy land thou canst offer with pride.

"[90]To these triumphs must be added the lately foiled plunder-raid of the Alamanni, so checked in its very first attempts that their entrance and exit were almost one event, like a wound well and opportunely cauterised. Thus were the excesses of the presumptuous invader punished, and the subjects of our King were saved from absolute ruin. I might indeed enumerate to you what crowds of the enemy fell in other places, but I turn rather-such is human nature-to more joyful themes, and revert to the point with which I at first commenced, namely that the Sovereign who has saved you from the hostile sword is determined now to avert from your Province the perils of famine.

"In this new war the citadels are well-stored granaries; Starvation is the dreaded foe: if they are closed she [525] enters; by opening them wide she is put to flight. I know not what the world in general may think of the relative merit of these two campaigns of our King. For my part, though I recognise it as the mark of a brave man

---

[88] 'Ut Gothi ad belli stadium geminâ se fortitudine contulerunt.' These words perhaps allude to the necessity of fighting two enemies at once, Belisarius and the Burgundians; or perhaps to the existence of two Gothic armies, whose combined operations are indicated by the following words, 'prospera concertatione.'

[89] 'Quasi inde nudos hinc stare contigisset armatos.' 'Hinc' and 'inde' refer to geographical position, not to the order of the words in the sentence.

[90] See von Schubert's 'Unterwerfung der Alamannen,' pp. 57-59, for a careful analysis of the following paragraph.

to have fought a winning battle, I think it is something above mere human valour to have conquered penury.

"In addition to these benefits the King has remitted one-half of the taxes of the Province, that he might not sadden with the one hand those whom he was gladdening with the other. Herein he compares favourably with Joseph, who sold corn to the Egyptians, but on such terms that they lost their personal freedom. Doubtless that holy man was placed in a dilemma between the necessity of satisfying a covetous King on the one hand, and that of rescuing a starving people on the other. Still I must think that the Egyptian, whose life was preserved, groaned over the loss of his liberty; and if I may say so, with all respect to so great a patriarch,[91] far nobler is it to sell corn to freemen who remain freemen, and to lighten their taxes on account of poverty. This is really a gratuitous distribution, when both the money with which to buy is handed over to you [by the abatement of tribute], and a price is fixed on purpose to please you.

"The generosity of the State therefore will sell 25 modii, when the peasant has lost his crops, at the price at which 10 are usually sold.[92] Humanity has altered the usual course of affairs, and by a strange kind of chaffering, but one which truly becomes a King, just when the famished peasant is willing to offer us an [526] enhanced price for food, we are directed to offer it to him for a smaller one.

"The King himself had seen your calamity, and thereupon bestowed on you previously one favour. Now, on hearing of its continuance, he adds to it a second. Happy calamity, which forced itself on the notice of such an eye-witness!

"Now, oh Ligurian, rejoice in the good fortune which has come to thee. Compare thy lot with the Egyptian's

---

[91] 'Pace tanti patris dixerim.'

[92] Probably one solidus: making the largesse price 15s. 4d. a quarter (about four shillings less than the price named in the preceding letter for millet); while the market price was 38s. 4d. a quarter. I read these sentences thus: 'Vendit itaque largitas publica vicenos quinque modios, dum possessor invenire non posit, ad denos. Ordinem rerum saeculi mutavit humanitas.' The construction is harsh and elliptical, but this makes sense, which the ordinary punctuation, throwing 'ad denos' into the following sentence, does not.

and be happy. He was fed, but lost his freedom; thou art fed, and at the same time defended from thy enemies. Joseph gave back the purchase-money to his brethren in their sacks, showing a greater kindness to his kindred than to his subjects. Our King shows no such partiality, but bestows on all the taxpayers larger benefits than he did on his brethren. Happy age! in which Kings may be likened, not to Kings, but to Prophets, and yet bear away the palm.

"But that we may not longer detain you from the desired enjoyment of the Royal benefits, know that our commands have been given to those whose business it is to attend to this affair, that, according to the tenour of this edict, the generosity of the Sovereign may penetrate into your homes."

["The same considerations which were applied to the date of the preceding letter seem to require that this also be dated in 537. After the raising of the siege of Rome (March, 538), by the despatch of Imperial troops into Liguria, and the enthusiastic adherence of that Province to the Imperial cause, a new state of things was established, and one to which the language of this letter would have been utterly inapplicable.

["There are two events of which we have no other knowledge than that furnished by this letter: the invasion of the Burgundians, and the ravages of the Alamanni in the Province of Liguria.

["(1) The invasion of the Burgundians seems, as stated [527] in a previous note, to have occurred in the spring or early summer of 536; so that Cassiodorus could represent the invaders as surprised and disheartened by learning of the elevation of Witigis. It no doubt formed part of those hostile operations of the Frankish Kings described by Procopius (De Bello Gotthico i. 13), the termination of which was purchased by Witigis by the cession of Provence and the payment of a subsidy. It is interesting to observe, however, that the Burgundians, notwithstanding their subjugation in 534, and their incorporation in the Frankish monarchy, are still spoken of as conducting an invasion on their own account. This is just like the invasion of Italy in 553 by the Alamannic brethren, and is quite in keeping with the loosely compacted character of the Merovingian monarchy, in which it was copied by the Anglian and Saxon Kingdoms.

["(2) For the ravages of the Alamanni consult, as before stated, von Schubert's monograph. This passage quite confirms his view of the events connected with the overthrow of the Alamannic Kingdom by Clovis. A remnant of the people, settled as refugees in Raetia under Theodoric's protection, now, in the decline of the Ostrogothic monarchy throw off their allegiance to his successors, and press forward over the Alps to share the spoil of Italy. Witigis, however, notwithstanding his struggle with Belisarius, is still able promptly to repel this incursion; but it co-operates with the Burgundian invasion and the inclement spring and summer of 537 to bring about the famine in Liguria in the autumn of that year."][93]

The End.

[In this same section we have called number **(02)**, we will address just one more issue before we move into number **(03)**:

(Regarding the Visigoths, Heiks believes they were the first of three horns to be plucked up by the roots when Clovis defeated the Visigoths at the Battle of Vouille in 507 AD (He also claimed the latest academic scholarship supported the 508 AD date.);[94] however, since his book was published, more recent scholarship has upheld 507 AD,[95] scholarship that actually comes to us from one of Heiks' highly touted sources."[96]) NL

[The source you mention I have not read, at this point, but I do know that the deadly wound of the papacy took place in 1798. That is indisputable and according to

---

[93] Thomas Hodgkin, *The Letters of Cassiodorus* (London: Henry Frowde, 1886), 523-527.
[94] Heidi Heiks, AD 508 Source Book, 40.
[95] Ralph W. Mathisen & Danuta Shanzer, eds., *The Battle of Vouillé, 507 CE: Where France Began* (Boston/Berlin: Walter de Gruyter, 2012).
[96] Heidi Heiks, *AD 508 Source Book,* xvii-xviii.

the Scriptures. Twelve hundred ninety years from 1798 brings one to 508, not 507, according to the Scriptures. I welcome anyone to take the specifications from the Scriptures to try to prove that the deadly wound did not take place in 1798. I am curious, though. Have the authors of that source you mention addressed the following primary documents by Cassiodorus: one dated June 24, 508—found in my AD 508 Source Book, chapter 2—and another on page 79? After all, the reports received by Cassiodorus were not just eyewitness "journalistic" accounts, but were from those literally involved, informing us of the ongoing war. Please explain.] HH

[*See Chapter 2 for the reply to the above, since it was not sent to NL when I replied to his **(20)** questions because I did not have that book at that time.*] HH

(03).

"'We shall exert Ourselves in every way' is legally confirmed by the legislative support from the state that the church canons received. Codex I.3.44 of Justinian's law codes, for example, was implemented on October 18, A.D. 530, thereby giving total authority to the canons of the synods." 2:280-1.

"Whatever the holy canons prohibit, these also by our own laws forbid."

"This codex alone was sufficient to elevate the laws of the church to equality with the laws of the state. Having been accorded this political backing, church canons had to be obeyed by all." 2:180-1.

(Not just any church canons, but the ones contained within the body of canon law at the time. Those were the laws of the church that Justinian elevated to the level of the state, and to which he gave total authority. Regarding the excerpt shown above, the emperor was referring to Canon 26 of the Holy Apostles that had become Canon 14 of the Council of Chalcedon.[97] It was an edict stipulating

---

[97] Andre J. Queen, *Old Catholic: History, Ministry, Faith & Mission* 172: "As to bachelors who have entered the clergy, we allow only anagnosts (Readers)

that only readers and chanters among the single clergy were allowed to marry.

(Heiks seems to be suggesting *(and you have confirmed in your own writings)*[98] that *"whatever the holy canons prohibit"* extended to any subsequent church canon when he said *"church canons had to be obeyed by all,"* but that couldn't possibly have been Justinian's meaning, especially since the emperor would never grant local councils the power to enact canons that might supercede or nullify his own legislation. This can be illustrated by looking at the third Council of Orleans; it produced a canon in 538AD forbidding Sunday rural labor within the Frankish domain. Heiks refers to this canon several times in his <u>A.D. 538 Source Book</u> (pgs.269-271*)*, but the canon would have directly contradicted Constantine's 321AD edict protecting Sunday rural labor.[99] Justinian had already incorporated Constantine's edict into his Code by the time Orleans III convened, and Heiks confirmed that Justinian's legislation was *"never altered or retracted in any way from 534 to the end of Justinian's reign in 565."*[100] In fact, Constantine's protection of Sunday rural labor was upheld in the Eastern Empire until the 10th Century when Emperor Leo VI repealed it.[101] So although the prohibitions of Orleans III may have been binding within the Frankish kingdom, Justinian did not give total authority to the church canons of just any synod.

(Ironically, my understanding on this issue appears to coincide with Le Roy Froom, of all people. His commentary on Novel 131 recognized that Justinian *"meant to enforce the canons of all the councils in the ancient collection as current in his day,* <u>up to and including Chalcedon.</u>*"* [102] Froom's view was that, through Novel 131, *"Justinian also*

---

and psalts (Chanters) to marry, if they wish to do so." (Canon XXVI of the Holy Apostles, Canon XIV of the Council of Chalcedon)

[98] Marcos S., article *Historicism & the 1260 Year Interpretation of Protestantism*, 10: "From October 18, A.D. 530, onward, whenever the church passed any canon law in one of its synods, it was IMMEDIATELY supported and enforced by the civil authorities, according to the edicts of Justinian's law codes in the Corpus Juris Civilis."

[99] Scott, S. P., trans., ed., *The Civil Law* [of Justinian], Book 3.12.3.

[100] Heidi Heiks, *AD 538 Source Book*, 178.

[101] Scott, S. P., trans., ed., *The Civil Law* [of Leo], Constitution 54.

[102] LeRoy Froom, *Prophetic Faith of Our Fathers*, Vol. I, 934-935.

A Reply to the Allegations

incorporated into the imperial Civil Law the body of canon law recognized in the church."[103] Froom did not connect this elevation of church law to the 530AD codex, and if the emperor's desire to forbid whatever the holy canons forbade had been satisfied by his 530AD law, then their elevation in Novel 131 was redundant and unnecessary.) NL

[Quoting NL: "Not just any church canons, but the ones contained within the body of canon law at the time." That is exactly right, and my entire book was about how the legislative branch of the church and the legal aspirations of the state (the "setting up" of this diverse kingdom) were progressing steadily from AD 508 to 538 in *all* the provinces she had conquered in her thirty-year crusade. Having documented the union of the church with the state's legislative branch in the West, with such a union already in place in the East, as well, there was and is nothing else that needs to be said. Your comment about Novel 131 being "redundant and unnecessary" was unwarranted, because in Justinian's *Corpus Juris*, Justinian was redundant in numerous other places. On a side issue:

["The emperor would never grant local councils the power to enact canons that might supersede or nullify his own legislation." While this is not even the subject matter, I will comment on that statement. Of course he wouldn't grant that. Any historian who reads anything about Justinian knows that no-one would be permitted to supersede Justinian, including the pope. History itself attests with this example:

> "**A.D. 528** The Decree that laid the Foundation for the Political Power of the Papacy as described by Gregorovius:
> "As Arians remained outside the Roman Church, it came to pass that the Pope, as head of Catholic Christendom, felt himself raised above the heretical kings, and thus, standing between them and the orthodox Emperor (*whom they recognized at the same time as their Imperial overlord*), he gradually became a man of importance, and finally acquired a greater degree of

---
[103] Ibid..

influence in the internal affairs of the city...." 2:176-177 (Emphasis mine.) HH]

(04).

"This serves as the only explanation as to why the papacy claims that Justinian's *Corpus Juris Civilis* is the basis of all Roman Catholic canon law." 2:195.

(Here is more of what the same *Catholic Encyclopedia* had to say about canon law in relation to civil law:

(Law entry, subsection "Sources of Canon Law")
("The sources or authors of this positive ecclesiastical law are essentially the episcopate and its head, the <u>pope</u>, the successors of the Apostolic College and its divinely appointed head, Saint Peter. <u>They are, properly speaking, the active sources of canon law.</u> *Their activity is exercised in its most solemn form by the ecumenical councils, where* <u>the episcopate united with its head, and convoked and presided over by him, with him defines its teaching and makes the</u> *laws* <u>that bind the whole Church.</u>"[104]

(And...

("The civil law of different nations, and especially the Roman law, may be numbered among the accessory sources of canon law. But it is necessary to explain more exactly its role and importance. Evidently secular law cannot be, strictly speaking, a source of canon law, the State as such having no competence in spiritual matters; yet it may become so by the more or less formal acceptation of particular laws by the ecclesiastical authorities. We pass by in the first place the laws made by the mutual agreement of both parties, such as the legislation of the numerous assemblies in the Visigothic kingdom, and the Frankish kingdom and empire, where the bishops sat with the lords and nobles. Such also is the case of the concordats of later ages, real contracts between the two powers. In these cases we have an ecclesiastico-civil law, the legal force of which arose from the joint action of the

---
[104] Charles Herbermann, *The Catholic Encyclopedia*, Vol. 9, 59.

two competent authorities. It is in a different sense that Roman law, Germanic law, and in a lesser degree modern law, have become *a subsidiary source of canon law.*"¹⁰⁵

(So it seems that the episcopate are considered the *"active sources"* of canon law, whereas Justinian's Code, Germanic law, etc., are considered *"accessory sources."* Canon law borrowed the *"structure, general concepts and detailed rules"*¹⁰⁶ of various civil codes, with Justinian's being chief among them. That was the sense in which Charles Herbermann *(not "the papacy")* said, *"Justinian's Corpus is the basis for canon law."* It wasn't because Justinian's Code elevated the *"laws of the church to equality with the laws of the state."* The same entry informs us how the pre-Constantine church formed a *"nucleus of local canon law"* based on the disciplinary decisions of various bishops, and this universally disseminated collection initially became the *"basis of general canon law."*)¹⁰⁷ NL

[Legal historians refer to Justinian as "the Father of Jurisprudence," and for good reason:

"The activity in the realm of public law earned the emperor the title "Father of Jurisprudence."'¹⁰⁸

[Why did Justinian receive this title?

"This *Corpus* became the definitive form of Roman law for the empire, and soon for the barbarian West, as well."¹⁰⁹

"...It is this Justinian legislation which dominated all the middle ages and supplied modern Europe with the basis of law."¹¹⁰

---
¹⁰⁵ Ibid
¹⁰⁶ George Mousourakis, *The Historical and Institutional Context of Roman Law* 430.
¹⁰⁷ Charles Herbermann, *The Catholic Encyclopedia*, Volume 9, 60, "Law" entry.
¹⁰⁸ Knecht, August. *Die Religions-Politik: Kaiser Justinians I: Eine kirchengeschichtliche Studie*. (Dissert. Würzberg, 1896), 11. [Andreas Gobel, *The Religious Politics of Emperor Justinian I*, Wurzburg, 1896.]
¹⁰⁹ Warren Treadgold, *A History of the Byzantine State and Society* (Stanford: Stanford University Press, 1997), 185. [See 2:173.]
¹¹⁰ Ibid, 24. [See 2:174.]

[We rightly understood the *prophetic implications* of Justinian's *Corpus*. It provided the foundational blueprint for the little horn during its "setting-up" period and guided it throughout the Dark Ages, as well. It will soon be copied as the heroine model, in *principle*. Its principles will be utilized once more for the "setting-up" of the image to the beast of Revelation 13 and for the resurrection of the "Mother of Harlots" of Revelation 17. Rome will be permitted to carry out her last crusade against Heaven during the closing scenes of earth's history, before her eternal demise in the seven last plagues.] HH

(05).

"Procopius dates the beginning of the siege of Rome to February 21, 537. Procopius, *History of the Wars*. Translated by H. B. Dewing. Bks. 1–8. In Loeb Classical Library, edited by Jeffrey Henderson. Cambridge, MA: Harvard Univ. Press, 2000–2001, V. xvii. 12-14. And Procopius concludes the siege of Rome on March 1, 538: 'Now it was about spring equinox, one year had been spent in the siege and nine days in addition, when the Goths, having burned all their camps, set out at daybreak. And the Romans, seeing their opponents in flight, were at a loss how to deal with the situation.' Ibid, VI. x. 13-14. 2:141, Footnote 202."

(Procopius did not make any mention of the February date; he reported that the siege of Rome began on the first day of March. Here's what he said:

"In Rome, moreover, some of the patricians brought out the Sibylline oracles, declaring that the danger which had come to the city would continue only up till the month of July. For it was fated that at that time someone should be appointed king over the Romans, and thenceforth Rome should have no longer any Getic peril to fear; for they say that the Goths are of the Getic race. And the oracle was as follows:'In the fifth (Quintilis) month ... under... as king nothing Getic longer....' And they declared that the 'fifth month' was July, some because the

siege began on the first day of March, from which July is the fifth month, others because March was considered the first month until the reign of Numa, the full year before that time containing ten months and our July for this reason having its name Quintilis."[111]

(If the siege began on March 1, 537AD, a year and nine days would take us to the end of the siege on March 10, 538AD, a date that is reasonably close to the spring equinox according to the Julian calendar (*March 25, I believe*). Now Dewing's translation of Book 5 certainly mentions February 21, but it was Dewing or an editor who put the date in a sidebar, presumably because the *Liber Pontificalis* used it.[112] However, Procopius did not; he pointed us to March 1, 537AD. It's a little confusing to read Heiks support the February 21 date while on the same page he quoted Charles Diehl confirming that Vitiges went to Rome in March: *"Vainly, Vitiges, with 150,000 men, went to lay siege to Rome (March 537)."*

(So between Procopius and the *Liber Pontificalis*, which date is correct? Unfortunately, we may never know for certain. But from my point of view, it just seems reasonable that if the siege really had concluded on the Kalends of March, then Procopius would have said so, instead of vaguely referring to the day as *"it was about spring equinox...."*) NL

[Yes, NL is correct that there are two dates given *for* and *from* the two primary sources for the commencement of the battle of Rome against the Ostrogoths, but both dates terminated, as correctly stated by NL, in March of AD 538. However, I mistakenly placed the February 21, 537, date[113] under the authorship of Procopius instead of the translator Dewing, as NL noted. Because of the dating discrepancy and because I could not find any

---

[111] Procopius, *History of the Wars*, Book V, Ch. XXIV. [For the precise page reference see: Procopius. *History of the Wars*. Translated by H. B. Dewing. Bks. 1–8. In Loeb Classical Library, edited by Jeffrey Henderson. Cambridge, MA: Harvard Univ. Press, 2000–2001, V. xxiv 25-31.]

[112] Louise Ropes Loomis, trans., *The Liber Pontificalis*, Vol. I, 148.

[113] Procopius, *History of the Wars*, V, xvii, 12-18. [See sidebar in the original.]

documentation to definitively confirm one date over the other, I had no ethical choice as an author but to submit both dates to the reader. Nevertheless, I see I should have explained the primary sources of Procopius further.[114] It's rather a unanimous agreement among historians, NL and myself that the spring equinox, according to the Julian calendar, fell on March 25th in AD 538. Also, I take no issue with NL reasoning for the termination date of March 10, 538, over March 1, 538. Nevertheless, we do agree that the battle ended in March of AD 538. Below, the reader will find the complete listing of the other source mentioned by the *Liber Pontificalis*. In this way the reader now has in his possession the two primary sources that give us this historical account:

> [147] "Then he heard that the Goths had chosen them a king contrary to the will of Lord Justinian Augustus and he marched into Campania toward the city of Naples and began to besiege the city with his army, because the citizens of Naples refused to open to him.[115] At that time the patrician fought against the city and entered it; and in his fury he slew both the Goths and all the inhabitants of Naples and sacked it and spared not even the churches from the sack. He killed husbands with the sword in the presence of their wives and he put to death the captive sons and wives of the nobles; he spared none, neither priests nor servants of God nor consecrated virgins.[116]
>
> "Then there was a terrible war, for Witiges marched against the patrician Vilisarius and against the city of

---

[114] "Now it was about the spring equinox, and one year had been spent in the siege and nine days in addition, when the Goths, having burned all their camps, set out at daybreak. And the Romans, seeing their opponent in flight, were at a loss how to deal with the situation." Ibid. VI. x. 8-14.

[115] The order of events here is uncertain. Procopius and the continuator of the *Chronicle of Marcellinus* describe the siege of Naples before the accession of Vitiges. Jordanes does the same in the *Romana* but in *Getica* he keeps the order of the *Lib. Pont.* Duchesne, *op. cit.*, p. 293, n. 5.

[116] Procopius says that the Massagetæ, who fought in the army of Belisarius, were chiefly guilty of the loot and sacrilege, that they cut down even the inhabitants who fled the churches for shelter and that Belisarius went up and down the city restraining them. *De Bello Gothico*, I, II; ed. Haury, vol, II, pp. 58-62.

Rome. For the patrician Vilisarius entered the city of Rome, December 10, and he surrounded the city with guards and fortifications and walls and repaired the trenches and strengthened it. The very night when the patrician Vilisarius entered, the Goths who were in the city or outside the walls fled and left all the gates open and escaped to Ravenna.[117] Then King Witiges collected a vast army of the Goths [148] and marched back against Rome, February 21, and pitched his camp by the Molbian bridge[118] and began to besiege the city of Rome. And the patrician Vilisarius, who defended the Roman name, shut himself up within the city and kept the city.

"In those days the city was besieged so that no man might go out or come in. And all the buildings, private and imperial and ecclesiastic, were consumed by fire and men died by the sword; some perished by the sword, some by famine and some by pestilence.[119] Likewise the churches and the bodies of the holy martyrs were destroyed by the Goths.[120] Within the city there was a great famine, so that water would have been sold for a price if the springs had not furnished deliverance.[121]

---

[117] Procopius says that Belisarius entered Rome by the gate called Asinaria on the same day that the Goths marched out by the Flaminian Gate. *De Bello Gothico*, I, 14; 77.

[118] The Mulvian bridge.

[119] Rome had suffered in the fifth century from barbarian invasion but without losing much of the outer semblance of her grandeur. With this terrible siege begins the real destruction of her orderliness and beauty, the transformation of the splendid capital of the ancient world into the scarred, crumbling, poverty-stricken medieval city of the popes. Lanciani, *Destruction of Ancient Rome*, 70-71, 79-87. Frothingham, *Monuments*, 76-85. Gregorovius, *History of Rome*, tr. Hamilton, vol. II, *passim*.

[120] Duchesne prints selections from inscriptions taken from martyrs' tombs and cemeteries along the Via Salaria, where the Gothic assaults were heaviest, recording the restoration of sacred monuments wrecked or damaged by the enemy. In one or two cases remains have been found both of the original epitaphs shattered by the Gothic soldiers and of the sixth century reproductions of the originals erected to fill the empty places. *Op. cit.,* 293-294, n. II.

[121] Procopius tells us that the aqueducts, which ordinarily gave the city its abundant supply of water, were cut by the invaders but that the springs within the walls together with the stream of the Tiber furnished enough for the reduced population. *De Bello Gothico*, I, 19, ed. Haury, vol. II, 96-100. Lanciani, *Destruction*

And the battles were fierce about the city. In those days the patrician Vilisarius fought against King Witiges and the host of the Goths and defended the Romans and with his army saved the city and the Roman name. Then the city and the harbor of Rome were besieged one year by the Goths.[122] But the patrician Vilisarius fought and conquered the Goths and at last, after one year, the Goths fled to Ravenna.

[149] "At that time there was a heavy famine throughout the whole world, as Datius, bishop of the city of Milan, has related fully in his report, so that in Liguria women ate their own children for hunger and want; some of them, he has said, were of the family of his own church."[123]] HH

(06).

"Yet, central to the prophecy was an issue not discussed by Diehl or other historians, though it was addressed by the ambassadors of the Ostrogoths and recorded by Procopius, the stenographer and bibliographer of Belisarius, who was present at those negotiations for peace over the battle of Rome in 538. The main

---

of Ancient Rome, 79-82.

[122] According to Procopius the siege lasted one year and nine days and ended just before the vernal equinox of 538. See Procopius' *De Bello Gothico*, II, 10, ed. Haury, vol. II, 192.

[123] Louise R. Loomis, trans., *Liber Pontificalis (The Book of the Popes)* (New York: Columbia University Press, 1916), 147-149. Procopius speaks of the desolating famine that fell upon Italy in 538 and of instances of cannibalism due to starvation. *De Bello Gothico*, II, 20, ed. Haury, vol. II, 236-239. He also says that Datius, bishop of Milan, and some of the leading citizens of the city came to Rome during that year to ask of Belisarius a small force of soldiers, with whose aid they proposed to reestablish the imperial government in the province of Liguria and to drive out the Goths. During his stay at Rome Datius may have reported on the famine in his diocese. Belisarius furnished the desired support, but in spite of it the Goths took and sacked Milan the following year. Datius escaped and fled to Constantinople, where he died in 552. The *Varia* of Cassiodorus contain a letter, written by himself as praetorian prefect to Datius between 534 and 539, regarding the opening of granaries for the relief of famine sufferers. See also Procopius' *De Bello Gothico*, II, 7; 180-185; and Hodgkin's *Letters of Cassiodorus*, 521-522.

contentious issue at hand was that of religious liberty. This is glossed over by Catholicism, historians, and the politically correct, yet it is central to the Scriptures, Ellen White, and the Ostrogoths." 2:145.

(Just based on prior research alone, I can easily count over a dozen historians—*at least one I can identify as Catholic*—who either discussed the issue of religious liberty/freedom among the Ostrogoths or openly wrote about how the Ostrogoths strengthened and protected the papacy, orthodox Christians, and Jews during their reign. The only way someone can reasonably conclude that historians *"gloss over"* Gothic support of religious liberty is if that person has a limited grasp of the subject matter—a deficiency Heidi Heiks certainly does not have.

(Now, I don't exactly see how religious liberty was the main issue in the above quote; the main issue raised by the Gothic ambassadors was the utter faithlessness of the Romans in allowing Belisarius to take the city unimpeded in 536AD.[124] The Ostrogoths felt that their staunch protection of the Roman civil and religious institutions should have earned Rome's loyalty, but they were infuriated because it had not been reciprocated. Granted, the slaughter of the Neapolitans following Belisarius' siege[125] heavily factored into the Romans' decision to admit the Byzantines into the city,[126] but regardless, the main contentious issue for the Goths was not *"Hey, we provided religious liberty for all people, so why did you betray us?!"* The issue was *"Hey, we protected the Roman bureaucracy and religion, and we had imperial sanction to rule Italy, so why did you betray us?!"*) NL

[The first chapter of my *AD 538 Source Book* presents the reason the topic of religious liberty has been introduced. While you speak the truth from your stated perspective, from my perspective I have not found any historian who references the Scriptures concerning the direct connection of the government of Heaven with

---

[124] Procopius, *History of the Wars*, Book VI, Ch. VI.
[125] Ibid., Book V, Ch. X.
[126] Ibid. Ch. XIV.

religious liberty and the Ostrogoths. Therefore, I wrote, "...It is central to the Scriptures, Ellen White, and to the Ostrogoths." 2:145. Viewed from your perspective, your argument is valid, honest and right when you said the main thrust was *"We protected the Roman bureaucracy and religion."* However, my reference point is first and foremost the Scriptures, as they alone define the issues at hand. The *Roman bureaucracy* = legislation and *religion* = religious liberty infringements was exactly the issue at hand. The issue of *religious liberty* strikes a chord, because someone with your knowledge of papal history knows full well the statements from popes and their attitude regarding the so-called "pestilential error" of religious liberty. In chapter one of my book we saw that religious liberty is nothing short of a cornerstone that upholds the government of Heaven. That cornerstone the "little horn" (papacy) would war against, as we're told in Daniel 7:25, along with the specification of a change in laws. The conflict is first and foremost vertical, and then we are able to see and understand the horizontal repercussions from history, as each member of humanity decides upon which side of the issue he or she will stand. The consequences of those decisions are eternal. It tells us if our hearts are still in rebellion against the government of God, or if they are in harmony with that government.] HH

(07).

"We have also witnessed that historians recognized that important legislation was issued about Italy in 538 which established Justinian's judicial authority in the west:

"Justinian was already speaking of Italy as entirely under his arms,[127] already he was designating a prefect from the court as governor...."[128] 2:274.

---

[127] Nov. 69, epil. (Mai 538).
[128] Charles Diehl, *Justinien et la Civilization Byzantine au VIᵉ Siècle* (Paris: Ernest Leroux, 1901), 186. Taken from Procopius, *De Bello Gothico,* ed. De la Byzantine de Bonn., 101.

(If Heiks truly believes that Justinian's judicial authority in 538AD was evidenced in part by the designation of an Italian prefect, then his belief is undermined by the simple fact that, according to Procopius, the man in question *(Fidelis)* was designated the prefect of Italy in early 537AD before the Gothic siege even began:

> "But the Romans, being overcome by a great fear, sat in silence, and, even though they were abused by the envoys at length for their treason to the Goths, dared make no reply to them, except, indeed, that Fidelis saw fit to taunt them. <u>This man was then praetorian prefect</u>, having been appointed to the office by Belisarius, and for this reason he seemed above all others to be well disposed toward the emperor."[129]

(Justinian certainly may have <u>spoken</u> of Italy as entirely under his arms by 538AD, but his words did not reflect reality, and the continuation of the war bore that truth out. Heiks' source for the above quote, Charles Diehl, recognized in another work that although Justinian's optimistic mind considered the war to be over in 540AD, "...*the issue disappointed his anticipations.*"[130] The Ostrogoths reorganized through the efforts of kings Hildibad and Totila, and under the latter, by the end of 541AD, "*the work of the imperial restoration was undone in a few months.*"[131] In Diehl's opinion, it took 20 years to put Italy entirely under Justinian's arms.[132]

(I'd also like to quickly point out that, between page 151 and the end of the chapter, the only legislation Heiks provided that mentioned Italy was Novel 69, but in no way was that piece of legislation actually <u>about</u> Italy.) NL

[First, we must recognize the fact that we do have authentic primary sources that state that there was indeed the designation of an Italian prefect to Italy in AD 538 by Justinian. Secondly, we have already proven by Hodgkin

---

[129] Procopius, *History of the Wars*, Book V, Ch. XX.
[130] Charles Diehl, Article, *The Cambridge Medieval History*, Vol. 2, 16.
[131] Ibid.
[132] Charles Diehl, *History of the Byzantine Empire*, 25.

and Mommsen that the legislative branch (the headship) of the Ostrogothic government met its demise in the year AD 538. Thirdly, the quote you provided certainly provides no substantive evidence for Procopius' designation of Fidelis as an Italian prefect to Italy in early 537AD, *before the Gothic siege had even begun*! After all, we have proof that Cassiodorus was still sending letters out of his official office throughout the entire year of AD 537.] HH

(08).

"The primary documents from Justinian himself confirm that it was not December 10, 536, (when King Vitiges abandoned Rome without a fight and Belisarius simply went in and occupied Rome) that established Justinian's judicial authority in the west. No, the deciding factor that would establish Justinian's judicial authority in the west would be the outcome of the first siege of Rome that began on February 21, 537, and ended one year and nine days later in a massive defeat of the Ostrogoths on March 1, 538. It was the outcome of that battle alone that secured for Justinian his judicial authority in the west." 2:274.

(At most it shows that Justinian was a bit premature in adding the prefecture of Italy to his legislation.

(Of course, the tragic irony here is that the Italian prefect Fidelis, the man whose elevation was supposed to be evidence of Justinian's secured judicial authority in the west, was dead at the hands of the Goths within a few weeks of the failed siege of Rome,[133] while his successor, Reparatus, shared his predecessor's fate after the Goths took Milan the following year.[134] Within a few years, Procopius admitted that Roman power in Italy, rather than being secured, was instead *"utterly destroyed within a short time."*[135] Justinian was forced to spend the next decade looking on in frustration as Italy *"fell*

---

[133] Procopius, *History of the Wars*, Book VI, Ch. XII.
[134] Ibid., Ch. XXI.
[135] Ibid., Book VII, Ch. I.

back into the hands of the barbarians,"[136] his Italian possessions reduced to just four coastal cities by the end of 549AD.[137] I think if Heiks were truly honest with himself, he would recognize that the deciding factor that secured Justinian's *"judicial authority"* in Italy was nothing less than the end of the Ostrogothic War.

(Incidentally, I am unaware of any writer who argues that Justinian established "judicial authority in the west" on December 10, 536AD, but I can't say I've read anyone who claimed it happened in 538AD, either. What is commonly understood, though, is that the city of Rome was taken and became subject to Byzantine authority on December 9 or 10, *536AD*, after sixty years of barbarian rule, and this is based primarily on the testimonies of Procopius[138] and Belisarius,[139] as well as mirrored by at least two dozen writers, including Edward Gibbon,[140] John Moorhead,[141] and Claire Sotinel.[142] *Heiks' A.D. 538 Source Book* even contains Charles Diehl's acknowledgement that Belisarius "reestablished Justinian's authority in the eternal city" on December 10, 536AD.[143]) NL

[Let's analyze the following legitimate statements:

"I think if Heiks were truly honest with himself, he would recognize that the deciding factor that secured Justinian's "judicial authority" in Italy was nothing less than the end of the Ostrogothic War. Incidentally, I am unaware of any writer who argues that Justinian established "judicial authority in the west" on December 10, 536AD, but I can't say I've read anyone who claimed it happened in 538AD, either."

---

[136] Ibid., Ch. XI.
[137] Thomas Hodgkin, *Theodoric the Goth*, 362.
[138] Procopius. *History of the Wars*, Book V, Ch. XIV.
[139] Ibid., Ch. XXIV.
[140] Edward Gibbon, *Decline and Fall of the Roman Empire* Vol. III, 61.
[141] John Moorhead, Article, *The New Cambridge Medieval History*, Vol. I, 129.
[142] Claire Sotinel, Article, *The Cambridge Companion to the Age of Justinian*, 279.
[143] Heidi Heiks, *AD 538 Source Book* 140.

[The issue (according to the Scriptures) is not about Justinian's "judicial authority" in Italy or when it was secured, but when the third and last kingdom's "judicial authority" was "up rooted" or removed before AD 539, given in its specified time and place. I admit I have spent perhaps too much time and effort on a non-essential that carries with it no scriptural support whatsoever, because there is no such specification given, other than for its historical value. However, the specifications of the Scriptures most emphatically predict that between the years AD 508 and 538, the legislative branches of government of three kingdoms would terminate, with the aid of the little horn, no later than by the end of AD 538. And for that, we have previously detailed an impeccable interpretation for the fulfillment of the Scriptures in (02) and we need not go any further.] HH

(09).

"Novel 69, issued June 1, 538, confirms that this was the first time in 62 years that a Catholic Emperor had held legal jurisdiction in Italy." 2:274-275.

(Why does that novel confirm this? Like I mentioned in the previous paragraph, Procopius tells us that Rome became subject to the Romans in December 536AD after a 60-year absence (*a reunion Diehl recognized had "reestablished Justinian's authority" in the city*), an Italian prefect was designated by early 537AD, and, according to John Moorhead, a *comes sancti patrimonii per Italian (a financial official)* was operating in the conquered regions of Italy by the end of 537AD.[144] Justinian's legal jurisdiction was reestablished in Rome, southern Italy and Sicily before 538AD for a period of time. But because the prefecture of Italy was included in a 538AD law concerning the regulation of court cases (*a law that he never actually had the chance to publish*), we're suddenly supposed to believe that June 1, 538, was the first time in 62 years a Catholic Emperor held legal jurisdiction in Italy? I think the historical record confirms otherwise.) NL

---

[144] John Moorhead, Article, *The New Cambridge Medieval History*, Vol. I, 129

A Reply to the Allegations

[Was Justinian, along with the full support of the little horn, responsible for the overthrow of the Ostrogothic legislative branch of government that we witnessed was terminated in AD 538? Yes, of course. Then why would it be wrong, biblically speaking, to acknowledge Justinian, technically, as overlord of the Ostrogothic monarchy in AD 538?] HH

(10).

"In conclusion, it has been rightly stated by Procopius that the Arian kingdoms did use the same laws and did practice a common religion, for they were all of the Arian faith and did not differ in anything else at all.[145] They were all unified under the legal ideology of religious liberty until A.D. 538. Hence, the best kept secret of the Dark Ages remains a secret no more." 2:62.

(In his history of the Vandal War, Procopius identified four barbarian tribes as *"Goths"* that shared the Arian faith *(the Visigoths, Ostrogoths, Vandals, and Gepids)*, and they supposedly *"did not differ in anything else at all."* However, history clearly shows that one way the Vandal tribe <u>did</u> differ from the others was their habitual persecution of the Catholic Church in North Africa. Gibbon pointed out that, of all the Western barbarian kingdoms, *"... the cruel and absurd enterprise of subduing the minds of a whole people was undertaken by the Vandals alone."*[146]

(It surprises me that Heiks could be familiar with the history of the Vandals and still come away concluding that all of the Arian kingdoms were *"unified under the legal ideology of religious liberty."* Now on page 56, he does try to cover his bases by admitting that they were *"not all free from some entanglements of church and state,"* but then he makes the mistake of claiming *"they never crossed the red line by resorting to force in religious matters against the will of an individual whether he be of the Arian or Catholic*

---

[145] Procopius, *History of the Wars*. Translated by H. B. Dewing. Bks. 1–8. In Loeb Classical Library, edited by Jeffrey Henderson. (Cambridge, MA: Harvard Univ. Press, 2000–2001), III. ii. 1-8.

[146] Edward Gibbon, *Decline and Fall of the Roman Empire*, Vol. III, 365.

faith." I'm sorry, but the Gothic tribes definitely crossed that line at times, and the Vandals did so quite extensively. A contemporary 5th-Century African cleric named Victor of Vita testified to the many crimes perpetrated against his countrymen in a 90-page account,[147] and although there have been a few modern challenges to the idea that systematic persecution was involved,[148] there can be no denying that the Catholic Church in Africa suffered greatly under Vandal rule. An Ibero-Roman bishop named Hydatius spoke of the crimes of King Geiseric who persecuted the orthodox *"in order to force them into the Arian impiety."*[149] Even Procopius wrote briefly about the violent actions taken by the Vandals against Catholics,[150] so whatever he meant by the Gothic tribes not differing in anything, he definitely did not have religious liberty in mind. Also, I'm sure Heiks must have noticed Justinian recounting how the Vandals re-baptized Catholics who were unable to bear the various *"tortures and punishments"* they suffered under the Vandal yoke.[151] In fact, the only Vandal king who wasn't known to oppress the church was Hilderic. Of course, that was due to his own adherence to the Nicene Creed.

(One objection that could be raised is the idea that Vandal persecution against Catholics occurred for economic/political reasons rather than religious ones, and upon their initial invasion into Africa that may very well have been the case. John Moorhead concurs, saying that the Vandals' early actions against Catholics were motivated primarily by greed. However, he continued, *"If Geiseric's persecution of Catholics was motivated by economic considerations, one would have expected it to have lessened as the Vandals increasingly gained control of their wealth. Yet the reverse happened, and from the period beginning with the death of bishop Deogratias, which occurred before the end of 457, persecution based on religion predominates."*[152]

---

[147] John Moorhead, *Victor of Vita, A History of Vandal Persecution.*

[148] Hohan Leemans, *Episcopal Elections in Late Antiquity*, 480.

[149] R.W. Burgess, *The Chronicle of Hydatius and the Consularia Constantinopolitana*, 95.

[150] Procopius, *History of the Wars*, Book III, Ch. VIII.

[151] S. P. Scott, trans., ed. *The Civil Law* [of Justinian], Book 1.27.1.2-4.

[152] John Moorhead, *Victor of Vita, A History of Vandal Persecution*, pg. xi.

A Reply to the Allegations 61

(Now Heiks claims that religious liberty was a *"legal ideology"* of all Arian tribes, as well as an *"Arian principle;"* on page 24 he also stated that it was *"legally promoted."* But where can it be shown in the extant Vandal legal texts that their laws promoted religious liberty? Heiks certainly does not provide any examples in his book. Is he basing this idea solely on Procopius' claim that the Gothic tribes used *"the same laws"* and *"didn't differ in anything else at all"*? Wouldn't successive persecutions under Geiseric, Huneric, Gunthamund, and Thrasamund undermine such a claim? Wouldn't Procopius' testimony of Vandal persecution do the same? In fact, Victor of Vita testified that on February 25, 484AD, King Huneric published Roman laws that were originally aimed at heretics, but he turned those statutes against the Catholic faithful, instead. The king then ordered all Catholic bishops to convert to the Arian religion by June 1st of that year.[153] Wouldn't that be a clear case of legally promoted religious intolerance?

(If the extant manuscripts dealing with Vandal law do not promote religious liberty, and if the historical record shows that the Vandals frequently used force or coercion in religious matters against the will of individuals, then religious liberty was <u>not</u> a universal Arian principle, and Heiks' unified *"legal ideology of religious liberty"* between the three chief Arian kingdoms simply did not exist. The truth is, religious persecution was exercised within those three kingdoms, albeit to varying degrees; it was almost non-existent under the Ostrogoths *(although Theodoric may have tolerated persecution of the Manicheans in Rome, thanks to the popes)*,[154] periodic under the Visigoths,[155, 156, 157] and commonplace under the Vandals *(except under Hilderic).*) NL

[Our Scriptural context under discussion is <u>time</u>—"in the presence of the little horn"—and <u>place</u>—"the

---

[153] Ibid., 64-69.
[154] Louise Ropes Loomis, *The Liber Pontificalis*, Vol. I, 111, 119-120.
[155] William Sumruld, *Augustine and the Arians*, 30.
[156] Charles Herbermann, *The Catholic Encyclopedia*, Vol. XI, 705.
[157] John Foxe, *Foxe's Book of Martyrs*, 54.

location of the little horn" between the years AD 508-538. Historical events before and after have no bearing on our topic or the prophecy. But first, for the record, has NL correctly stated the state of affairs under the Vandal kingship of Geiseric (AD 428-477) and Huneric (AD 477-484)? Yes, absolutely, but to lump the Vandal king Thrasamund in the same camp of Geiseric and Huneric will not withstand investigation. Let's return to our specifications, please. We begin by revisiting, in full, the eyewitness account of Procopius from his perspective of *time* and *place*:

> "...There were many Gothic nations in earlier times, just as also at the present, but the greatest and most important of all are the Goths, Vandals, Visigoths and Gepaedes. In ancient times, however, they were named Sauromatae and Melanchlaeni;[158] and there were some too who called the nations Getic. All these, while they are distinguished from one another by their names, as has been said, *do not differ in anything else at all*. For they all have white bodies and fair hair, and are tall and handsome to look upon, *and they use the same laws and practice a common religion. For they are all of the Arian faith*, and have one language called Gothic; and, as it seems to me, they all came originally from one tribe, and were distinguished later by the names of those who led each group."[159]

[Procopius's account is extremely credible, for the fact that he was with Byzantine General Belisarius during the entire sieges of the Vandals and the Ostrogoths. He would therefore have firsthand knowledge of the events and issues surrounding those two Arian kingdoms, and he communicated that understanding in his *History of the Wars*. History also shows us that from AD 496 to 523, Thrasamund was the king of the Vandals. History additionally confirms that Thrasamund ended many years of Catholic persecution that had begun under his uncle Huneric. Because of Huneric's cruelty, he was little mourned by either the Vandals or their subjects. In fact, this move on the part of Vandal King Thrasamund

---

[158] "Black-Coats"
[159] Procopius, *History of the Wars*, III. ii. 1-8. [Emphasis mine.]

greatly improved relations with the Byzantine Empire. Procopius tells us that

> "He [Thrasamund or Trasamundus] became also a very special friend of the emperor Anastasius."[160]

[When Thrasamund died in AD 523, Hilderic became the Vandal king, reigning from AD 523 to 530. Hilderic's reign and history is known to all, and was noteworthy for the kingdom's excellent relations with the Eastern Roman Empire. Procopius writes that he was "a very particular friend and guest-friend of Justinian, who had not yet come to the throne."[161] Procopius also said that "Hilderic and Justinian made large presents of money to each other."[162] Hilderic allowed a new Catholic bishop to take office in the Vandal capital of Carthage, and many Vandals began to convert to Catholicism, to the alarm of the Vandal nobility. After seven years on the throne, Hilderic was dethroned during a revolt led by his cousin Gelimer. Gelimer then became king of the Vandals and Alans, reigning from AD 530 to 534. He restored Arianism as the official religion of the kingdom. He imprisoned Hilderic, along with Hoamer and his brother Euagees, but did not kill them. Justinian protested Gelimer's actions, demanding that Gelimer return the kingdom to Hilderic. Gelimer sent away the envoys who had brought him this message, blinding Hoamer and putting both Hilderic and Euagees under closer confinement, claiming that they had planned a coup against him. When Justinian sent a second embassy protesting these developments, Gelimer replied, in effect, that Justinian had no authority to make these demands. Angered at this response, Justinian quickly concluded his ongoing war with Persia and prepared an expedition against the Vandals in 533.[163] Once Gelimer learned of the arrival of the Roman army, he had Hilderic murdered, along with Euagees and other supporters of Hilderic that he had

---

[160] Ibid., viii. 9-15.
[161] Ibid., ix. 3-8.
[162] Ibid.
[163] Ibid. III. ix. 3-8 to III. ix. 23.

imprisoned.[164] The closing scenes of the Vandal kingdom were described in my book as such:

> "...Gelimer and his people were established at Ticameron.... [26] [B]y the end of the winter Gelimer being forced to his last asylum, touched above all by the deprivations without number, he yielded to his destiny and put himself in the hands of Belisarius, depending on the promise that his life would be saved and he would have honorable treatment (March 534). The emperor's representative promised with willingness all that the overthrown king demanded. [According to Procopius the promise was made good and Gelimer lived to be an old man in ancient Galatia with his family, now modern Turkey. Procopius continues,] However, Gelimer was by no means enrolled among the patricians, since he was unwilling to change from the Arian faith of Arius."[165] 2:94.

[As one can clearly see, in the everyday life of the Vandals during the prophetic period of AD 508-538, diversity of religion was tolerated and upheld until King Hilderic made a fatal mistake. Thinking to transform an Arian province into one of the orthodox faith, against the wishes of his subjects, he crossed a line and the rest was history.] HH

(11).

[Two paragraphs of NL are in reduced marginal format below. His comments were previously responded to in number (02). However, there is one issue left that deserves a reply.] HH

> (...Heiks also recognized that Justinian overthrew the Vandals in 534AD. Again, it did not matter that the tide-turning battles took place in 533AD, or that Justinian was proclaiming Africa's reclamation in

---
[164] Ibid. III. xvii. 10-16.
[165] Procopius, *History of the Wars*. IV. ix, 11-16.

A Reply to the Allegations

December of that year;[166] what matters is the Vandals were overthrown when the war ended in 534AD.

(Now all Heiks has to do is apply that same reasoning to the Ostrogothic War. Did the Ostrogoths surrender in 538AD? No. Did the war come to an end in 538AD? No. As with the battles of Adda and Ad Decimum, did it matter that the failed siege of Rome was a tide-turning event early in the conflict? Again, no. And unlike the 7-month Vandal War, the Gothic War lasted 18 years, with the war's momentum swinging in the Goths' favor at times. But regardless, the last Ostrogothic king perished in 553AD and the remains of the Gothic military negotiated an end to the conflict with General Narses shortly thereafter.[167] 553AD was the year the Ostrogoths were overthrown, not 538AD.

(The key being "when the Ostrogoths were overthrown." Regarding Odoacer and his feodorati, Heiks clearly recognized they were overthrown in 493AD, the date when the war came to an end. On that, Heiks and I are in agreement. Despite Odoacer's decisive loss at the Battle of Adda in August of 490AD,[168] and despite the fact that, for two and a half years, the only Italian strongholds left in his possession were Ravenna, Caesena, and Rimini,[169] Heiks understood that the "long, fierce battle finally ended on March 5, 493," when Odoacer negotiated his surrender.[170] It didn't matter that Theodoric sent a patrician to the emperor in late 490AD seeking the royal mantle.[171] Odoacer's kingdom was overthrown when the war ended in 493AD.

(We can also see an apt parallel in Justinian's legislative policy; North Africa was liberated in March 534AD, and Justinian issued an edict in April of that year to reorganize the prefecture of Africa.[172] Likewise, after the capture of both the Gothic capital and King Vitiges in 540AD, Justinian saw fit to issue an *edictali programma* between

---

[166] Heiks, *AD 538 Source Book*, 94.
[167] Procopius, *History of the Wars*, Bk. VIII, Ch. XXXV.
[168] Thomas Hodgkin, *Italy and Her Invaders*, Vol. IV, 225.
[169] Ibid., pg. 226.
[170] Heidi Heiks, *AD 538 Source Book* 59.
[171] Thomas Hodgkin, *Italy and Her Invaders*, Vol. IV, 227-228.
[172] S. P. Scott, trans., ed., *The Civil Law* [of Justinian], Book 1.27.

540-541AD in an attempt to put the *Corpus Juris Civilis* into force throughout Italy.[173] However, the efforts of kings Hildibad and Totila gave the Ostrogothic kingdom a second life, and the continuation of the war brought Justinian's edict to no effect. After thirteen more years of war, the conflict ended in 553AD following the battle of Mons Lactarius, and at that point Justinian took the opportunity to issue a pragmatic sanction in 554AD to reestablish his jurisdiction in the re-conquered provinces and to put the revised code of Roman law into effect.[174]

(However, there were no such sanctions issued for Italy in 538AD, no codex reorganizing the Italian prefecture at that time. At most, all the emperor did was prematurely include the Italian prefect at the end of Novel 69. That was it. The novel wasn't even written for or about Italy in particular; it was simply a general edict forbidding a change of venue in court cases, along with a few other legal matters. There's no evidence to suggest that the novel was issued because of Belisarius' successful defense of Rome or that it wouldn't have been published if the siege had continued through June 538AD, so there's no real reason why Novel 69 should be credited with establishing Justinian's *"judicial"* authority in Italy in 538AD.) NL

[Anyone who studies the history of the man Justinian knows he does not legislate with presumptuous or idle words. With the decisive defeat of the Ostrogoths at Rome in 538, both emperor and pope believed the war was over. Novel 69 certainly expressed that belief in the circumference of the jurisdiction it now claimed, as well as by the territorial gains Justinian had now gained. Had Justinian spoken prematurely, as assumed by NL, or did Belisarius and Justinian recognize the fact that they had truly broken the back of the Ostrogoths' *military* and *legislative branch of government* in AD 538? Of course they had, as they would be first and foremost to know this, and it was "in their presence" that the head of Ostrogothic *legislative branch of government* abdicated his position in AD

---

[173] David Walker, *The Oxford Companion to Law* pg. 976.
[174] Frederick Pollock, *The History of English Law Before the Time of Edward I*, pg 11.

538 with no provision in place for a successor. Imagine, if you can, Justinian setting up legislation beside a rival government still in operation in the same "location" that Justinian had claimed as his own? We all know that would be unthinkable.

[Are we also to believe that Novel 79 was just presumptuous words of Justinian? The confusion of the issue comes in because many have not allowed the Scriptures to be their own interpreter. As I showed previously, the uprooting of a prophetic horn or kingdom "is the uprooting of a kingdom's legislative and judicial branches of government." Also, we saw and understood from the primary sources, which were acknowledged and so stated by Hodgkin and Mommsen, that the office of Cassiodorus, the Praetorian prefect of the Ostrogothic government, was still in operation in AD 536-537, but it ceased to exist in AD 538 after the decisive battle at Rome! So much for the argument of a Praetorian prefect sent to the West by Justinian in 536 or 537.

[NL also wants us to believe "there were no such sanctions [or authorizations] issued for Italy in 538AD...." We shall let the reader decide the truth of that matter by now submitting Novel 69 for the reader to judge for himself:

TITLE XXIV.

ALL PERSONS SHALL OBEY THE PROVINCIAL JUDGES IN BOTH CRIMINAL AND PECUNIARY CASES, AND PROCEEDINGS SHALL BE CONDUCTED BEFORE THEM WITHOUT ANY EXCEPTION BASED UPON PRIVILEGE, AND PROVINCIALS SHALL NOT BE SUED HERE UNLESS THIS IS AUTHORIZED By AN IMPERIAL PRAGMATIC SANCTION.

SIXTY-NINTH NEW CONSTITUTION.

The Emperor Justinian to the People of Constantinople.

PREFACE.

[262] "One of the most perfect of all human virtues is that which dispenses equity, and is designated

justice, for no other virtue, when accompanied with this, is worthy of the name; therefore We do not praise fortitude, which is not united with justice, and although the Roman language calls virtue courage in battle, if justice is excluded from it, it becomes a vice, and is productive of no good.

"As we have ascertained that justice is treated with contempt in Our provinces, We have deemed it necessary to re-establish it in a proper condition, by means of a law which will be acceptable to God...."

EPILOGUE.

[266] "Therefore, as soon as Our Most Glorious Imperial Pretorian Prefects appointed throughout the extent of the entire Roman Empire receive notice of this law, they will publish it in all the departments of their government, that is in Italy, Libya, the Islands, the East, and Illyria; in order that all persons may know how greatly We have their interests at heart. We dedicate this law to God who has inspired Us to accomplish such great things, and who will recompense Us for having enacted this constitution for the security of Our subjects. It shall also be communicated to Our citizens of Constantinople. Given at Constantinople, on the Kalends of June, during the twelfth year of the reign of Justinian, and the Consulate of John."[175] 2:152-153.

[NL also tells us that there was "no codex reorganizing the *Italian prefecture* at that time" (emphasis mine). How is that supposed to prove your point, please, since the situation with the Vandals hardly resembled the situation with the Ostrogoths? Justinian was a wise and cunning legislator; he learned from previous successes and errors. The legislation he had issued at the end of the Vandal war on behalf of the African clergy

---

[175] S. P. Scott, trans., ed., *The Civil Law* [of Justinian], 2001. Justinian, *The Novels*-69. Vol. 16: 262, 266, June 1, 538. [The definitive dating used here was taken from the work of a French Doctor of Law: Pierre Noailles, *Les Collections de Novelles de L'Empereur Justinien: Origine et Formation sous Justinien* (Paris: Recueil Sirey, 1912).]

had generated strong support and gained momentum throughout his newly-claimed province, as my book illustrated. Justinian therefore simply repeated that same strategy regarding the Ostrogoths; he again built upon the existing frenzy of the citizens—this time the excitement that was generated when the Romans greeted Belisarius as a liberator (Procopius tells us that the Romans hated the Ostrogoths.)—as they shared the same vision with Justinian and were exuberant over the prospect of a united Roman Empire. Further cementing this fact was that "[t]he dedication of the Great Church [Haghia Sophia] took place"[176, 177] in AD 538 (2:155-156). (And all the while the populace was freely giving over their Heaven-ordained rights to a tyrannical government. Revelation 13:12-18 tells us a similar scenario is to be repeated on a global scale.) Thus at the end of AD 538 we have the accomplishment and territorial extent gained by the "little horn" in the east during the very thirty-year period that biblical prophecy specified for the "setting up" or establishment of her political-religious kingdom, as can be verified from Novel 79:

[The issue we wish to highlight is regarding the *Italian Prefects* of *all dioceses, Praetors of the People, and the magistrates of the provinces in Italy and the entire West and those of both Romes,* as so stated in Novel 79 by Justinian and so quoted in my book:

> "However, by the end of the year 538 and just ten days into the New Year, Justinian's jurisdiction was declared by Justinian himself to encompass Italy, the

---

[176] Elizabeth Jeffreys, ed., *The Chronicle of John Malalas.* A Translation by Elizabeth Jeffreys, Michael Jeffreys, and Roger Scott (Melbourne: Australian Asso. for Byzantine Studies, 1986), 285.

John Malalas was a Byzantine chronicler that lived during the reign of Justinian. (A.D. 491-578). The three consular lists are these: (1) Theodor Mommsen, *Chronica Minora SAEC. IV.V.VI.VII* (Berlin: Verlag Hahnsche Buchhandlung (www.hahnsche-buchhandlung.de), vols. 1, 2, 3; 1892, 1894, 1898, respectfully; (2) Carl Frick, *Chronica Minora* (Leipzig: B. G. Teubneri, 1892); (3) Roger S. Bagnall, *Consuls of the Later Roman Empire* (Atlanta, GA: Scholars Press, 1987). See also Elizabeth Jeffreys, Brian Croke and Roger Scott, *Studies in John Malalas* (University of Sydney N.S.W.: Australian Association for Byzantine Studies, Department of Modern Greek, 1990), 143.

[177] Theophanes, *Chronographia,* ed. C. de Boor (Leipzig: n.p., 1888).

entire West and those of both Romes, meaning Rome and Constantinople:

BEFORE WHOM THE CASES OF MONKS AND ASCETICS SHALL BE TRIED.

SEVENTY-NINTH NEW CONSTITUTION.

CHAPTER II.

CONCERNING THE ENFORCEMENT AND OBSERVANCE OF THIS CONSTITUTION AND THE DETERMINATION OF THE LEGAL CONTROVERSIES IN WHICH MONKS ARE CONCERNED.

"Litigation in which monks are involved shall be speedily disposed of. This law is of general application, and its enforcement shall be committed to the Most Glorious *Prefects having jurisdiction in all dioceses, namely: those of Illyria,* Italy, the entire West *and* those of both Romes, *as well as by the Most Glorious Praetors of the People, and the magistrates of the provinces, with their subordinates*; and it shall not be evaded in any way but must be observed unchanged for the honor of the most reverend monks."[178] 2:283. (Emphasis mine.)

[Now back to Novel 69. NL continues, "The novel wasn't even written for or about Italy in particular." No, the novel was written first and foremost for Italy as well, and was not mentioned prematurely, as NL assumes, as Novel 79 reiterates. NL continues with "there's no real reason why Novel 69 should be credited with establishing Justinian's *'judicial'* authority in Italy in 538AD." Did Justinian overthrow the Ostrogothic government in AD 538? Yes! Did Justinian overthrow the Ostogothic military in a decisive battle in AD 538 that determined the outcome of the fighting? Yes! To what extent was that defeat of the Ostrogths in AD 538?

---

[178] S. P. Scott, trans., ed., *The Civil Law* [of Justinian], 17 vols (Union, NJ: Lawbook Exchange, 2001), 16:294-5 (March 10, 539).

A Reply to the Allegations 71

"So ended the long siege of Rome by Witigis, a siege in which the numbers and prowess of the Goths were rendered useless by the utter incapacity of their commander. Ignorant how to assault, ignorant how to blockade, he allowed even the sword of Hunger to be wrested from him and used against his army by Belisarius. He suffered the flower of the Gothic nation to perish, not so much by the weapons of the Romans as by the deadly dews of the Campagna. With heavy hearts the barbarians must have thought, as they turned them northwards, upon the many graves of gallant men which they were leaving on that fatal plain. Some of them must have suspected the melancholy truth that they had dug one grave, deeper and wider than all, the grave of the Gothic monarchy in Italy."[179]

"The whole nation of the Ostrogoths had been assembled for the attack, and was almost entirely consumed in the siege of Rome."[180] 2:150-151.

[It is true the fighting continued beyond 538, but in reality the outcome of the war was all but decided at the battle of Rome in AD 538. Is there really any wonder why Novel 69 should not be credited with establishing Justinian's *"judicial"* authority in Italy in 538AD? No! Was the emperor's inclusion of the Italian prefect at the end of Novel 69 truly premature, as NL claims? No!] HH

(12).

"With Rome known to the world at that time as "the capital of the world...."[181] 2:261.

(Of course, Heiks knows full well that the city of Rome was not actually the capital of the world in 538AD, regardless of Justinian's flattery, nor was it even the capital

---

[179] Thomas Hodgkin, *Italy and Her Invaders*. 8 vols., 1st ed. published 1880–1889. (New York: Russell and Russell, 1967), 4:285.
[180] Edward Gibbon, *The History of the Decline and Fall of the Roman Empire* (ed. J. B. Bury) (London: Methuen, 1909), 4:346.
[181] S. P. Scott, trans., ed., *The Civil Law* [of Justinian], Codex I. 17. 10. 12:92.

of the Ostrogothic kingdom. The Ostrogoths maintained their king, their government, their capital, and numerical superiority following the siege of Rome; their failure to retake the city did not dethrone the Gothic government, but it did serve to weaken the Goths' militarily and swing momentum in the Byzantines' favor.) NL

[Yes, and, of course, Rome was not the capital of the world at that time; I was simply allowing Justinian to speak for himself, to reveal the clear *intent* in the mind of Justinian to make it so once again. NL claims the following without qualification: "The Ostrogoths maintained their king, *their government*, their capital, and numerical superiority following the siege of Rome; their failure to retake the city did not dethrone the *Gothic government....*" [Emphasis mine.] However, we have already and amply shown that the Ostrogoths *did not* maintain their legislative government after the battle of Rome in AD 538.] HH

(13).

"We now proceed by presenting to the reader the primary definitive historical sources that will sustain the foretold biblical account of how the papacy orchestrated a universal Sunday law that was legislated throughout all of Christendom in the year A.D. 538." 2:266.

(And yet none of the sources Heiks provided between pages 167-197 made any mention of the papacy actually orchestrating a universal Sunday law throughout all of Christendom in the year A.D. 538. Heiks claims his sources *"sustain"* this idea, but it's hard to take that seriously when his sources are completely silent on the matter. Vigilius' letter to Eutherus doesn't mention a universal Sunday law, and Novel 69 doesn't mention it either. Nor does Malalas or Orleans III or Mary Ann Collins, or any of the important legislation Heiks listed.

(Frankly, I don't understand how his claim mirrors reality in 538AD. The Sunday laws contained within

Justinian's Code would have only applied to those territories the emperor had direct jurisdiction over; even at its height his empire never extended over the *"entire then-known world of Christendom"*. The Catholic Franks would have upheld Sunday observance on their own, but the Arian Visigoths were not obligated to enforce it since their kingdom in Spain and southern Gaul was not under the oppressive union of the Catholic church and state in 538AD. The same goes for the churches established in Northern Italy still within the Ostrogothic kingdom, or what few churches would have been found within the Suevic kingdom. In fact, Judith Herrin confirmed that the pagan practice of celebrating Thursday as the weekly day of rest persisted in Europe throughout the sixth and seventh centuries.[182] So how exactly was the universality of this Sunday law demonstrable when roughly a third of Western Europe was still ruled by Arian or pagan kingdoms following the siege of Rome in 538AD?

(In order for Heiks' Sunday law to have truly been universal throughout Christendom in that year, it needed to be a canon included in one of the four general councils. Of course, all of the Sunday legislation in Book III Title XII of the Code was secular in origin and was limited to the Byzantine Empire. The Orleans III Sunday law in 538AD was definitely religious in nature, but that council was not ecumenical and its canons only represented church law for certain Gallic ecclesiastical provinces.) NL

[Brother L, everything you have just said is historically true and I take no issue with you here at all, because we are precisely on the same page. I will take responsibility for not clarifying my position more clearly, as I had taken for granted that we all knew and understood we were dealing with the thirty-year "setting up" period alone. That is as I had stated earlier, that *all* the specifications of the prophecy that were given to take place between the years 508-538— including, of course, the uprooting of the three horns—must and did take place *only* in the "presence" of the papacy, and thus *only* in the

---
[182] Judith Herrin, *The Formation of Christendom*, 222.

"location" where she was able to stretch her tentacles far enough to secure her dominion during her thirty-years' crusade for power. I think any honest and free-thinking individual would have to agree with the Bible's logic and definition. In this context, do we find what is to be classified as "universal Christendom" up to the year AD 538, if you please? The answer is yes. I am more than aware of the extensiveness of Christendom, per se, in the world at that time, but we must stay within the confines of the prophecy. That includes the geographical "location" of the little horn during this thirty-year period only. If we stay within the specifications of Scripture, then wherever the papal tentacles could reach with the support of the state during the biblical time period given to her for setting-up—i.e., wherever she could extend her legislative power—this would encompass "universal Christdom." Since AD 538 her reach is open-ended until the Second Coming. In fact, at some point after AD 538, Revelation 13:3 tells us that "all the world wondered [will wonder] after the beast."

[We documented that in AD 316 Pope Sylvester I decreed a change from Sabbath to Sunday. Soon thereafter, the state added its influence in support of the altered law through Constantine's edict in AD 321. The rest is history, as you well know. In this thirty-year "setting-up" period, we witnessed two main players that helped to establish the little horn. There were Clovis in the West and Justinian in the East. The Sunday laws I have submitted in my book are open to all. Under Clovis for the Franks (French) in the West, we have the Council of Orleans III, canon 28. This Sunday law pertained to the Frankish jurisdiction alone. In the East, Justinian's Sunday laws were enforced only in his jurisdiction, as well. According to the boundaries put upon us by the specifications of the Scriptures, this is what constituted "universal Christendom" at that *time* and *place* in history. It is immaterial whether some of these Sunday laws were pagan, because the papacy is not a church; she is a political entity with a religious veneer, for she is pagan through and through. As I have proven in my book, she is the source for Sunday worship in Christendom then and today. So, was there a mandatory Sunday law throughout (and for no better word)

Christendom by the year AD 538 in all the provinces that Clovis and Justinian had control and jurisdiction over? Yes. Were there three kingdoms that had their legislative branches uprooted between the years AD 508 and 538 (and for no better word) throughout all of Christendom under the territorial jurisdiction of either Clovis or Justinian? Yes. At the end of the thirty-year prophecy in AD 538, did the "little horn" *"speak* [through legislation] great words against the most High" by thinking "to change times and laws"? Yes. Only by changing God's law could the papacy exalt itself above God Almighty. If one would just take a moment to stand back and look at the big picture, the specifications would begin to link with historical facts so obviously that the deductions would be trustworthy.] HH

(14).

> "We have already established the fact that the Ostrogoths were uprooted from Rome on March 1, 538, and that Justinian was the first Catholic Emperor since A.D. 476 to have held legal jurisdiction in Rome by designating a prefect from the court to be governor of Rome."[183] 2:266.

(No, the established facts are that the Ostrogoths were uprooted from the city of Rome in December of 536AD on account of Procopius' testimony *("Rome became subject to the Romans again after a space of sixty years")*, as well as Belisarius' testimony *("We have arrived in Italy, as thou didst command, and we have made ourselves masters of much territory in it and have taken possession of Rome also, after driving out the barbarians who were here....)*,[184] and the praetorian prefect that supposedly confirmed Justinian's *"legal jurisdiction"* over the re-conquered regions of Italy was designated in 537AD just prior to the siege of Rome.

(However, what hasn't been established yet is the starting point of the Ostrogoth's siege, and this is due to two

---

[183] Charles Diehl, *Justinien et la Civilization Byzantine au Vie Siècle,* 186. Taken from Procopius, *De Bello Gothico,* ed. De la Byzantine de Bonn, 101.
[184] Procopius, *History of the Wars,* Book V, Ch. XXIV.

conflicting dates; March 1 and February 21. Procopius wrote that the siege began on March 1, and we know that he was in Rome at the time and had first-hand knowledge of the event, whereas we do not know who penned the first part of Silverius' entry in the *Liber Pontificalis*, although he was believed to have been a contemporary).[185] NL

[Any Praetorian prefect that Justinian may have sent to Rome prior to the uprooting of the Ostrogothic legislative branch of government and before the decisive battle at Rome in AD 538 would be of no consequence to the prophecy whatsoever. However, having a Praetorian prefect sent by Justinian in AD 538 after the decisive battle at Rome, when Justinian was already speaking of Italy as entirely under his arms with the removal of Cassiodorus's legislative branch of government, the implications would be prophetic. Did such an event transpire? Let's revisit a primary document from my book:

> "Justinian was already speaking of Italy as entirely under his arms,[186] already he was designating a prefect from the court as governor...."[187] 2:274.

[The sources speak for themselves. Next, NL states the following: "...What hasn't been established yet is the starting point of the Ostrogoths' siege, and this is due to two conflicting dates: March 1 and February 21." As I commented previously, this is a true statement by NL. He and I are in agreement that the spring equinox was on March 25th and, weighing the arguments of NL and others, I would tend to side with NL that Procopius is probably closer to the actual date than the author of the *Liber Pontificalis*. That author has February 21, 537, to March 1, 538, for the battle of Rome against the Ostrogoths, whereas Procopius has it from March 1, 537, to March 10, 538. Although neither one of us can be definitive, I do think NL is on more solid ground by siding with

---

[185] Louise Ropes Loomis, *The Liber Pontificalis* Vol. I, 148, footnote #2.
[186] Nov. 69, epil. (Mai 538).
[187] Charles Diehl, *Justinien et la Civilization Byzantine au Vie Siècle*, 186. Taken from Procopius, *De Bello Gothico*, ed. De la Byzantine de Bonn., 101.

Procopius, since we know he was there in person and March 10, 538, would naturally be closer to the spring equinox date that fell on March 25th of 538.] HH

(15).

"On May 1, 538, we witnessed how Justinian clearly prohibited 'the practice of unlawful religious rites,' meaning, of course, that only the 'one and true Catholic faith' was to be recognized among all of humanity as religious liberty was banned and made illegal in the west, as well. Procopius, in other writings, confirms that it was Justinian who ended religious freedom for the Arian Christians, and we believe he is here quoting Novel 67 that was issued on May 1, 538, which we just reviewed:

"He [Justinian] seized the best and most fertile estates, and prohibited the Arians from exercising the rites of their religion."[188] 2:268.

(Novel 67 starts off as an edict prohibiting people from building new monasteries, churches, or oratories without a bishop's consent and preventing lawful churches from falling into disrepair and misuse. Although Scott's translation has Justinian mentioning that certain individuals pretended to build houses of worship for the practice of unlawful religious rites, whatever those rites were, they were already *"unlawful" (meaning that the prohibition against practicing them had been declared previously)*. What were new were the regulations for the building and maintenance of orthodox churches, etc. The novel was written for Patriarch Menas of Constantinople and to the other patriarchs and metropolitans *"under your* [Menas'] *jurisdiction."* It wasn't a law directed toward *"the west,"* at least not at that point.

(Now, concerning Heiks' belief that Procopius was quoting Novel 67; the excerpt Heiks provided from *Secret History* was specifically describing the conditions in

---

[188] Procopius, *The Secret History of the Court of Justinian* (Boston: IndyPublish.com, n.d.), 62.

North Africa about a year after the Vandal War. Procopius tells us that the emperor sent commissioners to North Africa, imposed new taxes, seized the best and most fertile estates, and prohibited the Arians from exercising the rites of their religion.[189] Although he later turned his attention to Italy in subsequent paragraphs, the part about seizing estates and prohibiting the Arian religion was all dealing with the post-Vandal situation in North Africa.

(If Procopius really was describing the aftermath of one of Justinian's Novels *(and Heiks gives no evidence of this other than his own "belief," on page 168)*, then I think it would be far more reasonable to conclude that Procopius was referring to Novel 37, enacted on August 1, 535AD. In it, Justinian declared that the African Church was entitled to all ecclesiastical property taken by the Arians in previous generations *(up to a point)*, no Christian heretic was allowed to have a house of worship or prayer, and he charged the praetorian prefect, Salomon, that no Arian should *"share in any manner in ecclesiastical rites."* Well, that's almost exactly what Procopius described: the seizure of property and the prohibition of Arian rites in North Africa. Seems like a near perfect match to me. Menas' Novel 67? Not so much. There's nothing in that novel about Africa, or taking estates away, or prohibiting the rites of Arians in particular. Fred H. Blume's translation of Novel 67 seems to make a connection with Procopius' passage even more tenuous since Blume replaced *"rites"* with *"grottos:"* *"For many about to build chapels, look after their own disease (heresy), not becoming builders of orthodox churches, but of unlawful grottos."*[190]) NL

[It is true, as NL claims, that Novel 67 was written for Patriarch Menas of *Constantinople* for territories under Menas' jurisdiction. That vital piece of information I overlooked. It was not a law directed toward the West at that point in time. Also, I wrote the following: "...And we *believe* he is here quoting Novel 67 that was issued on May 1, 538...." In that partial quote of mine (emphasis

---

[189] Procopius, *The Secret History of Procopius*, 64.
[190] http://uwacadweb.uwyo.edu/blume&justinian/AJCNovels2/Novel%2067%20copy.pdf

A Reply to the Allegations

mine), I chose the word "believe" because I did not go back to the original sources to confirm my findings, since I knew that I was not dealing with the first time Justinian used this stipulation. As NL rightly said, *"[T]he prohibition against practicing them had been declared previously."* As I have mentioned previously, this is not the first time Justinian has been found to be redundant in his *Corpus Juris,* although since NL brought this matter regarding Menas to my attention, I've looked through the primary sources again. I believe I stand to be corrected here. I believe NL has the correct interpretation.] HH

(16).

"It is significant that the third synod of Orleans, France, in AD 538, was not merely a provincial synod, meaning a local one, narrow or limited in scope." 2:270.

(Ok, but in what way is this significant? Heiks' source, Charles Hefele, likened Orleans III to the second council of the same name, which he described as a *"kind of national synod."*[191] Heiks seems to be implying that since provincial synods were local, narrow, and limited in scope, and since Orleans III was not *"merely a provincial synod,"* then the council was not local, narrow or limited. The fact is that even a national synod—*although larger than a provincial*—still has a narrow, limited scope because it is only authoritative for the church body within a particular nation or kingdom, not the church universal. The Catholic Encyclopedia states that the canons of national councils represent local law: *"Next to the pope, the bishops united in local councils, and each of them individually, are sources of law for their common or particular territory;* <u>canons of national or provincial councils, and diocesan statutes, constitute local law.</u>"[192]) NL

---

[191] Charles Hefele, *A History of the Councils,* Vol. IV, 185.
[192] George Herbermann, *The Catholic Encyclopedia,* Vol. IX, 59, "Law" entry.

[In my book I said:

"Then on May 7, 538, the Catholic Church takes her boldest step yet in the history of her church councils. A deliberate frontal attack on the law of God was witnessed as *all of Gaul came under an ecclesiastical Sunday law.*" (Emphasis mine.) 2:269.

[That is, it could be enforced in *all* of Gaul that was under the control and jurisdiction of Clovis. No discrepancy here.] HH

(17).

"The power and extended authority of a church council may be better understood from Mary Ann Collins, a former Catholic nun, in her remarks on infallibility in reference to the *Catechism of the Catholic Church*, 891:

"According to Roman Catholic doctrine, popes and Catholic Church councils are infallible. This means that whenever they make official declarations concerning matters of faith or morals, God supernaturally protects them from making errors. Infallibility applies to all Roman Catholic popes and church councils: past, present, and future."[193] 2:271-272.

(I don't see why appealing to an ex-Catholic like Mary Ann Collins would lead us to a better understanding of a church council's authority. It would be like suggesting we might better understand the Investigative Judgment doctrine by reading about it in Russel Earl Kelly's book *Exposing Seventh-Day Adventism*. In both cases, why not skip the polemics and stick to the source materials? In my opinion, Heiks' decision to appeal to an anti-Catholic writer feels entirely out of place and counterproductive.

(The catechism Ms. Collins quotes from adds these

---

[193] Mary Ann Collins (a former Catholic nun), *The Spirit of Roman Catholicism: What Lies Behind the Modern Public Image?* (2002) 31, note 17, PDF, "Infallibility."

A Reply to the Allegations 81

rather important provisos to the subject of infallibility: *"The Roman Pontiff, head of the college of bishops, enjoys this infallibility in virtue of his office, when, as supreme pastor and teacher of all the faithful—who confirms his brethren in the faith—*<u>he proclaims by a definitive act a doctrine pertaining to faith or morals</u>.... The infallibility promised to the Church is also present in the body of bishops <u>when, together with Peter's successor, they exercise the supreme Magisterium</u>, above all <u>in an Ecumenical Council</u>."[194]

(Simply put, Orleans III was not a general council, it was not convened or presided over by the pope or his representatives, the Bishop of Rome did not proclaim the canons of that council to be definitive acts of faith and morals, and the bishops in attendance certainly did not represent the *"supreme Magisterium."* The synod was a quasi-national Gallic council whose canons would have been limited to the churches under the jurisdiction of the metropolitans involved (*namely Lyons, Vienne, Sens, Bourges, and Rouen—all of which were within the Merovingian Frankish kingdoms*).

(Orleans III did not meet any of the conditions to make its canons infallible, and Roman Catholic doctrine does not state that infallibility applies to all church councils. A former nun like Collins should know that, and a seasoned researcher like Heiks should know better than to rely on ex-Catholics to accurately communicate Catholic doctrine. I mean, really, if Heiks is resourceful enough to track down and translate an obscure 6th-Century papal letter out of the *Corpus Scriptorum Ecclesiasticorum Latinorum*, then he should have little difficulty locating a more suitable source to communicate Catholic teaching than an ex-nun and anti-Catholic like Collins.) NL

[Quoting NL, "...Why not skip the polemics and stick to the source materials? In my opinion, Heiks' decision to appeal to an anti-Catholic writer feels entirely out of place and counterproductive." My purpose at the time was not to sling mud, but to show that sometimes what is understood within the church structure and what is on

---

[194] Heidi Heiks, *AD 538 Source Book*, 272.

the books are two different things. However, your point is valid, and your constructive criticism well-received. At least you now know what my intentions were.] HH

(18).

"However, let us not forget how Justinian's ecclesiastical legislation comes to fruition. From Codex I. 1. 4., we have read the letter by Justinian that he wrote to Pope John II on March 15, 533, as follows:

"'For we do not suffer anything which has reference to the state of the Church, even though what causes the difficulty may be clear and free from doubt, to be discussed without being brought to the notice of Your Holiness, because you are the head of all the Holy Churches, for We shall exert Ourselves in every way (as has already been stated), to increase the honor and authority of your See.'"[195] 2:280.

"There was nothing which had reference to the state of the Church in ecclesiastical matters that did not come first before the pope for approval. This procedure was already established when Justinian declared, "We shall exert Ourselves in every way," and was legally confirmed by the legislative support from the state that the church canons received." 2:280-281.

(If Justinian did make the Bishop of Rome aware of the state of ecclesiastical matters in the Church, it was almost always after the fact. Ironically, the 533AD letter Heiks used as his proof-text in the above quote serves to validate my point; Justinian wrote that letter in order to get Pope John II's approval of the Theopaschite formula, but he only did so <u>after</u> making it the accepted doctrine in the East;[196] Justinian did not wait to get the pope's approval first. In reality, the only reason he even made the pope aware of the situation was because a group of Eastern ecclesiastics, called the Sleepless Monks, rejected the formula, and they had sent a delegation to Rome hoping that

---

[195] S. P. Scott, trans., ed., *The Civil Law* [of Justinian], 12:12 (March 15, 533).
[196] Milton Anastos, *Studies in Byzantine Intellectual History*, 3.

John would agree with Pope Hormisdas' earlier ruling on the matter.[197] The Monks' delegation made Justinian feel pressured to send one of his own to Rome, and the letter in question was sent with the Byzantine ambassadors.[198] So if the monks hadn't opposed Justinian, there would not have been a 533AD "headship" letter to Pope John II seeking his advice on the formula. As Littledale recognized, the letter was actually a *"confession of faith which Justinian forced on the Pope*, compelling him to alter the ruling of the Roman Church *on a point of doctrine, in order to bring it into conformity with the teaching of the Eastern Church."*[199]

(Then there is the Origenistic controversy in which Justinian issued 10 anathemas against Origen and some of his teachings. Did he consult with Pope Vigilius first and get his approval before issuing his judgment? No; he promulgated the edict against Origen, then sent letters to the Pope and various patriarchs encouraging them to procure anathemas in their own synods.[200] Now the decision to condemn Origen had been supported by Patriarch Menas and the papal legate Pelagius prior to Justinian issuing his sentence,[201] but regardless, Hefele clearly understood that Justinian's edict was *"one of those many and great, even if well-meant, Byzantine encroachments, which does not disappear even when we assume that the Emperor acted in agreement with Menas and Pelagius."*[202]

(Lastly, there is the Three Chapters controversy, arguably the most important theological conflict of Justinian's career. Did the emperor obtain Vigilius' approval first before issuing an edict condemning the writings of Theodore, Theodoret, and Edessa? No, of course not; he condemned them first around 544AD, then went about a 9-year process of trying to coerce Vigilius and the Western Church into accepting his decision. In fact, instead of acquiescing to papal authority during the Council of Constantinople in 553AD, Justinian rejected the pope's

---

[197] Richard McBrien, *Lives of the Popes*, 89.
[198] R. F. Littledale, *The Petrine Claims*, 292-293.
[199] Ibid., 293-294.
[200] Charles Hefele, *A History of the Councils of the Church*, Vol. 4, 219.
[201] Ibid., 217-218.
[202] Ibid., 220.

Constitutum on the Chapters and declared to the council that *"the very religious pope of old Rome had made himself an alien to the catholic church by defending the impious chapters, and by putting himself out of the communion (of the fathers)."*[203] The council then proceeded to condemn the Chapters and depose Vigilius,[204] while Justinian broke communion with the pope until Vigilius finally capitulated several months later.[205] I think Milton Anastos and Charles Diehl summed up the situation succinctly;

> (*"Moreover, he* [Justinian] *issued his dogmatic decrees whenever he chose, and did not concern himself about securing the signatures of bishops and patriarchs until his decree was drafted. Then, after it was officially promulgated, he set about to procure whatever ecclesiastical sanction he saw fit, which on the part of the clergy amounted to no more than the purely administrative act of announcing the Emperor's theological decisions to the churches within their jurisdiction. In every instance, the priests, when asked to give their approbation to an imperial theological decree, were confronted with a fait accompli, and were powerless to resist, or to suggest changes."* [206]
>
> (*"Moreover, he* [Justinian] *proposed to rule the Church as its master, and in exchange for his protection and for the favors he had heaped upon it, he despotically and brutally imposed his will upon it, proclaiming himself curtly,* 'emperor and priest'."[207]

(I also don't understand how Heiks can claim that Justinian's letter to Pope John II shows us how the emperor's ecclesiastical legislation came to *"fruition."* His statement is a bit unclear; is he suggesting it was drawn up due to prior papal approval? If that is the case, then Claire Sotinel informs us that between 521-533AD, the emperors and popes had next to no communication with each other, with the exception of Pope John I's visit to Constantinople in 526AD:

---

[203] Claire Sotinel, article, *The Cambridge Companion to the Age of Justinian*, pg. 283.
[204] Ibid.
[205] Eamon Duffy, *Saints and Sinners*, 57.
[206] Milton Anastos, *Studies in Byzantine Intellectual History*, 518.
[207] Charles Diehl, *History of the Byzantine Empire*, 25.

"*For the next five years (521-526AD), there was no correspondence between popes and emperors, and for fifteen years after that Justinian, although actively trying to reconcile Chalcedonian and non-Chalcedonian, did not consult Rome about religious matters. No pope felt the need for a permanent representative in Constantinople before 533AD. The union had been proclaimed and the names of Roman popes and eastern patriarchs entered on the diptychs, but this was all.*"[208]

"*Despite the pontifical visit of 526, Constantinople and Rome went their separate ways until 533. The new pope Felix (526-530) had no dealings at all with the imperial court, a policy largely continued by his successor, Boniface (530-532). In 532, Boniface asserted the rights of Rome over Illyricum, in answer to an appeal by the bishop of Larissa, who had been deposed by the patriarch of Constantinople, which worsened relations with the East.*"[209]

(Also, S. P. Scott's translation of Novel 9 has Justinian declaring, "*(W)e [Justinian] are the source of both secular <u>and ecclesiastical</u> jurisprudence.*" If that is the correct translation, then Justinian wouldn't have believed he needed to receive the pope's prior approval concerning church law; the emperor would have seen himself as the divinely appointed arbiter of such legislation.

(Honestly, I can't really think of any instance in which Justinian or his successors took ecclesiastical matters before the bishop of Rome in order to get prior approval; even if examples did exist, they would be exceptions, not the rule. Now Justinian did submit to Pope Agapetus' decision to depose Anthimus, despite the emperor's prior protestations—but his acquiescence was not exercised in a vacuum. Since Justinian was about to embark on the Gothic War, I think it is reasonable to conclude that he handled Agapetus with kid's gloves because he simply could not risk alienating the Roman populace at such a critical hour. There was already a segment of the Italian population who had no interest in Greek rule, so mistreating the bishop of Rome would only reinforce their prejudices and give the Romans reason to shift their

---

[208] Claire Sotinel, *The Cambridge Companion to the Age of Justinian*, 273.
[209] Ibid., 274.

allegiance to their current rulers. Justinian understood this, and I believe he was willing to forfeit a minor battle within the church for the sake of a much larger war.) NL

[I have read a fair number of the letters from Pope Simplicius to Anastasius. I have also read almost all of the letters from Pope Symmachus to Vigilius, and have translated all of Pope Symmachus' letters. I am certainly familiar with the history you speak of concerning the next-to-nothing communication between popes and emperor; we are in agreement here. Also, I am fully abreast of Justinian's issues with Pope Vigilius and the Three Chapters controversy; again we are in agreement. I am vaguely familiar with the histories of popes John II, Felix and Boniface, of which you speak, but I found nothing there that addressed the specifications of what I was looking for, so I went no further. However, I am confident you are right in what you say. And, of course, there is no argument that Justinian did whatever he so desired. That's a given.

[All of what you say here I accept as true, but it has nothing to do with what I am talking about, if you please. My emphasis has been and is all about the Scriptures' specifications of the prophecy. My focus has been on the legislative establishment of the union of church and state during the prophesied thirty-year crusade to power, and their (church and state) handling of religious liberty and the law of God during that time period, along with the related *time* and *place* of the uprooting of the three horns of Daniel 7:8, to name just a few aspects of my inquiry. The legislation that I presented proves to the reader the service and support that the state renders to the church, though they are viewed as one entity—although in the eyes of Heaven, the apostate church has more guilt to atone for. The primary sources had already revealed who would have the upper hand, and although that fluctuated throughout history somewhat, Justinian became the man recognized by historians, as well by the pope at that time, as "Imperial overlord." That fact I quoted in 2:176-180, from the decree of AD 528 that laid the foundation for the political power of the papacy.] HH

(19).

"With the last of the three major Arian powers subdued judicially in A.D. 538 when they were forced to relinquish Rome, the capitol of the world as we have just witnessed, the oppressive union of church and state had successfully put down all major opposition and had outlawed religious liberty throughout all of Christendom. By this act, the church officially ushered in the horrors of the dark ages. This has been the best kept secret of the dark ages." 2:312-313.

(The Visigothic kingdom was still rooted in the West in 538AD, and that means the Ibero-Roman Catholic Church remained under the rule of one of Heiks' three major Arian powers. So no, religious liberty was not outlawed throughout all of Christendom at that time. Within a few years, the resurgence of the Ostrogothic kingdom was restored throughout most of Italy for another decade, and in 568AD, the Lombards migrated to Italy and established yet another Arian/pagan horn on Italian soil.) NL

[These issues were addressed in (02).] HH

(20).

"In 536 came the final establishment of the French monarchy in Gaul[210] and the possession of Provence, and this left the Franks in complete control to freely enforce the Lex Romana Visigothorum law code throughout all of Gaul." 2:312.

(No, not throughout *"all of Gaul;"* the Gallic province of Septimanie remained a Gothic possession until the beginning of the 8th Century; Heiks' *A.D. 538 Source Book* confirms this on page 316: *"Gothic countries:* <u>Septimanie which remained in Visigoth hands until 711</u> *and shared*

---

[210] Edward Gibbon, *The History of the Decline and Fall of the Roman Empire*, 4:128, margin, AMS edition.

the destiny of Spain and Province that belonged to the Ostrogoths.") NL

[The province of Septimanie was not something I had overlooked. I simply had not expressed the matter properly, as I meant that all the Franks' territorial gains in the West, including the possession of Provence in AD 536, would comprise her geographical boundaries in light of the Scriptures' specification of "location," and would remain so at least until AD 538. Throughout the territories of Gaul she had claimed as her own and over which she had jurisdiction, which comprised almost the whole of Gaul, she would be able to freely enforce the *Lex Romana Visigothorum* law code.] HH

[Below is a summary by NL of his main concerns that have been addressed in this discourse.] HH

(So my main points of disagreement are summed up as follows: the Visigothic kingdom withstood Heiks' Molotov litmus test and it remained an opposing Arian armament in Europe long past 508 or 538AD. Codex I.3.44 did not give total authority to the canons of *"the synods."* Justinian's legal jurisdiction was established in Italy prior to 538AD, and the notion that Belisarius' successful defense of Rome secured the emperor's *"judicial authority in the west"* is falsified by Procopius' continued account of the war. The Vandal kingdom was not *"unified under the legal ideology of religious liberty;"* that tribe crossed the red line on many occasions by resorting to force in religious matters, and for the most part the Visigothic and Ostrogothic kingdoms continued to uphold religious liberty after 538AD. The Ostrogoths were not dethroned in 538AD. Since the Third Synod of Orleans was not a general council, its canons were narrow, limited in scope, and constituted local ecclesiastical law. Roman Catholic doctrine does not state that infallibility applies to all *"church councils,"* and infallibility did not apply to canon 28 of Orleans III. Justinian never established a procedure in which all ecclesiastical matters were first brought before the pope for approval, nor did the emperor follow such a procedure himself, and the ecclesiastical legislation within his Code came to fruition as a result of his own ambition and genius, not through prior collaboration with the bishop of Rome.

(But most importantly, despite claiming that the papacy orchestrated a universal Sunday law throughout all of Christendom in 538AD, none of Heiks' *"primary definitive sources"* made any mention of a universal Sunday law or the pope's orchestration of it; the Christian Church within the Iberian Peninsula, Southern Gaul, and Northern Italy would have remained under the Goths' *"legal code of religious liberty"*[211] following the Ostrogoth's failed siege of Rome in 538AD, while at most the observance of Catholic Sunday laws would have been enforced upon those who were direct "subjects"[212] of Justinian or the Franks. In 538AD, Catholic "legal jurisdiction" in the West extended as far as North Africa, most of Gaul, and over half of Italy; therefore, the proposed Sunday laws would not have been universal throughout Christendom in 538AD.

(On a more conciliatory note, it is readily apparent that Heidi Heiks put a great deal of time and effort into his research, so although I may ultimately disagree with some of his conclusions, I respect his work ethic. I also appreciated that he took a little time to address a few common falsehoods that have plagued historicist apologetics for far too long; his correction of Nicholas Summerbell over the timing of Justinian's three-month ultimatum was a welcome admission,[213] as well as his recognition that the fall of Odoacer and his motley crew of mercenaries did not represent the uprooting of the Heruli tribe. On those and other issues, I will gladly tip my proverbial hat to Mr. Heiks on a job well done.) NL

[In closing, I would like to say a few words about my friend NL. I do not wish for anyone to think he is

---

[211] Heidi Heiks, *AD 538 Source Book*, 261.

[212] Ibid., 282-283.

[213] Ibid., 180.

my enemy. I have conversed with numerous Jesuit and Catholic historians and theologians; NL is one of the best historians I have run across in this era of history. I know well the documents he cites. He never veered to the left or right to sustain his position, but, as I have witnessed thus far, he has always stayed on the line. It was his honesty and tact that led to my decision to reply. As I have presented thus far, I believe NL has built upon some false premises that can easily be overlooked, which is not the case with deliberate falsehoods. Also, I recognize the strong probability of being misread, in part by my own poor choice of words, but NL is not to be faulted for this. As a historian, Brother L has gained my utmost respect and I wish him the very best!] HH

2

Clarifying the Issues

I have had opportunity to review a source NL had mentioned previously,[214] with which I had been unfamiliar. For the sake of the truth and for the reader, I now take the reader back to pg. 42 in Chapter 1 to review NL's charges before I more fully respond to NL, since I now have the source he cited in my hands.

Also, from the section we have called number **(02)**, we will address just one more issue before we move into number **(03)**. NL wrote:

(Regarding the Visigoths, Heiks believes they were the first of three horns to be plucked up by the roots when Clovis defeated the Visigoths at the Battle of Vouille in 507 AD (He also claimed the latest academic scholarship supported the 508 AD date);[215] however, since his book was published, more recent scholarship has upheld 507 AD,[216] scholarship that actually comes to us from one of Heiks' highly touted sources."[217]) NL

---

[214] Ralph W. Mathisen & Danuta Shanzer, eds., *The Battle of Vouillé, 507 CE: Where France Began* (Boston/Berlin: Walter de Gruyter, 2012).
[215] Heidi Heiks, AD 508 Source Book, 40.
[216] Mathisen & Shanzer, *The Battle of Vouillé, 507 CE: Where France Began.*
[217] Heiks, *AD 508 Source Book,* xvii-xviii.

(A) [It is true that latest academic scholarship has now generally agreed to place the battle of Vouille in AD 507. I have no problem with that, as the previous sources had lent credit to that conclusion to the extent that I acknowledged it as a strong possibility in my *AD 508 Source Book* on page 41. Primary sources and historians are also agreed that the war itself continued into AD 508, but again that was not the prophetic marker that commenced the prophetic period. The battle and war were means to an end, but not the end. The prophetic marker was the "setting up" of a "kingdom" (Dan. 11:31) that would be the first kingdom after the demise of the Western Roman Empire in AD 476 to lend its military might to the "little horn" to enforce the dogmas of the apostate church through legislation. In order for all of that to take place, there would *first* have to be the crowning of a king, and that was precisely what happened in AD 508. That historical event and prophetic marker was established in my *AD 508 Source Book*, as follows:

> "After Clovis received the titles and dignity of Roman Patricius and consul from the Greek Emperor Anastasius, the diadem and purple robe in the Church of St. Martin, and baptism at Rheims in 508, he was then on his way to Paris to his royal residence and capital. Henceforth, from his coronation in 508, it was the Breviary law code that was in place and implemented as the official law code in the provinces of the Gallo-Romans and also in those provinces that were conquered by the Franks. As already established by legal historians, that same law code remained in use until the twelfth century.
>
> "Thus, there is indisputable historical confirmation and legislative documentation that 'the one and true Catholic faith was indeed 'set up' or established, as prophesied. With 'Catholic law' 'commanded' to be 'preserved unimpaired,' and with the exclusivity of the bishops' jurisdiction in ecclesiastical affairs legally fixed, Clovis had become the first Catholic king of the ten symbolic horns of the Western Roman Empire dating from A.D. 476. His ascension to the throne in 508 brought in its train the first instituted 'National' religion. All other

faiths were outlawed. Then began the long chain reaction in prophetic history until every European nation accepted the one and true Catholic faith and was led to follow the example of the Franks in using the civil power to enforce the church's dogmas!"[218]

[Ironically, the same source and author referenced by NL above[219] to my implied discredit will actually be proven to be my strongest collaborator. Danuta Shanzer is joint editor of the book cited by NL; she wrote the foreword and there stated the following, which confirms Clovis' kingship commencing in the year AD 508:

> "The immediate international consequences of the battle in Gaul are discussed by *Ralph Mathisen* in a detailed analysis of the ceremony at Tours in 508 in which Clovis received from the Byzantine emperor Anastasius the patriciate, the honorary consulate, and a golden crown. It is suggested that the Roman recognition of his role as a Roman client king resulting from his vicrory at Vouille gave Clovis the political and personal capital that allowed him to incorporate the other Frankish peoples under his rule. As a result, he was able to create a Frankish kingdom that eventually would develop into the modern nation of France."[220]

[Mathisen,[221] in his article in the same book, also confirms the kingship of Clovis in the year AD 508 when he says this:

> "In the second book of his *Histories*, Gregory of Tours narrated the events that followed the defeat of the Visigoths and their king Alaric II by Clovis and the Franks at the Banle of Vouille in 507.[222] In *Hist.* 37, he

---

[218] Heiks, *AD 508 Source Book*, 60. Emphasis mine.
[219] Mathisen & Shanzer, *The Battle of Vouillé, 507 CE: Where France Began.*
[220] Danuta Shanzer in Mathisen & Shanzer, *The Battle of Vouillé, 507 CE: Where France Began*, xvii.
[221] Ralph W. Mathisen, *Clovis, Anastasius, and Political Status in 508 C.E.: The Frankish Aftermath of the Battle of Vouille*, in Mathisen & Shanzer, *The Battle of Vouillé, 507 CE: Where France Began*, 79.
[222] An abbreviated and less well-developed French version of this study appeared as R. W. Mathisen, "Clovis, Anastase, et Gregoire de Tours: Consul, patrice et

reported, for the year 508, 'After that, when the victory was complete, he returned to Tours, where he gave many gifts to the basilica of Saint Manin.'[223] In the index, the title for the next chapter, 38, reads, *De patriciatu Chlodovechi regis* ('On the Patriciate of King Clovis'). The related text describes Clovis's visit to Tours (fig. I) as follows:

"Therefore he received from the emperor Anastasius codicils of the consulate and in the basilica of the blessed Martin, placing a diadem on his head, he was clothed in a purple tunic (*tunica blattea*) and the chlamys (*clamide*). Then, mounted on horseback, he dispensed gold and silver with great generosity along the route that lies between the city gate and the church of the city,[224] scattering it with his own hand to people who were present, and from that day he was addressed as if he were a consul or emperor (*tamquam consul aut augustus*). Then he departed from Tours and came to Paris, and there he fixed the seat of the kingdom."[225]

[Mathisen then concludes his lengthy article with the following:

"In this model, the significance of Clovis's victory at Vouille cannot be overstressed. It was of much greater

---

roi," in *Clovis, le Romain, le chretien, l'Europeen*, ed. M. Rouche (Paris, 1998), 395-407. Pace Bachrach (in this volume), this earlier study in fact suggested that Clovis received the patriciate, honorary consulate, and recognition as king, and did not present "an either/or interpretation."

[223] *Peracta victoria, Turonos est regressus, multa sanctae basilicae sancti Martini munera offerens* (Greg. *Hist.* 2.37). For the battle, see the essays in this volume by Mathisen (Location), Bachrach, and Shanzer.

[224] That is to say, the cathedral inside the walls of the city, not the basilica of Saint Martin, which was outside the walls.

[225] Igitur ab Anastasio imperatore codicillos de consolato accepit, et in basilica beati Martini tunica blattea indutus et clamide, inponens vertice diadema.
Tunc ascensoequite, aurum argentumque in itinere illo, quod inter portam atque [ms. Atrii] ecclesiam civitatis est, praesentibus populis manu propria spargens, voluntate benignissima erogavit, et ab ea die tamquam consul aut augustus est vocitatus. Egressus autem a Toronus, Parisiis venit ibique cathedram regni constituit (Greg. *Hist.* 2.38). For Clovis's visit to Tours, sec also Bachrach's essay in this volume.

importance, for example, than Clovis's defeats of either Syagrius or the Alamanni. As a result of Vouille, Clovis did much more than merely defeat his Visigothic rival Alaric II. He also put himself on the Byzantine radar and was acknowledged not only as a barbarian chieftain worthy of receiving Roman honors, but also as a Byzantine client king. That status, coupled with the religious unity that he also shared with the Byzantine emperor, gave him a political status that placed him on a whole different playing field from the other Frankish petty kings and must have been a prime factor in the ease with which the other Frankish peoples accommodated themselves to his rule. Thus, even though Clovis's adoption of Nicene Christianity usually is cited as one of the primary reasons, if not the primary reason, for his success, one also must appreciate the significance of the political credit that he gained as a result of his victory over the Visigoths."[226]

[Here we see, contrary to the claim put forth by NL, that the latest input from the international academic community still fully supports the chronological sequence of events as designated by the Scriptures and history, as found in my books.] HH

(B) Another aspect that needs clarification is the two groups of people that come under scrutiny in the investigative judgment. The two chapters of Daniel 7-8 must be viewed as a unit. Both reveal the righteous judge distinguishing between the sheep and the goats, between the wheat and the tares, and between lip service and heart service, and removing all that are without a wedding garment. Yes, we have witnessed in my book[227] that *all* who profess Jesus Christ—including the "little horn," because she professes Jesus Christ, as well—will have their names come before this tribunal to receive their just verdicts.

---

[226] Mathisen, "Clovis, Anastasius, and Political Status in 508 C.E.: The Frankish Aftermath of the Battle of Vouille," in Mathisen and Shanzer, *The Battle of Vouillé, 507 CE: Where France Began*, 79, 107.

[227] Heidi Heiks, *The "Daily" Source Book* (Ringgold, GA: Teach Services, 2010), 142-3.

Those who have never professed Jesus Christ will not be judged in the investigative judgement; their cases are examined during the thousand year millennium after the second coming. The confusion comes in on how the text in Daniel 8:12 is translated in some of the Bibles of today and therefore how it is interpreted. The KJV, along with the NKJV, literally translates Daniel 8:12 this way:

> "And a host will be given over the continuance causing transgression, and it throws the truth down to the earth; and it practiced, and prospered."

The NASB translates it as such:

> "And on account of transgression the host will be given over *to the horn* along with the regular *sacrifice*"

The KJV translates "host" as referring to the host of the little horn (i.e., the host of papal priests) which is given over to the "little horn" causing transgression.

The NASB represents "host" as God's people, who are being given over into the hands of the little horn along with the "daily," because of transgression of God's people.

Do you comprehend the ramifications of what the NASB is saying? We will come back to this. We must always remember this very important point: the text can have only one correct interpretation—only one translation. Multiple translations have resulted in multiple interpretations for Daniel 8:9-12 even among Adventists; they have affected our confidence in the specifications establishing the commencement of the 1290- and 1260-day/year prophetic periods of AD 508 and 538. I will now prove my point.

The honest in heart, I think, are in agreement that Daniel 7-8 is an investigative judgement scene. We have seen previously that the "little horn" came from one of the four winds, not from the Grecian Empire or from one of the four horns after it was divided, and it started out small.[228] The vision of Daniel 8:9-12 concerns the

---

[228] Richard M. Davidson, Graduate-level sanctuary textbook commissioned by the Biblical Research Institute. Sent to the author on Feb. 2015 by email from an unfinished draft of 28 chapters. I would highly recommend to the reader the sections

"little horn" (papacy) and this vision is *solely* about the papacy until verses 13-14. Daniel 8:13-14 moves into the all-inclusive and final procedure and outcome for both parties. The problem arises when some try to include the righteous saints in the condemnation of the "little horn" in verses 10-12, concerning the "daily," "host" and "transgression."

How can we be so sure? In Daniel 7:22, 27, for example, we have the genuine Christian being vindicated. There is not the slightest implication of condemnation whatsoever. Why?

> Because "there is therefore now no condemnation to them which are in Christ Jesus, who walk not after the flesh, but after the Spirit." Rom. 8:1.

However, Daniel 8:10-12 reeks with condemnation! It is a stark warning to Rome and all who follow her lead in walking away from the "Scripture of truth" (Dan. 10:21), to follow Rome in her circle of tradition and in the commandments of men. But it is a time of Heaven's vindication and eager anticipation to welcome the saints into the Heavenly throng. The NASB translation of 12a misrepresents the character of God and perverts the gospel. The Scriptures reveal Him running as a Father to meet his erring child that has turned about-face, humbly heading homeward to his Father. The Father does not pile on more baggage or punishment for him or her to carry, for the load is already too heavy to carry. God forbid! No, rather, when that child "returns home," the God that I know is presented in the Scriptures as expressing nothing but love and forgiveness. He is so delighted to bestow mercy that, when we fully surrender to Him, He takes away the heart of stone and fills the vessel with a heart of flesh. It's a gift of peace and love so fulfilling that the recipient wants to follow the Lamb whithersoever He goeth. That is the God that I serve and share! That is the God of those "who walk not after the flesh, but after the Spirit."

I am sure we are in agreement that staying with the text renders the absolutely best interpretation, unless the

---

pertaining to Daniel 8:9 regarding the rise and identity of the "little horn" in his chapter 21.

text calls us to go elsewhere. I will show that the text in the context of Daniel 8:10-12; 11:31; 12:11 is not asking us to go outside of this context for its interpretation. To do so would be to superimpose an unqualified private interpretation. Let us now confirm the one and only translation and its interpretation.

In my previous books, we clearly witnessed in Daniel 8:10 a vertical shift toward Heaven and away from the horizontal activities of the successive kingdoms described from Daniel 8:1 and onward. In Daniel 8:10 we saw it was the "little horn" (papacy) that was persecuting the "host" or "saints" of the Most High. By understanding aright that there are the two distinct visions of the *khazon* and *mar'eh* in Daniel 8,[229] as told to Daniel, we now understand that Gabriel was told to make Daniel understand the first part (the *mar'eh*) (Dan. 8:16) of the full vision (the *khazon*), *from its commencement*. Gabriel began by retracing Daniel 8:1 and moving onward. In Daniel 8:23-25, Gabriel described the horizontal activities of pagan Rome. The *mar'eh* concluded with the crucifixion of Christ in Daniel 8:25. Gabriel then informed Daniel in Daniel 8:26 that remainder of "the vision of the evening and the morning [the *khazon*]," which extended to October 22, 1844, was to be "shut up" "for many days," and "none understood it" at that time (Dan. 8:26-27), for the latter part of the *khazon* was to be understood only by those people living at the end of the vision's timespan, circa 1844. The remainder of the *khazon* began in Daniel 8:10 with the vertical activities of the "little horn" (papacy) commencing immediately after the crucifixion of Christ, according to Chapter 8. Also, in Daniel 8:11 we witnessed that it was the little horn who unlawfully took away, or usurped, the "daily" from Christ (the high-priestly ministry of Christ) and cast down the "place" of His sanctuary to this earth. This was so clearly illustrated in my books that I felt no need to reiterate it here again. However, regarding the next clause, I see I did not connect the dots as securely as I should have done; it has left too much to assumption on the part of the reader.

If we hold to the translation and interpretation that the "host" of v. 12a is of the "little horn," then it must

---

[229] See section **(D)** of this chapter.

be proven that such a "host" of priestly intercessors had come onto the world stage and was in place sometime after AD 476, along with a much-overlooked specification that this "host" had to appear only during the little horn's thirty-year crusade to power between the years AD 508–538, when the "little horn" was being "set up" or established by legislation (See Dan. 11:31; 12:11; 7:25). At this point, we need to first verify whether Heaven uses the term "host" to identify a priesthood of believers or a group of people in religious garb, thus representing themselves to be priestly intercessors.

> "Take the sum of the sons of Kohath from among the sons of Levi, after their families, by the house of their fathers, From thirty years old and upward even until fifty years old, all that enter into the host,^{6635} to do the work in the tabernacle of the congregation." Numbers 4:2–3

Clearly, these sanctuary priests were the "host," so we find Heaven indeed uses "host" in a context of religious ministry. Thus the host of verse 12 finds its fulfillment only in papal Rome."[230]

Again, a literal translation of this verse reads thus:

> "And a host will be given over the continuance causing transgression, and it throws the truth down to the earth; and it practiced, and prospered." Daniel 8:12

Next we must ask if history confirms just such a biblical specification concerning the "host." We know that the "location" and "presence" of the papacy during this "setting up" period during her thirty-year rise to power between AD 508–538 was secured by two civil entities: Clovis in the west and Justinian in the east. Therefore, we would expect to see enabling legislative actions by both civil parties, in fulfillment of these biblical specifications. In the west Clovis was under the *Lex Romana Visigothorum* law code; in the east Justinian was under the *Corpus Juris* law code. In my *AD 508 Source Book*, we saw just such legal documentation for the "setting up" of

---
[230] Heiks, *The "Daily" Source Book*, 114–5.

the "little horn" by Clovis through legislation in the west. In that same book, page 27, we also have historical proof of a "host" in religious garb given over to the papacy:

> [27] "Clearly, these sanctuary priests were the "host," so we find Heaven, indeed, uses "host" in a context of religious ministry. Thus, the host of verse 12 finds its fulfillment only in papal Rome. In the context of Daniel 8:11–12, the supposition that the "host" is in reference to the barbarians that invaded and subverted the Roman Empire has no biblical or historical support whatsoever.
>
> "It is of interest to mention that Pope Symmachus (AD 498–514), the bishop of Rome who reigned through the time period of 508, has been recognized by Catholic historians for one of his great feats. During his pontificate, through ordination, he created:
>
>> " 'One hundred and seventeen bishops, ninety-two priests, and sixteen deacons.'[231]"

Fulfilled! Next we will show how Justinian in the east fulfilled the Scriptures to the very letter. Was a "host" set up between the allotted years of AD 508–538 through legislation in the east, as well? Yes! The following document was legislated into effect on AD March 16, 535, and can be found in my *AD 538 Source Book* on pages 217-8. Novel 3, also called Constitution 3, will give a glimpse into the *vast* "host" given over to the priesthood in Constantinople at that time for the church that Justinian had built, Hagia Sophia, which was also the "Great Church" dedicated in AD 538. See pages 155-6.

---

[231] Chevalier Artaud De Montor, "Pope Symmachus" [A. .D. 498-514], *The Lives and Times of the Popes* (n.p.: Catholic Publication Society, 1911), 1:150. Imprimatur.

THE NOVELS

CONCERNING THE NUMBER OF ECCLESIASTICS ATTACHED TO THE PRINCIPAL CHURCH AND THE OTHER CHURCHES OF CONSTANTINOPLE.

THIRD NEW CONSTITUTION.

PREFACE.

[17] "...We have ascertained that on this account the principal church of this Imperial City, the Mother of Our Empire....

CHAPTER I.

[18] "(1) Wherefore We order that not more than sixty priests, a hundred deacons, forty deaconesses, ninety sub-deacons, a hundred and ten readers, or twenty-five choristers, shall be attached to the Most Holy Principal Church, so that the entire number of most reverend ecclesiastics belonging thereto shall not exceed four hundred and twenty in all, without including the hundred other members of the clergy who are called porters. Although there is such a large number of ecclesiastics attached to the Most Holy Principal Church of this Most Fortunate City, and the three other churches united with the [19] same, none of those who are now there shall be excluded, although their number is much greater than that which has been established by Us, but no others shall be added to any order of the priesthood whatsoever until the number has been reduced, in compliance with the present law."[232]

Fulfilled! We have proved historically that indeed a "host" of papal priests in religious garb was "set up" legislatively between the years AD 508–538, just as the Scriptures has said it would be, and as I had previously revealed in my *Daily Source Book*. Now let's take this a step further.

---

[232] S. P. Scott, trans., ed. *The Civil Law [of Justinian],* 17 vols. (Union, NJ: Lawbook Exchange, 2001), *The Novels*, 3. Preface, Chapter I, Vol. 16:17-19, March 16, 535.

> "And it cast down the truth to the ground; and it practised, and prospered." Daniel 8:12

There are two major clues that determine the chronology of these last two phrases. The first is "the truth"[571] (*emeth*). What is the "truth" that the papacy cast down? Certainly, it was the truth concerning the "daily" and the "place" of his sanctuary, among all the other truths that papal Rome has cast down or obscured throughout the ages, but the Bible has a specific focus in mind in harmony with Dan. 7:25, for it says:

> "Thy righteousness is an everlasting righteousness, and thy law is the truth.[571] Psalms 119:142

The first clue is that the Bible says the "law is the truth." So why is the law of God introduced in Daniel 8:12? Before we answer, we must disclose the second clue, which will define the chronology of verse 12.

After the papacy "cast down the truth to the ground"—cast down *the law of God* (Daniel 8:12)–thus proceeding in "transgression" in the fullest sense), it is then that the Bible says it "practiced, and prospered." Daniel 7:25 confirms this and reveals again the emphasis being put on the law of God:

> "And he shall speak great words against the most High, and shall wear out the saints of the most High, and think to change times and laws: and they shall be given into his hand until a time and times and the dividing of time."

It was after the man of sin had thought to change times and laws that the Bible says he was to begin his reign, to practice and to prosper for "a time and times and the dividing of time"—that is, for 1260 long years. This began, as we have witnessed, in AD 538 and extended to 1798.

As we shall also see from the confirming prophetic pen of Ellen White, "the papal power cast down the truth to the ground" (a direct quote from Daniel 8:12). Notice, though, that the law of God was to be cast down and trampled in the dust at a specific time in earth's history.

"Among the leading causes that had led to the separation of the true church from Rome was the hatred of the latter toward the *Bible Sabbath. As foretold by prophecy, the papal power cast down the truth to the ground. The law of God was trampled in the dust,* while the traditions and customs of men were exalted. The churches that were under the rule of the papacy were early compelled to honor the Sunday as a holy day. Amid the prevailing error and superstition, many, even of the true people of God, became so bewildered that while they observed the Sabbath, they refrained from labor also on the Sunday. But this did not satisfy the papal leaders. They demanded not only that Sunday be hallowed, but that the Sabbath be profaned; and they denounced in the strongest language those who dared to show it honor. It was only by fleeing from the power of Rome that any could obey God's law in peace."[233]

Next is the phenomenal statement that fully confirms our application and interpretation of Daniel 8:12 and the prophetic event that Heaven declared to have commenced the beginning of the 1260-year prophecy:

"*The change in the fourth commandment exactly fulfills the prophecy.* For this the only authority claimed is that of the church. Here the papal power openly sets itself above God."[234]

In Daniel 7:25 we find another clarification, this time given to us by Brother Davidson:

"But the most audacious work of the little horn power, as foretold in Daniel 7, was the attack upon God's law: the "attempt to change the times [*zimnin*] and law [*dat*]." The Aramaic word *zimnin* is plural of *zeman*, and refers to the repetitious nature of "specific, appointed times," while the word *dat* refers to a "royal law (or decree)." These two terms are probably used

---

[233] Ellen White, *The Great Controversy*, (Nampa, Idaho: Pacific Press, 1911), 65, emphasis mine.
[234] Ibid., 446, emphasis added. (See *AD 538 Source Book* for all additional documentation, including the uprooting of the three horns.)

here as hendiadys for one concept: "the recurring specific appointed times [in] the royal law." The "royal law" in the context of vs. 25 is clearly a reference to the divine law of God, the Ten Commandments, and the only reference to "appointed time" in the Decalogue in the fourth commandment, with regard to the seventh-day Sabbath."[235]

Therefore, the true translation and interpretation of these Scriptures has been made plain by clarifying that the transference of the "daily," the "host" and the "transgression" of Daniel 8:10-12 all are designated solely to Rome and no other. All the other clauses and issues that were previously and sufficiently addressed in my books, and every specification, have been proven to have met their fulfillment in this allotted time span. Clearly then, the "host" of Daniel 8:12 cannot be God's true people. If the "host" of Daniel 8:12 were truly God's people, then the specification given for the allotted time period of thirty years between AD 508–538 for this "host" to come on the stage of action through legislation could apply only to those people that lived during those thirty years. Of course, one can clearly see that will not withstand investigation. The same failure to withstand investigation can be said for the many arguments for the so-called dual interpretations for the "daily" and the "transgression" of verses 11-12, as well, because all three clauses must go outside the text to bring, at best, a superimposed interpretation, whereas by staying with the text, nothing is eclipsed or forced.

Without question, history has confirmed every Scriptural specification of time and place as being fulfilled to the very letter! Daniel 7 clearly reveals God's investigative judgement in behalf of His purchased possession. Even a fifth-grader could read and understand its meaning. Would we not do well to embrace the obvious when sharing outside our faith with those who deny an investigative judgement? As the righteous Judge of all the earth (Gen. 18:25) presides before ten thousand

---

[235] Davidson, Graduate-level sanctuary textbook commissioned by the Biblical Research Institute. Sent to the author on Feb. 2015 by email from an unfinished draft of 28 chapters, 20:18.

Clarifying the Issues 105

times ten thousand, and the books are opened, He reveals both mercy and justice. His true character is open before all (Rom. 3:4). Verdicts of mercy go out from the throne room, granting entrance into His everlasting dominion. At the same time, verdicts of eternal guilt are pronounced upon those in whose hearts rebellion is still found, even as they falsely claim Him as their own while trying to climb up some other way by their own merits. We need no apology for advocating what is clearly written and documented in the "Scripture of truth" for all to see for themselves.

(C) Another issue that needs a sufficient clarification is number **(16)**, to which NL objected. I had written the following in my *AD 538 Source Book*, page 270:

> "It is significant that the third synod of Orleans, France, in AD 538, was not merely a provincial synod, meaning a local one, narrow or limited in scope."

The gist of NL's argument is that there is no historical evidence that its decrees had any impact beyond the borders of the Frankish kingdom.

Concerning the extent of the synod's decrees, a Brother I'll identify as EY, an honest seeker of truth, emailed me a letter that I now present in part. It exposes the flaw in NL's reasoning that has kept many from not recognizing the Sunday law of the Synod of Orleans III, France, in AD 538, for its time and place as another prophetic marker for the beginning point of the 1260 years. EY stated the following:

> "Last April I met Dr. Edwin Cook at the ATS Spring Symposium at SAU where he conducted a breakout session entitled 'Modern Roman Catholicism: Beast or Benefactor?' If you do not know Dr. Cook, here is his bio: received his PhD in Church-State Relations from the J. M. Dawson Institute of Church-State Studies, Baylor University, Waco, TX, 2012; founder and Director of Liberty 21st Century, Inc. (a corporation "dedicated to advancing religious freedom for

people of all faiths whose actions are non-violent;" http://liberty21stcentury.com/Index.html; conducts seminars on religious liberty issues; written numerous articles for *Liberty* magazine; pastors the English and Spanish SDA churches in Waco, TX; does PARL work for the Texas Conference.

"Given Dr. Cook's credentials in church-state relations, I explained to him the issue and asked him what he thought. He recently emailed me his response, and with his permission I will share it with you:

" '... [T]here really is no need for historical evidence that the decrees had any impact beyond the borders of the Frankish kingdom for two main reasons:

" '1) Any time that we analyze issues within the Catholic Church, we must recognize that its history is one of a developing power. Its doctrines, many of which are erroneous, did not come into existence in many cases except over decades, or in a few cases, over several hundred years (such as the idea of the Immaculate Conception, the sacredness of Mary, until finally she is accepted as a Co-Mediatrix with Jesus!) So, the Sunday law of 538 can certainly serve as a marker, albeit with limited geographical application, of the nature of the Beast as it began to receive political power and develop into a coercive institution.

" '2) Whether the Synod of Orleans was or was not provincial, really does not matter when we consider Catholic claims to jurisdiction. The Church claims authority to obligate the consciences of men and such power still exists, even when the Church is not exercising it. I would refer you to a careful reading of Jacques Maritain, whom I footnote in my book (footnote #178 or 180, or thereabouts *[sic, is actually #638]*). He asserts that the right to coerce is a right retained by the Church, even though she may not use it for centuries. Likewise, the portion of the Sunday law you quote, "If anyone be found doing the works forbidden above,... but as the ecclesiastical powers may determine," does not limit the threat to a geographical location, meaning that it would have universal application, especially since it refers to "the ecclesiastical powers," without limiting the jurisdiction (i.e., the ecclesiastical powers existed wherever the Church's presence existed).'

"The book he [Cook] references is *Roman Catholic Hegemony and Religious Freedom: A Seventh-day Adventist Assessment of Dignitatis Humanae* (2012)."

(D) In this section I wish to inform the reader of a work that I highly recommend that pertains to Richard Davidson's latest work on the chronological accuracy pertaining to Oct. 22, 1844.[236] Davidson references and quotes Michael Oxentenko's work entitled, "The Two Distinct Visions of *khazon* and *mar'eh* in Daniel 8 and the Relationship of the 2300 Evenings and Mornings of Daniel 8:14 to the Seventy Weeks of Daniel 9:24-27," an unpublished manuscript in progress (in 2014). Oxentenko's comments in regard to Daniel 8:15b-26 and Dan. 11 and 12, concerning the two parts of the "vision of *khazon* and *mar'eh*," are very convincing, as Davidson acknowledges:

"Hence, the entire *mar'eh* of Dan 8:16-26 deals with the *first part* of the *khazon*, the part from the time of the Medo-Persian empire to the death of Christ during the period of pagan Rome.... The *khazon* is the entire vision involving the full sweep of the 2300 days—all that is encompassed in Dan 8:1-14."[237]

Another issue that I wish to bring to light that was not discussed in Davidson's textbook is a significant biblical hermeneutic that is being reiterated at the end of the *horizontal* vision of the *mar'eh* with the death of Christ in Daniel 8:25. This hermeneutic is also under attack by even some Adventists of today in their futuristic interpretations of Daniel 11-12. Let me explain:

Daniel chapters 11-12 covers the same ground as

---

[236] Richard Davidson, Graduate-level Sanctuary textbook commissioned by the Biblical Research Institute. An unfinished draft of 28 chapters sent on Feb. 2015 to the author.
[237] Ibid.

Daniel chapters 7-8, with additional specifications given to Daniel by the angel Gabriel as he again interprets the events of Daniel 8:1 and onward. These events, we saw, were part of the *mar'eh*, the horizontal part of the *khazon* that concluded with the death of Christ at the hand of pagan Rome in Daniel 8:25. There, with the events of the cross, is where the literal/local language stops. After the cross, we interpret the symbols as spiritual/worldwide, just as we have always done with Daniel 8:10-12. The death of Christ at the cross is also clearly stated in Daniel 11:22, ending again the *mar'eh*. Therefore, the second, vertical part of the *khazon* must naturally and instantaneously follow the concluded first part. But when the vertical vision of the *khazon* did so, we witnessed earlier that it commenced with the "little horn" (papacy) of the events of Daniel 8:10-12 rising to power, while the horizontal vision of the *mar'eh* (pagan Rome) ceased to exist at the crucifixion of Christ in Daniel 8:25. However, the symbols and specifications of the vision that take us to the end of the *khazon*, to October 22, 1844, are also reiterated in Daniel chapters 11-12 with additional specifications not found in Daniel 7-8. Would not Daniel 11:23 straightway commence, then, with the remainder of the *khazon* concerning the "little horn" (papacy), perhaps with further specifications concerning her actual infamous, but initially small, rise in time, place and intent? After all, Daniel 11:23-30 clearly reveals an entity fighting vertically against Heaven. This conflict does not abate in behalf of the saints until Daniel 12:1. Please look closely at v. 23:

> "And after^{H4480} the league^{H2266} *made* with^{H413} him he shall work^{H6213} deceitfully:^{H4820} for he shall come up,^{H5927} and shall become strong^{H6105} with a small^{H4592} people."^{H1471} Dan. 11:23

Could it be that this text was foretelling the "league," ^{H2266} or union of church and state, under the pagan Roman Empire by the edict[238] of the Emperors Gratian, Valentinian II and Theodosius I that established Catholicism as the state religion on February 28, AD 380?

---
[238] Original Latin text in Mommsen, *Theodosiani libri XVI*, vol. 1-2, "De fide catholica," p. 833.

After all, the "little horn" is not recognized by Heaven as in a state of prophetic growth without her adulterous and forbidden marriage to the state. After that alliance, then the "little horn" works "deceitfully" [H4820] and "comes up" [H5927] or ascends "strong" [H6105] or mightily with a "small" (*Strong's Concordance* renders [H4592] as "a little") "people" (*Strong's Concordance* renders [H1471] as "Gentile, heathen nation or people").

Does the Bible ever refer to the "little horn" or papacy as Gentile or heathen? Yes. Consider Revelation 11:1-2:

> "And there was given me a reed like unto a rod: and the angel stood, saying, Rise, and measure the temple of God, and the altar, and them that worship therein." Rev. 11:1

> "But the court which is without the temple leave out, and measure it not; for it is given unto the <u>Gentiles</u> [papacy]: and the holy city shall they tread under foot forty *and* two months." Rev. 11:2

But I am getting ahead of myself. As I have amply illustrated the true biblical hermeneutic/method of interpreting the Scriptures in my other books,[239] I see no need to repeat myself here, except for a simple illustration. The biblical hermeneutic of interpreting the symbols in their time and place is simply this. Before the cross, we interpret the symbols to mean literal/local. After the cross, we interpret the symbols to mean spiritual/worldwide. Take the "daily" of Daniel 8:11-12, for example. It is a symbol representing the high-priestly ministry of Christ. Even if one wants to say the "daily" is paganism, it is still a symbol, although there is no Scripture or Spirit of Prophecy support for the pagan interpretation whatsoever. For symbolic language regarding events after the second coming, we interpret the symbols to mean literal/local again, just as it reads. This means that after Daniel 11:22, with the crucifixion of Christ on the cross, the biblical method of interpreting the symbols from henceforth

---

[239] Heidi Heiks, *Satan's Counterfeit Prophecy* (Ringgold, GA: Teach Services, 2013); *King of the North* (Brushton, New York: Teach Services, 2009).

until the second coming is that we now interpret the symbols to apply spiritually/worldwide. All biblical language spoken of after the second coming and during the millennium is literal, not symbolic. Those who follow after the hermeneutics of the Jesuits, who continue to use them to counter the reformation, declare that we must interpret the symbols of Daniel 11:23 to the end of Chapter 12 and elsewhere literally. However, those who misapply the prophetic symbolic specifications for events designated before the second coming follow in the footsteps of Rome and grossly misrepresent the "Scripture of truth."

(E) In closing, I will share one last, but significant, observation. As Timothy Hullquist, my publisher as well as manager of TEACH Services, was giving me some good pointers on my forthcoming book, our conversation moved to the topic of the demise of the Ostrogoths. I was sharing with him the historical documentation concerning how Cassiodorus, being the last Praetorian prefect that held the highest position of office for the Ostrogothic legislative and judicial branches of government, after the siege of Rome in 538, was witnessed packing up his office, as his official work was now finished. Timothy suggested a simple but profound explanation that could drive the point home. He said (I am paraphrasing), "Consider a dandelion out in the field, or even a rose in the garden. Once it is 'plucked up,' *it's dead*. It may still look alive and well, at least for a while, but the fact of the matter is, it was dead the moment it was plucked up. So were the Ostrogoths in the eyes of *Heaven*, when their legislative and judicial branches of government permanently stopped functioning in AD 538!

Appendix I

AD 508
Source Book
Bibliography

Acta Conciliorum et Epistolae Decretales ac Constitutiones Summorum Pontificum, vols. 2, 4. Paris: Typographia Regia, 1714.

Acton, Lord. *The States of the Church*. Reprinted from *The Rambler*, March 1860. Newport, RI: Remington Ward, 1940.

Akademie der Wissenschaften Philosophisch-Historische Classe, ed. *Sitzengsberichte der Kaiserlichen*. 134 Band. Jahrgang 1895. Wien: Druck Von Adolf Holzhausen, 1896.

Altendorf, Erich. *Einheit und Heiligkeit der Kirche*. (Arbeiten zur Kirchengeschichte published by Emanuel Hirsch and Hans Lietzmann Bd. 20), 1932.

Angenendt, Arnold. *Imperial Reign and Baptism of Kings: Emperor, Kings and Popes as Spiritual Patrons in the Occidental Missionary History*. Berlin: Walter de Gruyter, 1984.

Archives d'Histoire Doctrinale et Littéraire du Moyen Age. Paris: Librairie Philosophique J. Vrin, 1956.

Ardagh, John, with Colin Jones. *Cultural Atlas of the World.* Alexandria, VA: Stonehenge Press, 1991.

Askowith, Dora. "The Toleration of the Jews under Julius Caesar and Augustus," pt. 1. PhD diss., Columbia University, 1915.

Ayerst, David, and A. S. T. Fisher. *Records of Christianity,* vol. 2. Oxford: Basil Blackwell, 1977.

Bachrach, Bernard S. *Liber Historiae Francorum.* Lawrence, KS: Coronado Press, 1973.

Barion, Hans, Das fränkisch-deutsche Synodalrecht des Frühmittelalters (Kanonistische Studien und Texte ed. By A.M. Koeniger Bd. 5 u. 6), 1931;

Barnes, Timothy D. *Constantine and Eusebius.* Cambridge, MA: Harvard University Press, 1981.

Barnwell, P. S. "Emperors, Jurists and Kings: Law and Custom in the Late Roman and Early Medieval West." *Past and Present,* no. 168 (August 2000): 6–29.

Baronio, Cesare. *Annales Ecclesiastici,* bks. 8, 9. Lucae: Typis Leonardi Venturini, 1741.

Baus, Karl. *From the Apostolic Community to Constantine.* 2 vols. of *Handbook of Church History,* ed. Hubert Jedin and John Dolan. New York: Herder and Herder, 1965.

Baus, Karl, H-G. Beck, E. Ewig, and H. J. Vogt. *The Imperial Church from Constantine to the Early Middle Ages.* Vol. 2 of *History of the Church,* ed. Hubert Jedin and John Dolan. Translated by Anselm Biggs. New York: Seabury Press: 1980.

Baynes, Norman H. *Constantine the Great and the Christian Church.* Vol. 15 of *The Proceedings of the British Academy.* London: Humphrey Milford Amen House, 1929.

Baynes, Norman H. *Constantine the Great and the Christian Church*, 2nd ed. Reprint of 1st publication: Vol. 15 of *Proceedings of the British Academy* (London: Humphrey Milford Amen House, 1929). London: Oxford Univ. Press, 1972.

Beale, S. Sophia. *The Churches of Paris from Clovis to Charles X*. London: W. H. Allen, 1893.

Beneŝeviĉ, V. N. *Sinagogá v 50 Titulov: I Drugie Juridiĉeskie Sborniki Joanna Scholastika*. Leipzig: Zentralantiquariat der Deutschen Demokratischen Republik, 1972.

Bergengruen, Alexander. *Vierteljahrschrift für Sozial- und Wirtschaftsgeschichte: Adel und Grundherrschaft im Merowingerreich*. Weisbaden: Franz Steiner Verlag, 1958.

Berkhof, Hendrik. *Church and Emperor: An Inquiry into the Origin of the Theocratic Byzantine Concept of State in the 4th Century*. Trans. Gottfried W. Locher. Zollikon-Zurich: Evangelic Pub., 1947.

Bernheim, Ernst. *Mittelalterliche Zeitanschauungen in ihrem Einfluß auf Politik und Geschichtsschreibung*, Teil I: Die Zeintanschauungen, 1918;

Beurlier, E. *Essae sur le culte rendu aux empereurs Romains*, Thèse Paris, 1890 ;

Andreas Biglmair, *Die Beteiligung der Christen am öffentlichen Leben in vonconstantinischer Zeit* (Veröffentlichungen aus dem kirchenhistorischen Seminar München I. Reihe 8. Heft), 1902;

Binii, Rev. D. Severini. *Concilia Generalia, et Provincialia*, bk. 2. Coloniae Agrippinae: Apud Ioannem Gymnicum, und Antoinum Heirat, 1606.

Birks, Peter, and Grant McLeod, trans. *Justinian's Institutes*. Ithaca, NY: Cornell Univ Press, 1987.

Blakeney, E. H., trans. *The Tome of Pope Leo the Great*. Latin and English texts. London: Society for Promoting Christian Knowledge, 1923.

Bordonove, Georges. *Les Rois qui Ont Fait la France: Clovis*. Paris: Pygmalion, 1988.

Boretius, Alfredus. *Capitularia Regum Francorum*, bk. 1. In *Legum Section II. Capitularia Regum Francorum*, bk. 1. In *Monumenta Germaniae Historica*, edited by Societas Aperiendis Fontibus. Hanover: Impensis Bibliopolii Hahniani, 1883.

Brehaut, Ernest, trans. *(Gregory of Tours') History of the Franks*, selections. New York: Columbia Univ. Press, 1916.

Louis Bréhier et Pierre Batiffol, *Les survivances deu culte impérial romain*, 1920 ;

Bremond, Henri. *Historie Littérature du Sentiment Religieux en France*, vol. 1. Paris: Bloud and Gay, 1924.

Brieger, Theodor D., ed. *Zeitschrift für Kirchengeschichte*. Band 8. Gotha: Friedrich Andreas, 1886.

Bright, William. *A History of the Church D. 313–451*, 4th ed. Oxford: Parker and Co., 1881.

Brown, Elizabeth A. R. *"Franks, Burgundians, and Aquitanians" and the Royal Coronation Ceremony in France*. Vol. 82, pt. 7, of *Transactions of the American Philosophical Society*. Philadelphia: American Philosophical Society, 1992.

Bury, J. B. "The End of Roman Rule in North Gaul." *Cambridge Historical Journal* 1, no. 2 (1924): 197–201.

Bury, J. B. *A History of Freedom of Thought*. London: Oxford Univ. Press, 1949.

Bury, J. B. *The Invasion of Europe by the Barbarians*. New York: W. W. Norton, 1967.

Cameron, Averil. *Christianity and the Rhetoric of Empire.* Berkeley: Univ. of California Press, 1991.

Cameron, Averil, and Stuart G. Hall, trans. *Eusebius: Life of Constantine.* Oxford: Clarendon Press, 1999.

Cameron, Averil. *The Mediterranean World in Late Antiquity AD 395–600.* London: Routledge, 1993.

Carlyle, R.W. and A. J. Carlyle. *A History of mediaeval political theory in the west,* Vol. I, 1903;

Caspar, Erich. *Geschicthe des Papsttums,* Bd. I and II, 1930/1933;

Caspar, Erich. *Geschichte des Papsttums,* Bd. II, 1933;

Chadwick, Henry. "Faith and Order at the Council of Nicaea: A Note on the Background of the Sixth Canon." *The Harvard Theological Review* 53, no. 3 (July 1960): 171–195.

Charanis, Peter. *Church and State in the Later Roman Period: The Religious Policy of Anastasius I.* Madison: University of Wisconsin Press, 1939.

Chaunu, Pierre, and Eric Mension-Rigau. *Baptême de Clovis, Baptême de la France.* Paris: Balland, 1996.

Chevallier, Béatrice. *Clovis un Roi Européen.* Paris: Brepols, 1996.

Clauss, Manfred. *Der magister officiorus in der Spatantike (4.–6. Jahrhundert).* Munich: C. H. Beck'sche Verlagsbuchhandlung, 1980.

Cloché, Paul. *Les élections épiscopales sous les Mérovingiens* (Le Moyen-age T. 35 [2e Série T. 26] p. 203 sqq.), 1924.

Coleman-Norton, P. R. *Roman State and Christian Church: A Collection of Legal Documents to A.D. 535,* 3 vols. London: S.P.C.K., 1966.

Corpvs Christianorvm, Series Latina CXVII, (Gundlach, W; Epistvlae Avstrasicae)

Conrat (Cohn), Max, "comp". *Breviarium Alaricianum.* N.p.: Scientia Verlag Aalen, 1963.

Crehan, J. H. "Canon Dominicus Papae Gelasi." *Vigiliae Christianae* 12, no. 1 (May 1958), 45–48.

Crisp, Ryan Patrick. "Marriage and Alliance in the Merovingian Kingdoms, 481–639." PhD diss., Ohio State Univ., 2003.

Currier, John W. *Clovis, King of the Franks.* Milwaukee: Marquette Univ. Press, 1997.

Dahn, Felix. *Die Könige der Germanen,* Abt. V und VI, 1870/1871;

Dahn, Felix. *Die Könige der Germanen,* Bd. VII 1-3: *Die Franken unter den Merovingen,* 1894/1895;

Daly, William M. "Clovis: How Barbaric, How Pagan?" *Speculum* 69, no. 3 (July 1994): 619–664.

D'Arcy, M. C., S.J.; Maurice Blondel; Christopher Dawson; Etienne Gilson; Jacques Maritain; C. C. Martindale, S.J.; Erich Przywara, S.J.; John-Baptist Reeves; B. Roland-Gosselin; and E. I. Watkin. *St. Augustine.* Reprint. Cleveland: World Publishing, 1969.

Darras, M. L'Abbe J. E. *A General History of the Catholic Church.* 1st Am. trans. from last Fr. ed. New York: P. O'Shea, 1867.

Deanesly, Margaret. *A History of Early Medieval Europe 476– 911.*London: Methuen, 1956.

Dearden, Rev. H. W. *Modern Romanism Examined,* 3rd ed. London: Chas. J. Thynne, 1909.

De Bonnechose, Emile. *History of France*. London: Routledge, 1854.

Deissman, Adolf. *Licht vom Osten*, 2nd edition, 1909

Delorme, Philippe, and Luc de Goustine. *Clovis 496–1996*. Paris: Règnier, 1996.

De Sismondi, J. C. L. Simonde. *The French under the Merovingians and Carlovingians*. Trans. William Bellingham. Reprinted from original (London: W. and T. Piper, 1850). New York: AMS Press, 1976.

Diehl, Charles. *Justinien et la Civilisation Byzantine*, vol. 1. New York: Burt Franklin, 1901.

Dill, Sir Samuel. *Roman Society in Gaul in the Merovingian Age*. London: MacMillan, 1926.

Diplomata Regum Francorum E Stirpe Merovingica, 2 bks. In *Monumenta Germaniae Historica*, edited by Societas Aperiendis Fontibus. Hanover: Impensis Bibliopolii Hahniani, 1901.

Dods, Marcus, trans. *The City of God by Saint Augustine*. New York: Modern Library, 1950.

Doerries, Hermann. *Constantine and Religious Liberty*. Trans. Roland Bainton. New Haven: Yale Univ. Press, 1960.

Dolan, Rev. Thomas S. *The Papacy and the First Councils of the Church*. St. Louis: B. Herder, 1910.

Donini, Guido, and Gordon B. Ford, Jr., trans. *Isadore of Seville's History of the Goths, Vandals, and Suevi*, 2nd rev. ed. Leiden: E. J. Brill, 1970.

Dopsch, Alfons. *Wirtschaftliche und soziale Grundlagen der europäischen Kulturentwicklung aus der Zeit von Caesar bis auf Karl den Großen*, II. Teil, 2nd edition, 1924;

Drake, H. A. *Constantine and the Bishops*. Baltimore: Johns Hopkins Univ. Press, 2000.

Drew, Katherine Fischer, trans. *The Laws of the Salian Franks*. Philadelphia: Univ. of Pennsylvania Press, 1991.

Drew, Katherine Fischer, trans. *The Lombard Laws*. Philadelphia: Univ. of Pennsylvania Press, 1996.

Duchesne, Mons. Louis. *Early History of the Christian Church*. 3 vols. Translated into English from the 4th ed. London: John Murray, 1957.

Duchesne, Mons. Louis. *L'Église au VIe Siècle*. Paris: Fontemoing (de Boccard), 1925.

Duchesne, L'Abbé Louis. *Fastes Épiscopaux de L'Ancienne Gaule*, 3 bks. Paris: Thorin et Fils, n.d. (1); 1900 (2). Paris: Fontemoing (de Boccard, Successeur), 1915 (3).

Duchesne, L'Abbé Louis. *Le Liber Pontificalis*, bk. 1. Paris: E. de Boccard, 1955.

Dvornik, Francis. *The Ecumenical Councils*. New York: Hawthorn Books, 1961.

Dvornik, Francis. "Emperors, Popes, and General Councils." *Dumbarton Oaks Papers* 6 (1951): 1, 3–23.

Eichmann, Eduard. *Acht und Bann im Reichsrecht des Mittelalters* (Görres-Gesellschaft, Veröffentlichungen der Secktion für Rechts- und Sozialwissenschaft, 6. Heft), 1909;

Eusebius, *The History of the Church from Christ to Constantine*. Translated by G. A. Williamson. New York: Barnes and Noble, 1965.

Fear, A. T., trans., ed. *Lives of the Visigothic Fathers*. Vol. 26 of *Translated Texts for Historians*. Liverpool: Liverpool University Press, 1997.

Ferreiro, Alberto. *The Visigoths in Gaul and Spain A.D. 418–711*. A bibliography. Leiden: E. J. Brill, 1988.

Five Great Encyclicals: The Condition of Labor, Christian Education of Youth, Christian Marriage, Reconstructing the Social Order, Atheistic Communism. New York: Paulist Press, 1944.

Foakes-Jackson, F. J. *The History of the Christian Church to A.D. 461*, 6th ed. Cambridge, UK: J. Hall and Son, 1914

Frend, W. H. C. *The Donatist Church*. Oxford: Clarendon Press, 1952.

Frend, W. H. C. *The Early Church*. Minneapolis: Fortress Press, 1991.

Friedberg, Emil. *De Finium inter Ecclesiam et Civitatem Regundorum Judicio*. N.p.: Scientia Verlag Aalen, 1965.

Funk-Bihlmeyer, *Kirchengeschichte auf Grund des Lehrbuches* von F. X. Von Funk re-worked by Karl Bihlmeyer, I. Teil, 9th edition, 1931;

Gaudemet, Jean. *Ius Romanum Medii Aevi*, pts. 1, 2 b aa β. Milan, It.: Typis Giuffrè, 1965.

Gaudemet, Jean, and Brigitte Basdevant, trans. *Les Canons des Conciles Mérovingians (VIe–VIIe Siècles)*. 2 vols. Paris: Les Éditions du Cerf, 1989.

Geary, Patrick J. *Before France and Germany*. New York: Oxford University Press, 1988.

Geffcken, Johannes. *The Last Days of Greco-Roman Paganism*. Translated by Sabine MacCormack. Vol. 8, *Europe in the Middle Ages, Selected Studies*, edited by Richard Vaughan. Amsterdam: North-Holland, 1978.

Gerberding, Richard A. *The Rise of the Carolingians and the Liber Historiae Francorum*. Oxford: Clarendon Press, 1987.

Gilliard, Frank D. "The Senators of Sixth-Century Gaul." *Speculum* 54, no. 4 (October 1979): 685–697.

Gobry, Ivan. *Clovis le Grand*. Paris: Regnier, 1995.

Gonestal, R. *Les origines du privilege clerical (Nouvelle Revue historique de droit français et étranger*, 3lZe AnDee p. 161 sqq.), 1908.

Gorce, M. M. *Clovis 465–511*. Paris: Payot, 1935.

Gore, Rev. Charles. *Leo the Great*. London: Society for Promoting Christian Knowledge, 1897.

Görres, Franz. *Kritische Untersuchungen über den Aufstand und das Martyrium des westgothischen Königsohnes Hermenegild* (Zeitschr. F. *Die histor. Theologie* Bd. 43 p. 3 ff.), 1873;

Görres, Franz. *Kirche und Staat im Westgotenreich von Eurich bis auf Leovigild (466-567/69)* (*Theolog. Studien und Kritiken*, 66. Jahrgang p. 708 ff.), 1893;

Görres, Franz. *König Rekared der Katholische (586-601)* (Zeitschr. F. Wissenschaftl. *Theologie* Bd. 42 [N.F. Bd. 7] p. 270 ff.), 1899;

Görres, Franz. *Der spanisch-westgotische Episkopat und das römische Papsttum von König Rekared dem Katholischen bis Wamba* (ebd. Bd.45 (N. F. Bd. 10] S. 41 if.), 1902;

Grant, Robert M. *Augustus to Constantine*. New York: Harper and Row, 1970.

Grayzel, Solomon. "Jews and the Ecumenical Councils." *The Jewish Quarterly Review*, n.s., 57 (1967): 287–311.

Greenslade, S. L. *Church and State from Constantine to Theodosius*. London: SCM Press, 1954.

Gregory of Tours. *The History of the Franks*, 2 vols. Translated by O. M. Dalton. Reprint authorized by Clarendon Press; republished in Farnborough, Eng.: Gregg Press, 1967.

Gregory of Tours. *The Merovingians*. Translated by Alexander C. Murray. Orchard Park, NY: Broadview Press, 2005.

Griffe, Élie. *La Gaule Chrétienne a L'Époque Romaine*. Paris: Letouzey and Anè, 1964.

Grisar, Hartmann. *Rom und die fränkische Kirche vornehmnlich im sechsten Jahrhundert* (Zeitschr. F. Kathol. Theologie Bd. 14 p. 447 ff.), 1890;

Guenther, Otto, Ed. *Epistulae Imperatorum Pontificum Aliorum, Avellana Quae Dicitur Collectio*, 2 pts. In *Corpus Scriptorum Ecclesiasticorum Latinorum*, vol. 35. Prague: F. Tempsky, 1895 (1); 1898 (2).

Guichard, Réne. *Essay sur L'Histoire du Peuple Burgonde*. Paris: A. and J. Picard, 1965.

Guizot, François P. G. "Clovis Founds the Kingdom of the Franks: It Becomes Christian." In *Great Events by Famous Historians*. N.p.: n.p., 1914.

Guttman, Allen. "From Brownson to Eliot: The Conservative Theory of Church and State." *American Quarterly* 17, no. 3 (Autumn, 1965): 483–500.

Gwatkin, H. M. "Guenther's Epistulae; Tischendorf's Synopsis; Butler's Lausiac History; Gelzer's, Hilgenfeld's and Cuntz's Nicene Council." Review of *Corpus Scriptorum Ecclesiasticorum Latinorum*, by Ottonis Guenther; *Synopsis Evangelica*, by Tischendorf; *Texts and Studies*, by J. Armitage Robinson; *Patrum Nicaenorum Nomina*, by H. Gelzer, H. Hilgenfeld; O. Cuntz. *The Classical Review* 13, no. 2 (March 1899): 134–135.

Haenel, Gustavus, ed. *Lex Romana Visigothorum*. Sientia Aalen, 1962.

Hardy, E. G. *Christianity and the Roman Government*. Reprint of 1st ed., 1894. London: George Allen and Unwin, 1925.

Harnack, Adolf. *Kirche und Staat bis zur Gründung der Staatskirche* (Internat. Wochenschrift 2. Jahrg. Nr. 49-52), 1908;

Harries, Jill and Ian Wood, eds. *The Theodosian Code*. Ithaca, NY: Cornell Univ. Press, 1993.

Hashagen, Justus. Über die Anfänge der christlichen Staats- und Gesellschaftsanschauung (Zeitschr. F. Kirchengesch. Bd. 49 [N.F. Bd. 12] p. 131 ff.), 1930.

Hauck, Karl, ed. *Arbeiten zur Frühmittelalterforschung*. Bd. 15. Berlin: Walter de Gruyter, 1984.

Hauck, Albert. *Kirchengeschichte Deutschlands*, Bd. I 3rd and 4th edition, 1904;

Hauck, Karl, ed. *Works to Early Medieval Research*, vol. 15. Berlin: Walter de Gruyter, 1984.

Hayward, Jane. "Sacred Vestments as They Developed in the Middle Ages." *The Metropolitan Museum of Art Bulletin*, n.s., 29, no. 7 (March 1971): 299–309.

Heather, Peter. "The Huns and the End of the Roman Empire in Western Europe." *The English Historical Review* 110, no. 435 (February 1995): 4–41.

Heather, Peter, ed. *The Visigoths from the Migration Period to the Seventh Century*. Woodbridge, Eng.: Boydell Press, 1999.

Heinzelmann, Martin. *Gregory of Tours*. Trans. Christopher Carroll. Cambridge, UK: Cambridge Univ. Press, 2006.

Hen, Yitzhak. *Culture and Religion in Merovingian Gaul A.D. 481–751*. Leiden: E. J. Brill, 1995.

Hillgarth, J. N. *The Conversion of Western Europe 350–750*. Englewood Cliffs, NJ: Prentice-Hall, 1969.

Hodgkin, Thomas. *The Letters of Cassiodorus: Being a Condensed Translation of the Variae Epistolae of Magnus Aurelius Cassiodorus Senator*. London: Henry Frowde, 1886.

Holmes, J. Derek, and Bernard W. Bickers. *A Short History of the Catholic Church*. Tunbridge Wells, UK: Burns and Oates, 1987.

Hughes, Philip. *The Church in Crisis: A History of the General Councils, 325–1870*. New York: Hanover House, 1961.

Hunt, Bro. Edmund, trans. *St. Leo the Great: Letters*. Vol. 34 of *The Fathers of the Church*. New York: Fathers of the Church, 1957.

Hyde, Walter W. *Paganism to Christianity in the Roman Empire*. Philadelphia: Univ. of Pennsylvania Press, 1946.

Ingram, Scott. *Attila the Hun*. San Diego: Blackbirch Press, 2002.

IVRA: Rivista Internationale di Diritto Romano e Antico, vol. 18. Napoli: Jovene, 1967.

Jaffé, Philippus. *Regesta Pontificum Romanorusm*, bk. 1. Graz: Akademische Druck- U. Verlagsanstalt, 1956.

Jaffé, Philippus. *Regesta Pontificum Romanorum*, bk. 1. Leipsic: Veit, 1885.

James, Edward. *The Franks*. Oxford: Basil Blackwell, 1988.

James, Edward, trans. *Gregory of Tours: Life of the Fathers*, 2nd ed. Vol. 1 of *Translated Texts for Historians*. Liverpool: Liverpool Univ. Press, 1991.

James, Edward. *The Origins of France from Clovis to the Capetians 500–1000*. London: MacMillan, 1994.

Jervis, Rev. W. Henley. *The Gallican Church to the Revolution*, 2 vols. London: John Murray, 1872.

Jervis, Rev. W. Henley. "Mr. Jervis on the Jansenistic and Gallican Movement." Art. 4, *Dublin Review*, 1874.

Juster, Jean. *Les Juifs dans L'Empire Roman: Leur Condition Juridique, Économique et Sociale*, 2 vols. New York: Burt Franklin, 1914.

Kampers, Franz. *Rex et sacerdos* (*Histor. Jahrbuch* Bd. 45p. 495 ff.), 1925.

Kattenbusch, Ferdinand. *Lehrbuch der vergleichenden Confessionskunde*, Bd. I: *Die orthodoxe anatolische Kirche*, 1892;

Katz, Solomon. *The Jews in the Visigothic and Frankish Kingdoms of Spain and Gaul*. Cambridge, MA: Medieval Acad. of America, 1937.

Kern, Fritz. *Gottesgnadentum und Widerstandsrecht im früheren Mittelalter*, 1914;

King, P. D. *Law and Society in the Visigothic Kingdom*. London: Cambridge Univ. Press, 1972.

King, Anthony. *Roman Gaul and Germany*. Berkeley: Univ. of California Press, 1990.

Kirsch, J. F. *Kirchengeschichte*, Bd. I: *Die Kirche in der antiken griechisch-römischen Kulturwelt*, 1930;

Kissling, Wilhelm. *Das Verhältnis zwischen Sacerdotium und Imperium nach den Anschauungen der Päpste von Leo d. Gr. Bis Gelasius (440-496)* (Görres-Gesellschaft, Veröffentlichungen der Sektion für Rechts- und Sozialwissenschaft 38. Heft), 1921.

Klingshirn, William E., trans. *Caesarius of Arles: Life, Testament, Letters.* Vol. 19 of *Translated Texts for Historians.* Liverpool: Liverpool Univ. Press, 1994.

Klingshirn, William E. *Caesarius of Arles.* Cambridge, UK: Press Syndicate of the Univ. of Cambridge, 2004.

Knabe, Lotte. *The Gelasian Theory of Two Powers until the End of the Investiture Era.* Berlin: Emil Ebering, 1936.

Knabe, Lotte. *Die gelasianische Zweigewaltentheorie bis zum Ende des Investiturstreits.*Vaduz: Kraus Reprint, 1965.

Krusch, Bruno. *Fredegarii et Aliorum Chronica. Vitae Sanctorum.* In *Scriptores Rerum Merovingicarum,* bk. 2, in *Monumenta Germaniae Historica,* edited by Societas Aperiendis Fontibus. Hanover: Impensis Bibliopolii Hahniani, 1888.

Krusch, Bruno. *Gregorii Episcopi Turonensis Historiarum Libri X,* new ed. In *Scriptores Rerum Merovingicarum,* bk. 1, pt. 1, fasc. 1, in *Monumenta Germaniae Historica,* edited by Societas Aperiendis Fontibus. Hanover: Impensis Bibliopolii Hahniani, 1837.

Krusch, Bruno. *Scriptores Rerum Merovingicarum,* bk. 1, pt. 2, new ed. In *Monumenta Germaniae Historica,* edited by Societas Aperiendis Fontibus. Hanover: Impensis Bibliopolii Hahniani, 1885.

Krusch, Bruno, and Wilhelmus Levison. *Gregorii Episcopi Turonensis Libri Historiarum X,* bk. 1, pt. 1, new ed. In *Scriptores Rerum Merovingicarum,* bk. 1, pt. 1, new ed, in *Monumenta Germaniae Historica,* edited by Societas Aperiendis Fontibus. Hanover: Impensis Bibliopolii Hahniani, 1860 (1865).

Kurth, Godefroid. *Clovis*, 3rd ed, 2 bks. Brussels: Albert Dewit Library, 1923.

Ladner, Gerhart B. "Aspects of Mediaeval Thought on Church and State." *The Review of Politics* 9, no. 4 (October 1947): 403–422.

Laforest, Michele. *Clovis, un Roi de Légende*. Paris: Albin Michel, 1996.

Lambertini, Renzo. *La Codificazione di Alarico II*. Turin, It.: G. Giappichelli, 1990.

Lasko, Peter. *The Kingdom of the Franks*. New York: McGraw-Hill, 1971.

Lecky, William E. H. *History of European Morals*, 2 vols. New York: D. Appleton, 1929.

Leges Visigothorum, bk. 1. In *Legum Sectio I. Leges Nationum Germanicarum*, bk. 1, in *Monumenta Germaniae Historica*, edited by Societas Aperiendis Fontibus. Hanover: Impensis Bibliopolii Hahniani, 1902.

Lesbaupin, Ivo. *Blessed are the Persecuted*. Translated by Robert R. Barr. London: Spire, 1988.

Levine, Robert, trans. *France before Charlemagne: A Translation from the* Grandes Chroniques. Lewiston, NY: Edwin Mellen, 1990.

Liebs, Detlef. *Romische Jurisprudenz in Gallien (2. Bis 8. Jahrhundert)*, n.s. Bd. 38. Berlin: Duncker and Humblot,

Linder, Amnon, ed., trans. *The Jews in the Legal Sources of the Early Middle Ages*. Detroit, MI: Wayne State Univ. Press, 1997.

Linder, Amnon, ed., trans. *The Jews in Roman Imperial Legislation*. Detroit, MI: Wayne State Univ. Press, 1987.

Linder, Amnon. *The Myth of Constantine the Great in the West: Sources and Hagiographic Commemoration.* Spoleto: Centro Italiano di Studi Sull'Alto Medioevo, 1987.

Llewellyn, P. A. B. "The Roman Church during the Laurentian Schism: Priests and Senators." *Church History* 45, no. 4 (December 1976): 417–427.

Loening, Edgar. *Geschichte des deutschen Kirchenrechts,* Bd. II, 1878;

Loening, Edgar. *Geschichte des deutschen Kirchenrechts* Bd.II, 1878; l' a u I Hi n s chi u s, [las *Kirchenrecht der Katholiken und Protestauten in Deutschland,* Bd. III und IV, 1883/1886.

Maassen, Fridericus. *Concilia Aevi Merovingici,* bk. 1. In *Concilia,* in *Monumenta Germaniae Historica, Legum Sectio III Concilia,* bk. 1, edited by Societas Aperiendis Fontibus. Hanover: Impensis Bibliopolii Hahniani, 1893.

Maassen, Friedrich. *Sitzengsberichte der Kaiserlichen Akademie der Wissenschaften Philosophisch-Historiche Classe.* 35 Band. 2 Heft. Jahrgang, 1860. Wien: Aus der K. K. Hof- und Staatsdruckerei, 1860.

MacDowall, Simon. *Goths, Huns and Romans.* Hemel Hempstead, Eng.: Argus, 1990.

MacMullen, Ramsay, and Eugene N. Lane, eds. *Paganism and Christianity 100–425 C.E.* Minneapolis: Fortress Press, 1992.

Maenchen-Helfen, Otto J. *The World of the Huns.* Berkeley: Univ. of California Press, 1973.

Magnin, E. *L'Eglise wisigothique au VIIe siècle,* T. I (*Bibliothèque d'histoire religieuse*), 1912;

Malalas, Joannes. *Corpus Scriptorum Historiae Byzantinae.* Bonn: Impensis Ed. Weberi, 1831.

Mango, Cyril, and Roger Scott, trans. *The Chronicle of Theophanes Confessor.* Oxford: Clarendon Press, 1997.

Mansi, Joannes Dominicus. *Sacrorum Donciliorum Nova et Amplissima Collectio,* vol. 1. Graz: Akademische Druck- U. Verlagsanstalt. 1960.

Mathisen, Ralph W. "Barbarian Bishops and the Churches 'in Barbaricis Gentibus' During Late Antiquity." *Speculum* 72, no. 3 (July 1997): 664–697.

Mathisen, Ralph W. *Ecclesiastical Factionalism and Religious Controversy in Fifth-Century Gaul.* Washington, DC: Catholic Univ. of Am. Press, 1989.

Mathisen, Ralph W., ed. *Law, Society, and Authority in Late Antiquity.* Oxford: Oxford Univ. Press, 2005.

Mathisen, Ralph W., trans. *Ruricus of Limoges and Friends.* Vol. 30 of *Translated Texts for Historians*. Liverpool: Liverpool Univ. Press, 1999.

Mathisen, Ralph W., and Danuta Shanzer, eds. *Society and Culture in Late Antique Gaul.* Aldershot, Eng.: Ashgate, 2001.

Matthews, John, and Bob Stewart. *Warriors of Christendom.* Poole, UK: Firebird Bks., 1988.

Mausbach, Joseph. *Die Ethik des heil.* Augustinus, 2nd Edition, Bd. I, 1929;

McCabe, Joseph, The Contemporary Review, "The Church of Rome in Spain." (London, Horace Marshall & Son, Temple House, Temple Avenue, and 125 Fleet Street, E.C; Volume 83 (January–June 1903): 855–865.

McCabe, Joseph, *St. Augustine and His Age.* London: Duckworth, 1902.

McCabe, Joseph, The Contemporary Review, "St. Augustine and the Roman Claims." London: Horace Marshall & Son, Temple House, Temple Avenue, and 125 Fleet Street, E.C; Volume 82 (July–December 1902): 685–695.

McCabe, Joseph, *The Truth About the Catholic Church.* Girard, Kansas: Haldeman-Julius Company, 1926), 7-16, (Big Blue Book, No. B-27), chapters 1-2.

McCabe, Joseph, *St. Augustine and His Age*, (New York, G. P. Putnam's Sons, 1902). 431-435, 456-460.

McCabe, Joseph, "St. Augustine and the Roman Claims," *The Contemporary Review.* London: Horace Marshall & Son, Temple House, Temple Avenue, and 125 Fleet Street, E.C; Volume 82. July-December, 1902, 685-695.

McKitterick, Rosamond. "Constructing the Past in the Early Middle Ages: The Case of the Royal Frankish Annals." *Transactions of the Royal Historical Society*, 6th ser., 7 (1997): 101–129.

Mérowingici et Karolini, bk. 1. In *Epistolarum Tomus III*, 2nd ed., in *Monumenta Germaniae Historica*, edited by Societas Aperiendis Fontibus. Berlin: Apud Weidmannos, 1862.

Mitchell, Edwin K., ed. *The Canons of the First Four General Councils: Nicaea, Constantinople, Ephesus and Chalcedon*, rev. ed. Vol. 4, No. 2, of *Translations and Reprints from the Original Sources of European History.* Philadelphia: Dept. of History of the Univ. of Pennsylvania, 1908.

Mitchell, Kathleen, and Ian Wood, eds. *The World of Gregory of Tours.* Leiden: Brill, 2002.

Mitteilungen des Institute für Österreichische Geschichtsforschung. 75 Bd., 1 u 2 Heft. Graz: Hermann Böhlaus Nachf, 1967.

Mommsen, Th. *Theodosiani, Libri XVI cum Constitutionibus Sirmondianis*, vol. 1; pts. 1, 2. Dublin: Apud Weidmannos, 1971.

Moorhead, John. "The Laurentian Schism: East and West in the Roman Church." *Church History* 47, no. 2 (June 1978): 125–136.

Moorhead, John, trans. *Victor of Vita: History of the Vandal Persecution*. Vol. 10 of *Translated Texts for Historians*. Liverpool: Liverpool Univ. Press, 1992.

Mueller, Sis. Mary Magdeleine, trans. *Saint Caesarius of Arles*. Vol. 1 of *The Fathers of the Church*. New York: Fathers of the Church, 1956.

Mueller, Sis. Mary Magdeleine, trans. *St. Caesarius of Arles: Sermons*. Vol. 2 of *The Fathers of the Church*. Washington, DC: Catholic Univ. of America Press, 1963.

Murray, Alexander, ed., trans. *From Roman to Merovingian Gaul*. Peterborough, ON: Broadview Press, 2000.

Murray, Alexander C., ed., trans. *Gregory of Tours: the Merovingians*. Peterborough, ON: Broadview Press, 2006.

Mussot-Goulard, Renée. *Clovis*. Paris: Univ. of France Press, 1997.

Myers, Philip Van Ness. *Ancient History*, rev. 2nd ed. Boston: Ginn, 1916.

Myers, Philip Van Ness. *Mediaeval and Modern History*, rev. ed. Boston: Ginn, 1905.

Nelson's Encyclopedia, vol. 12. New York: Thomas Nelson, 1907.

Neumann, Karl Johannes. *Der römische Staat und die allgemeine Kirche bis auf Diocletian*, Vol. I, 1890;

Neumann, Karl Johannes. *Hyppolitus von Rom in siner Stellung zu Staat und Welt*, 1902;

Noailles, Pierre. *Les Collections de Novelles de L'Empereur Justinien: La Collection Grecque des 168 Novelles*. Paris: Recueil Sirey, 1914.

Noailles, Pierre. *Les Collections de Novelles de L'Empereur Justinien: Origine et Formation sous Justinien*. Paris: Recueil Sirey, 1912.

Noble, Thomas F. X., ed. *From Roman Provinces to Medieval Kingdoms*. London: Routledge, 2006.

Odahl, Charles M. *Constantine and the Christian Empire*. London: Routledge, 2004.

Odahl, Charles M. *Early Christian Latin Literature*. Chicago: Ares Publishers, 1993.

Offergelt, Franz. *Die Staatslehre des heil*. Augustinus nach seinen sämtlichen Werken, 1914;

O'Grady, Desmond. *Beyond the Empire*. New York: Crossroad, 2001.

Oliver, Lisi. *The Beginnings of English Law*. Toronto: Univ. of Toronto Press, 2002.

Oppenheimer, Sir Francis. *Frankish Themes and Problems*. London: Faber and Faber, 1952.

Parkes, James. *The Conflict of the Church and the Synagogue*. New York: Atheneum, 1969.

Peiper, Rudolfus. *Alcimi Ecdicii Aviti*. In *Avctorum Antiquissimorum Tomi VI pars posterior*, in *Monumenta Germaniae Historica*, edited by Societas Aperiendis Fontibus. Berlin: Apud Weidmannos, 1883.

Pelikan, Jaroslav. *The Excellent Empire*. San Francisco: Harper and Row, 1987.

Pellus, Daniel. *Clovis: Réalities et Légendes*. Amiens, Fr.: Martelle, 1996.

Perry, Walter C. *The Franks*. London: Longman, Brown, Green, Longmans, and Roberts, 1857.

Pharr, Clyde, trans. *The Theodosian Code and Novels and the Sirmondian Constitutions*. Union, NJ: Lawbook Exchange, 2001.

Pontal, Odette. *Histoire des Conciles Mérovingiens*. N.p.: Éditions du Cerf, 1989.

Pontal, Odette. *Die Synoden im Merowingerrich*. Paderborn, Ger.: Ferdinand Schöningh, 1986.

Porter, W. S. *The Gallican Rite*. London: A. R. Mowbray, 1958.

Pöschl, Arnold. *Bischofsgut und mensa episcopalis*, I. Teil, 1908;

Potter, John. "The Development and Significance of the Salic Law of the French." *The English Historical Review* 52, no. 206 (April 1937): 235–253.

Pride, Ellen Perry. "Ecclesiastical Legislation on Education, A.D. 300–254." *Church History* 12, no. 4 (December 1943): 235–254.

Rabello, Alfredo Mordechai. *The Jews in the Roman Empire: Legal Problems, from Herod to Justinian*. Aldershot, UK: Ashgate, 1999.

Rabello, Alfredo Mordechai. "The Legal Condition of the Jews in the Roman Empire." In *Aufstieg und Neidergang der Romischen Welt:Geschichte und Kultur Roms im Spiegel der Neueren Forschung*, vol. 2, 662–766. Berlin: Walter de Gruyter, 1980.

Rabello, Alfredo Mordechai. *The Legal Status of the Jews in Roman Empire and in Medieval Age*. Jerusalem: n.p., 1972. First published in *Israel Law Review* 11, no. 2 (1972): 216–589.

Rabello, Afred M. "The 'Lex de Templo Heirosolymitano,' Prohibiting Gentiles from Entering Jerusalem's Sanctuary," pt. 1.

Rabinowitz, Jacob J. "The Influence of Jewish Law upon the Development of Frankish Law." *Proceedings of the American Academy for Jewish Research* 16 (1946–47): 205–224.

Revue du Moyen Age Latin, bk. 4. Strasbourg: Societe Nouvelle D'Impression, 1948.

Reydellet, Marc. *Royalty in Latin Literature from Sidonius Appolinarus to Isadore of Seville*. Paris: Diffusion de Boccard, 1981.

Ribbeck, Konrad. *Die sog. Divisio des fränkischen Kirchengutes in ihrem Verlaufe under Karl Martell und seinen Söhnen*, Dissert. Leipzig, 1883.

Richards, Jeffrey. *The Popes and the Papacy in the Early Middle Ages 476–752*. London: Routledge and Kegan Paul, 1979.

Roberts, Rev. Alexander, and James Donaldson, eds. *The Ante-Nicene Fathers*, vol. 7. Trans. of *The Writings of the Fathers down to A.D. 325*; American reprint of Edinburgh edition. Grand Rapids, MI: Wm. B. Eerdmans, 1886.

Roberts, Ethel. "Notes on Early Christian Libraries in Rome." *Speculum* 9, no. 2: 190–194.

Rouche, Michel. *Clovis*. Fayard, 1996.

Rouche, Michel, ed. *Clovis, Histoire et Mémoire* (Actes du Colloque international d'historie de Reims), 2 vols. Paris: Univ. of Paris-Sorbonne Press, 1997.

Rouche, Michel. *L'Aquitaine des Wisigoths aux Arabes 418-781*. Paris: Jean Touzot, 1979.

The Sacramentary (The Roman Missal), rev., Eng. trans. New York: Catholic Book Pub., 1985.

Saki (H. H. Munro). *The Chronicles of Clovis*. New York: Viking Press, 1911.

Salin, Edgar. *Urchristentum und Staat* (Schmollers Jahrb. F. *Gesetzgebung, Verwaltung und Volkswirtschaft im Deutschen Reiche*, 55. Jahrg. I, p. 21 ff.), 1931;

Salin, Édouard. *La Civilisation Mérovingienne*, vol. 4. Paris: A. and J. Picard, 1959.

Sammarthani, Domni Dionysii. *Gallia Christiana in Provincias Ecclesisticas Distributa*, bk. 2. Paris: Apud Victorem Palmé, 1868.

Schäferdick, Knut. "The Church in the Empires of the Visigoths and the Suebi up to the Establishment of the Visigothic Catholic State Church." Diss., Rhenish Friedrick-Wilhelm-Univ., 1967.

Schaferdiek, Kurt von. *Die Kirche in den Reichen der Westgoten und Suewen bis zur Errichtung der westgotischen katholischen Staatskirche*. Berlin: Walter de Gruyter, 1967.

Schaferdiek, Kurt von. *Die Kirche in den Reichen der Westgoten und Suewen bis zur Errichtung der westgotischen katholischen Staatskirche*. Berlin: Walter de Gruyter, 1967. [The Church in the Empires of the Visigoths and the Suebi up to the Establishment of the Visigothic Catholic State Church].

Scherman, Katharine. *The Birth of France*. New York: Random House: 1987.

Schilling, Otto. *Die Staats- und Soziallehre des heil. Augustinus*, 1910.

Schilling, Otto. *Naturrecht und Staat nach der Lehre der alten Kirche* (Görres-Gesellschaft, *Veröffentlichungen der Sektion für Rechts- und Sozialwissenschaft* 24. Heft), 1914;

Schmidt, Ludwig. *Allgemeine Geschichte der germanischen Völker bis zur Mitte des sechsten Jahrhunderts,* 1909;

Scholz, Bernhard Walter, trans. *Carolingian Chronicles.* Ann Arbor, MI: Univ. of Michigan Press, 1970.

Schultze, Viktor. "Untersuchungen zur Geschichte Konstantin's d. Gr." In *Zeitschrift für Kirchengeschichte,* edited by Theodor Brieger. Bd. 8. Gotha: Friedrich Andreas Perthes, 1886.

Siebold, Martin. *Das Asylrecht der römischen Kirche mit besonderer Berücksichtigung seiner Entwicklung auf germanischem Boden,* Dissert. Münster, 1930;

Seidel, Bruno. *Die Lehre des heil. Augustinus vom Staate* [cover-titel: *Die Lehre vom Staat beim heil. Augustinus*] (Kirchengeschichtliche Abhandlungen ed. By Max Sdralek IX. Bd. 1. Heft), 1909;

Shanzer, Danuta. "Dating the baptism of Clovis: the bishop of Vienne vs the bishop of Tours." In vol. 1 of *Early Medieval Europe,* 29–57. Oxford: Blackwell, 1998.

Shanzer, Danuta, and Ian Wood, trans. *Avitus of Vienne: Letters and Selected Prose.* Vol. 38 of *Translated Texts for Historians.* Liverpool: Liverpool Univ. Press, 2002.

Sitzengsberichte der Kaiserlichen. 134 Band. Jahrgang 1895. Edited by Akademie der Wissenschaften Philosophisch-Historische Classe. Wien: Druck Von Adolf Holzhausen, 1896.

Smith, R. Payne, trans. *The Third Part of the Ecclesiastical History of John Bishop of Ephesus.* Oxford: Oxford Univ. Press, 1860.

Sonntag, Regine. *Studien zur Bewertung von Zahlenangaben in der Geschichtsschreibung des früheren Mittelalters: Die Decem Libri Historiarum Gregors von Tours und die Chronica Reginos von Prüm.* Bd. 4. Kallmünz, Ger.: Michael Lassleben, 1987.

Spencer, Mark. "Dating the baptism of Clovis, 1886–1993." *Early Medieval Europe* 3(2), 97–116. Oxford: Blackwell, 1994.

Stein, Simon. "Lex Salica, I." *Speculum* 22, no. 2 (April 1947): 113–134.

Stein, Simon. "Lex Salica, II." *Speculum* 22, no. 3 (July 1947): 395–418.

Steinen, Wolfram von den. *Chlodwigs Übergang Zum Christentum.* Bd. 103. Darmstadt, Ger.: Wissenschaftliche Buchgesellschaft, 1969.

Steinen, Wolfram von den. *Theoderich und Chlodwig.* Tübingen: J. C. B. Mohr (Paul Siebeck), 1933.

Stutz, Ulrich. *Arianismus und Germanismus* (Internat. Wochenschrift Jahrg. 1909, Sp. 1561 ff., 1615 ff., 1633 ff.), 1909.

Stutz, Ulrich. Artikel *Eigenkirche, Eigenkloster* (Herzog-Hauck, *Realencyklopädie für protestant. Theologie und Kirche,* 3rd edition, Bd. 23 p. 364 ff.), 1913.

Stutz, Ulrich. *Die Eigenkirche als Element des mittelalterlich-germanischen Kirchenrechtes,* 1895;

Stutz, Ulrich. *Geschichte des kirchlichen Benefizialwesens,* Bd. I, 1895;

Stutz, Ulrich. *Das karolingische Zehntgebot* (Zeitschr. Der Savigny-Stiftung f. Rechtsgeschichte Bd. 42 [N. F. Bd. 29], German. Abt. P. 180 ff., 1908;

Stutz, Ulrich. *Kirchenrecht* (von Holtzendorff-Kohler, *Encyklopädie der Rechtswissenschaft*, 7th edition, Bd. 5 p. 299 ff.), 1914;

Tcherikover, Victor A., ed. *Corpus Papyrorum Judaicarum*, vol. 1. Cambridge, MA: Harvard Univ. Press, 1957.

Tessier, Georges. *Le Baptême de Clovis*. N.p.: Gallimard, 1996.

Thiel, Andreas, ed. *Epistolae Romanorum pontificum genuinae*, bk. 1. Brunsbergae In Aedibus Eduardi Peter, 1868.

Thiel, Andreas, ed. *Epistolae Romanorum pontificum genuinae*, bk. 1. New York: Georg Olms Verlag, 1974.

Thomson, John A. F. *The Western Church in the Middle Ages*. London: Arnold Pub., 1998.

Tierney, Brian. "Religion and Rights: A Medieval Perspective." *Journal of Law and Religion* 5, no. 1 (1987): 163–175.

Tilley, Maureen A., trans. *Donatist Martyr Stories*. Vol. 24 of *Translated Texts for Historians*. Liverpool: Liverpool Univ. Press, 1996.

Townsend, W. T. "Councils Held under Pope Symmachus." *Church History* 6, no. 3 (September 1937): 233–259.

Townsend, W. T. "The Henotikon Schism and the Roman Church." *The Journal of Religion* 16 (January 1936): 78–86.

Troeltsch, Ernst. *Augustin, die christliche Antike und das Mittelalter* (*Histor. Bibliothek* Bd. 36), 1915;

Vacandard, E. *Les élections épiscopales sous les Mérovingiens* (*Revue des questions historiques* 32e Année p. 321 sqq.), 1898

Vacandard, E. *L'Inquisition. Etude historique et critque sur le pouvoir coercitif de l'église*, 1907;

Van Dam, Raymond, trans. *Gregory of Tours: Glory of the Confessors*. Vol. 5 of *Translated Texts for Historians*. Liverpool: Liverpool Univ. Press, 1988.

Van Dam, Raymond, trans. *Gregory of Tours: Glory of the Martyrs*. Vol. 4 of *Translated Texts for Historians*. Liverpool: Liverpool Univ. Press, 1988.

Van Dam, Raymond. *Leadership and Community in Late Antique Gaul*. Berkeley: Univ. of California Press, 1985.

van de Vyver, André. "La Chronologie du règne de Clovis d'après la Légende et d'après l'Histoire." Excerpt from *Le Moyen Age (*1947), nos. 3-4: 177–196.

van de Vyver, Andre. "L'unique victoire contre les Amalans et la Conversion de Clovis en 506" [The single victory against the Alamanni and the conversion of Clovis in 506]. Pts. 1–3. *Revue Belge de Philologie et D'Histoire* [*Belgian Review of Philology and History*] (1936): 859–914; 16, nos. 1–2 (January–June 1938): 35–94; 17, nos. 3–4 (July–December 1938): 793–814.

van de Vyver, Andre. *La Victoire Contre les Alamans et la Conversion de Clovis III-IV*. Excerpt from *Review Belge de Philologie et d'Histoire*. Brussels: n.p., 1937.

Verlinden, Charles. "Frankish Colonization: A New Approach." *Transactions of the Royal Historical Society*, 5th ser., 4 (1954): 1–17.

Verseuil, Jean. *Clovis ou la naissance des Rois*. Paris: Criterion, 1992.

von Campenhausen, Hans Freiherr. *Ambrosius von Mailand als Kirchenpolitiker* (ibid. Bd. 12), 1929

Villada, Zacarias Garcia, S. J. *Historia eclesiastica de Espana*, T. II 1 and 2, 1932/1933;

Vineyard, Clyde Dale. "The Origin, Development and Significance of the Roman Catholic Papal Tiara." MA diss., Seventh-day Adventist Theological Seminary, Washington, DC, August 1951.

Voigt, Karl. *State and Church from Constantine the Great to the End of the Carolingian Period.* New printing of Stuttgart ed., 1936. N.p.: Scientia Verlag Aalen, 1965.

Voigt, Karl. *Staat und Kirche: Von Konstantin dem Grossen Bis Zum Ende der Karolingerzeit.* Aalen. [*State and Church from Constantine the Great to the End of the Carolingian Period.*] New printing of Stuttgart ed., 1936. N.p.: Scientia Verlag Aalen, 1965

von Schubert, Hans. *Das älteste germanische Christentum oder der sogenannte "Arianismus" der Germanen*, 1909.

von Schubert, Hans. *Geschichte der christlichen Kirche im Frühmittelalter*, 1917/21.

von Schubert, Hans. *Staat und Kirche in den arianischen Königreichen und im Reiche Chlodwigs.* Bd. 26. Munich: Druck and Verlag von R. Oldenbourg, 1912.

von Schubert, Hans. *Staat und Kirche in den arianischen Königreichen und im Reiche Chlodwigs.* Bd. 26. (Munich: Druck and Verlag von R. Oldenbourg, 1912), 167-8. [*Nation and Church in the Aryan Kingdoms and in Clovis' Kingdom.* (Munich Press and Publishing House of R. Oldenbourg, 1912).

von Ullman, Walter. *Päpste und Papsttum: Gelasius I. (492–496).* Bd. 18. Stuttgart: Anton Hiersemann, 1981.

Wace, Henry, and William C. Piercy, eds. *A Dictionary of Christian Biography.* London: John Murray, 1911.

Wallace-Hadrill, D. S. *Eusebius of Caesarea.* London: A. R. Mowbray, 1960.

Wallace-Hadrill, J. M. *The Barbarian West: The Early Middle Ages A.D. 400–1000*. Revised. New York: Harper Torchbooks, 1962.

Wallace-Hadrill, J. M., *The Frankish Church*. Oxford: Clarendon Press, 1985.

Wallace-Hadrill, J. M. *The Long-Haired Kings*. New York: Barnes and Noble, 1962.

Wallace-Hadrill, J. M. "Review of *Chlodwigs Taufe: Riems 508* by Rolf Weiss." *The English Historical Review* 89, no. 350 (January 1974): 144–145.

Wallace-Hadrill, J. M. Untitled. Review of *Intitulatio: Lateinische Königs– und Fürstentitel bis zum Ende des 8. Jahrhunderts* by Herwig Wolfram. *The English Historical Review* 83, no. 329 (October 1968): 816.

Wallace-Hadrill, J. M. "The Work of Gregory of Tours in the Light of Modern Research." *Transactions of the Royal Historical Society*, 5th ser., 1 (1951): 25–45.

Warmington, B. H. *The North African Provinces from Diocletian to the Vandal Conquest*. London: Cambridge Univ. Press, 1954.

Wattenbach and Levison. *Deutschlands Geschichtsquellen im Mittelalter: Vorzeit und Karolinger*, 3 bks.

Weimar: Hermann Böhlaus Nachfolger, 1952 (bk. 1); 1953 (bk. 2); 1957 (bk. 3).

Weinel, Heinrich. *Die Stellung des Urchristentums zum Staat*, 1908;

Weise, Georg. *Königtum und Bischofswahl im fränkischen und deutschen Reich vor dem Investiturstreit*, 1912 ;

Weiss, Rolf. *Chlodwigs Taufe* [Baptism]*: Reims 508*. Bern: Verlag Herbert Lang, 1971.

Werminghoff, Albert. *Geschichte der Kirchenverfassung Deutschlands im Mittelalter*, Bd. I, 1905;

Weyl, Richard. *Das fränkische Staatskirchenrecht zur Zeit der Merowinger (Untersuchungen zur Deutschen Staats- und Rechtsgeschichte*, ed. By Otto Gierke Heft 27), 1888;

Whitby, Michael, trans. *The Ecclesiastical History of Evagrius Scholasticus*. Vol. 33 of *Translated Texts for Historians*. Liverpool: Liverpool Univ., 2000.

Whitney, J. P. "The Earlier Growth of Papal Jurisdiction." *Cambridge Historical Journal* 4, no. 1 (1932): 1–25.

Williams, George Huntston. "Christology and Church-State Relations in the Fourth Century." *Church History* 20, no. 3 (September 1951): 3–33.

Winston, Richard. *Charlemagne*. New York: American Heritage, 1968.

Wittmayer, Baron Salo. *The Jewish Community: Its History and Structure to the American Revolution*, vol. 1. Philadelphia: Jewish Pub. Soc. of Am., 1948.

Wolfram, Herwig. *Intitulatio: Lateinische Königs—und Fürstentitel bis zim Ende des 8. Jahrhunderts* [Latin kings' and princes' titles up to the end of the eighth century]. Graz: Böhlau, 1967.

Wolfram, Herwig. *The Roman Empire and Its Germanic Peoples*. Translated by Thomas Dunlap. Berkeley: Univ. of California Press, 1997.

Wood, Ian, ed. *Franks and Alamanni in the Merovingian Period: An Ethnographic Perspective*. Woodbridge, UK: Boydell Press, 1998.

Wood, Ian. *Gregory of Tours*. Gwynedd, Eng.: Headstart History, 1994.

Wood, Ian. *The Merovingian Kingdoms 450–751*. Harlow, Eng.: Pearson Ed., 1994.

Wood, James E., Jr. "Christianity and the State." *Journal of the Academy of Religion* 35, no. 3 (September 1967): 257–270.

Wormald, Patrick. "The Decline of the Western Empire and the Survival of its Aristocracy." Review of *Western Aristocracies and Imperial Court, A.D. 364–425*, by J. F. Matthews. *The Journal of Roman Studies* 66 (1976): 217–226.

Wyatt, Thomas. "Clovis the First." Chap. in *Great Men and Famous Women*. 1893.

Zarchin, Michael M. *From Constantine to Hitler*. San Francisco: United Council to Combat Anti-Semitism and Nazism, 1936.

Ziegler, Aloysius K. "Church and state in Visigothic Spain," Dissert. Washington: Catholic University of America, 1930.

Sources for the History of Clovis

Translated from the French by
Kurth, Godefroid. *Clovis*, 3rd ed, 2 bks.
Brussels: Albert Dewit Library, 1923.

I. Chronicles

Gregory of Tours (and his sources)

(p. 255:)
Gregory of Tours. *Historia Francorum*. Edited by Dom Ruinart. Paris, 1699.

Gregory of Tours. *Historia Francorum*. In *MGH Scriptores Rerum Merovingicarum*, edited by Arndt and Krusch, vol. I. Hanover, 1884.

Gregory of Tours. *Historia Francorum*. Edited by Omont and Collon. Paris, 1886-1893.

(p. 258:)
Lair. *Annuaire-bulletin de la Société de l'Histoire de France*, vol. XXXV. 1898. 4.

Monod, G. Études critiques sur les sources de l'Histoire mérovingienne. In *Bibliothèque de l'École des hautes études*. Paris, 1872. 161.

Arndt. *Historische Zeitschrift* of Sybel, vol. XXVIII. No date, 421.

(p. 259:)
Schubert. *Die Unterwerfung der Alamannen unter die Franken*. Strasbourg, 1884. 134-140.

Mabillon, ed. [*Life of Saint Maixent*]. In *Acta Sanctorum O.S.B.*, vol. I. No date.

Bollandists, eds. [*Life of Saint Maixent*]. In *Acta Sanctorum*, vol. V. No date.

(p. 260)
Fortunat. *Liber de Virtutibus sancti Hilarii.* In *MGH Auct. antiquiss.*, IV. No date.

Kurth, Godefroid. *Les Sources de l'Histoire de Clovis dans Grégoire de Tours.* In *Revue des Questions historiques*, vol. XLIV. 1888. Also in *Le Congrès scientifique international des catholiques, tenu à Paris du 8 au 13 avril 1888.* Paris, 1889.

Kurth, Godefroid. *Histoire poétique des Mérovingiens.* Paris-Brussels, 1893.

(p. 261:)
Arndt and Krusch. Preface to *MGH Scriptores Rerum Merovingicarum*, vol. I. Hanover, 1884.

Kurth, G. *De l'autorité de Grégoire de Tours.* No date.

Chronical of the so called Fredegar

[*Chronical of Fredegar*]. Edited by Ruinart. Paris, 1699.

[*Chronical of Fredegar*]. Edited by Monod. *Bibliothèque de l'Ecole des hautes études*, fasc. 63. Paris, 1885.

[*Chronical of Fredegar*]. Edited by Krusch. *MGH Scriptores Rerum Merovingicarum*, vol. II. Hanover, 1888.

Krusch. *Die Chronicae des sogenannten Fredegar. Neues Archiv der Gesellschaft fur aeltere deutsche Geschichtskunde*, vol. VII. 1882.

(p. 262:)
Schnürer, G. M. *Die Verfasser der sogenannten Fredegar-Chronik. Collectanea Friburgensia*, fasc. 9. Freiburg, 1900.

Ranke. *Weltgeschichte*, vol. IV. No date.

Kurth, G. *Histoire de Clovis d'après Frédégaire. Revue des Questions historiques*, vol. XLVII. 1890.

Liber Historiae

Liber Historiae. Edited by Dom Bouquet. In *Recueil des historiens de Gaule et de France*, v. III. No date.

Liber Historiae. Edited by Krusch. In *MGH Scriptores Rerum Merovingicarum*, vol. II. Hanover, 1888.

(p. 263:)
Kurth. Étude critique sur le Liber Historiae. No date.

(p. 264:)
Certain, ed. *Miracles de Saint Benoît*, books II and III. Paris, 1857.

Mabillon, ed. *Vie d'Abbon de Fleury*. In *Acta Sanctorum OSB*, vol. VI. No date.

Aimoin. *De Gestis regum Francorum libri IV*. Edited by A. Duchesne, vol. III. No date.

Aimoin. *De Gestis regum Francorum libri IV*. Edited by Dom Bouquet, vol. III. No date.

(p. 265:)
Roricon. *Gesta Francorum*. Edited by A. Duchesne, vol. I. No date.

Roricon. *Gesta Francorum*. Edited by Dom Bouquet, vol. III. No date.

Lebeuf. *Mémoires de l'Académie des Inscriptions*, vol. XVII. 1751.

II. Lives of Saints

(p. 266:)
Saint Arnoul of Tours (July 18)

Bollandists, eds. [*Life of Saint Arnoul of Tours*]. In *Catalogus codicum hagiographicorum... bibliothecae Parisiensis*, vol. I., 415-428. No date.

Translatio sancti Arnulfi. In *Analecta bollandiana*, vol. VIII. No date. 97.

(p. 267:)
Chevalier. *Les Origines de l'église de Tours.* In *Mémoires de la Société archéologique de Touraine*, vol. XXI. 1871.

Duchesne. *Les Anciens catalogues épiscopaux de la province de Tours.* Paris, 1890.

Saint Césaire of Arles (August 27)

Mabillon, ed. [*Life of Saint Césaire of Arles*]. In *Acta Sanctorum O.S.B.*, vol. I. No date.

Bollandists, eds. [*Life of Saint Césaire of Arles*]. In *Acta Sanctorum*, vol. VI. 1743.

Krusch, B, ed. [*Life of Saint Césaire of Arles*]. In *Scriptores Rerum Merovingicarum*, vol. III. No date.

Arnold, C.-F. *Caesarius von Arelate und die gallische Kirche seiner Zeit.* Leipzig, 1894.

Malnory. *Saint Césaire, évêque d'Arles. Bibliothèque de l'Ecole des hautes études*, fasc. 103. Paris, 1894.

Lejay. No title. *Revue du Clergé français*, vol. IV. No date.

Morin. *Le Testament de saint Césaire d'Arles et la Critique de M. Krusch. Revue bénédictine*, vol. XVI. 1899.

Morin. *Un écrit de saint Césaire d'Arles renfermant un témoignage sur les fondateurs des églises des Gaules. Mélanges*, vol. I. No date.

Chaillan. *Saint Césaire.* 1912.

Saint Clotilde (June 3)

Mabillon, ed. [*Life of Saint Clotilde*]. In *Acta Sanctorum O.S.B.*, vol. I. No date.

Bollandists, eds. [*Life of Saint Clotilde*]. In *Acta Sanctorum*, vol. I.

(p. 268:)
Krusch, B., ed. [*Life of Saint Clotilde*]. In *Scriptores Rerum Merovingicarum*, vol. II. No date.

Kurth. *Sainte Clotilde.* Paris, 1897.

Poulain. *Sainte Clotilde.* Paris, 1899.

(p. 269:)

Saint Éleuthère of Tournai (February 20)

Bollandists, eds. [*Life of Saint Eleuthère*]. In *Acta Sanctorum*, vol. III. No date.

Ghesquière, ed. [*Life of Saint Eleuthère*]. In *Acta Sanctorum Belgii*, vol. I. No date.

(p. 270:)

Saint Eptade (August 24)

Bollandists, eds. [*Life of Saint Eptade*]. In *Acta Sanctorum*, vol. IV. No date.

Krusch, B., ed. [*Life of Saint Eptade*]. In *Scriptores Rerum Merovingicarum*, vol. III. No date.

Pétigny. Études sur l'histoire, les lois et les institutions à l'époque mérovingienne, vol. II. No date. 647.

Binding. *Das Burgondisch-Romanische Koenigreich.* No date. 188 and 196.

Loening. *Geschichte des deutschen Kirchenrechts,* vol. II. Strasbourg, 1878. 176.

Kaufmann. *Forschungen zur deutschen Geschichte,* vol. X. No date. 391-395.

Arnold. *Caesarius von Arelate.* No date. 242.

Duchesne. *Bulletin Critique.* 1897. 451-455.

Jahn, A. *Die Geschichte der Burgundionen und Burgundiens,* vol. II. No date. 106-112.

Krusch. No title. In *Neues Archiv,* vol. XXV, 131-257. No date.

(p. 271:)
Thomas. *Sur un passage de la Vita sancti Eptadii.* In *Mélanges, Julien Havet,* 593. Paris, 1895.

(p. 272:)
Henry. *Vie de saint Eptade.* Avallon, 1863.

<u>Saint Genevieve of Paris (January 3)</u>

Bollandists, eds. [*Life of Saint Genevieve of Paris*]. In *Acta Sanctorum,* vol. I. 1643.

Kohler, C. Étude critique sur le texte de la vie latine de sainte Geneviève de Paris. In *Bibliothèque de l'École des hautes études,* fasc. 48. Paris, 1881.

Narbey. *Quel est le texte de la vie authentique de sainte Geneviève? Étude critique suivie de sa vie authentique et de la traduction.* In *Bulletin d'histoire et d'archéologie du diocèse de Paris.* 1884.

Krusch, ed. [*Life of Saint Genevieve of Paris*]. In *Scriptores Rerum Merovingicarum,* vol. III. 1896.

(p. 274:)
Valois, Adrien. *Rerum Francicarum, libri VIII*, vol. I. Paris, 1646. 317-319.

Molinet, Claude. *Histoire de sainte Geneviève et de son abbaye royale et apostolique*. Late 17th century.

Moulinet, Claude. *Lettre critique sur les différentes Vies de sainte Geneviève*. Late 17th century.

Wallin. *De sancta Genovefa...disquisitio historico-critico-theologica*. Wittenberg, 1723.

(p. 275:)
Krusch, B. *Die Faelschung der Vita Genovefae*. In *Neues Archiv*, vol. XVIII. No date.

Wattenbach. *Deutschlands Geschichtsquellen im Mittelalter*, vol. II. 6th ed. Berlin, 1894. 491.

(p. 276:)
Duchesne. *La vie de sainte Geneviève est-elle authentique?*. In *Bibliothèque de l'École des Chartes*, vol. 54. 1893.

Krusch. *Das Alter der Vita Genovefae*. In *Neues Archiv*, vol. XIX. 1894.

Kohler, C. *La vie de sainte Geneviève est-elle apocryphe?* In *Revue historique*, vol. 67. 1898.

(p. 277:)
Saintyves. *Vie de sainte Geneviève, patronne de Paris, et du royaume de France*. Paris, 1846.

Vidien. *Sainte Geneviève, patronne de Paris, et son influence sur les destinées de la France*. Paris, 1889.

Lesètre. *Sainte Geneviève*. Paris, 1900.

Florisoone. *La véritable légende de Sainte Geneviève*. *Correspondant*, vol. 202 (January 1901).

(p. 278:)
Saint Fridolin, abbot of Saeckingen (March 6)

Balther. [*Life of Saint Fridolin*]. In *Acta Sanctorum*, edited by the Bollandists, vol. I. No date.

Mone, ed. [*Life of Saint Fridolin*]. In *Quellensammlung der badischen Landesgeschichte*, vol. I. Karlsruhe, 1848.

Krusch, ed. [*Life of Saint Fridolin*]. In *Scriptores Rerum Merovingicarum*, vol. III. 1896.

Schultz. *Jahrb. für Schweiz. Geschichte*, vol. XVIII. 1893.

Malnory. *Quid Luxorinus monachi, etc.* No date. 52.

Saint Germier of Toulouse (May 16)

(p. 279:)
Papebroch, ed. [*Life of Saint Germier of Toulouse*]. In *Acta Sanctorum*, vol. III. No date. 592.

Douais, ed. [*Life of Saint Germier of Toulouse*]. In *Mémoires de la Société des Antiquaires de France*, vol. I. 1890.

Histoire générale du Languedoc. No date.

Duchesne. *Les Fastes épiscopaux de l'ancienne Gaule*. Paris, 1894. 296.

Saltet. Étude critique sur la vie de saint Germier. In *Annales du Midi*, vol. XIII. 1901.

Saint Gildard or Godard of Rouen (June 8)

[*Life of Saint Gildard or Godard or Rouen*]. In *Analecta Bollandiana*, vol. VIII. No date. 393-402.

(p. 281:)
Saint Hilary of Poitiers (January 14)

Fortunat. [*Life of Saint Hilary of Poitiers*]. In *M.G.H., Auctor. Antiquiss.*, edited by Leo and Krusch, vol. IV. No date.

(p. 282:)
Largent. *S. Hilaire.* Paris, 1902.

Saint Jean of Réomé (January 28)

Bobbio, Jonas. [*Life of Saint Jean of Réomé*]. Edited by Mabillon. In *Acta Sanctorum O.S.B.*, vol. I. No date.

Roverius. *Reomaus seu historia monasterii sancti Joannis Reomaensis.* Paris, 1637.

Bobbio, Jonas. [*Life of Saint Jean of Réomé*]. In *Acta Sanctorum*, edited by the Bollandists, vol. II. No date.

Bobbio, Jonas. [*Life of Saint Jean of Réomé*]. Edited by Krusch. In *Mittheilungen des Instituts für oesterreichische Geschichtsforschung*, vol. XIV. No date.

Jonas. *Vitae Sanctorum Colunbani vidastis Johannis.* 1905.

Stoeber. *Sitzungsberichte der phil. hist. Classe der K. Akademie der Wissenschaften.* Vienna, 1885.

Saint Leonard of Limousin

Arbellot. *Vie de saint Léonard, solitaire en Limousin.* Paris, 1863. 277-289.

Krusch, ed. [*Life of Saint Leonard of Limousin*]. In *Scriptores Rerum Merovingicarum*, vol. III. No date.

Bollandists, eds. [*Life of Saint Leonard of Limousin*]. In *Acta Sanctorum*, vol. III. No date.

Histoire littéraire de France, vol. VIII. No date.

Flahaut, R. *S. Léonard, ermite en Limousin, vénéré à Spycken*. Dunkirk, 1893.

Nimal. *L'ancienne légende de S. Léonard, etc.* Liège, 1901.

(p. 284:)

<u>Saint Maixent (June 26)</u>—see p. 259

(p. 285:)

<u>Saint Melaine (January 6)</u>

Bollandists, eds. [*Life of Saint Melaine*]. In *Acta Sanctorum*, vol. I. No date.

Bollandists, eds. [*Life of Saint Melaine*]. In *Catalogus codicum hagiographicorum bibliothecae nationalis Parisiensis*, vol. I. No date. 71

Bollandists, eds. [*Life of Saint Melaine*]. In *Catalogus codicum hagiographicorum bibliothecae nationalis Parisiensis*, vol. II. No date. 531.

Krusch, ed. [*Life of Saint Melaine*]. In *Scriptores Rerum Merovingicarum*, vol. III. No date.

Lippert. *Zur Vita Melanii*. In *Neues Archiv.*, vol. XIV. 1889.

Rivet. *Histoire littéraire de la France*, vol. III. No date.

Plaine. Étude comparative des trois anciennes Vies de saint Melaine. In *Revue historique de l'Ouest*, vol. V and VIII. No date.

Duchesne. *Saint Melaine, évêque de Rennes*. In *Recueil de Mém. de la Société des Antiq. de France*. 1904.

Loth, J. *L'émigration teutonne en Armorique.* No date. 42.

(p. 286:)
Borderie. *Revue de Bretagne, de Vendée et d'Anjou,* vol. III. 1891.

Saint Mesmin, abbot of Micy (December 15)

Mabillon, ed. [*Life of Saint Mesmin*]. In *Acta Sanctorum O.S.B.,* vol. I. No date.

Bollandists, eds. [*Life of Saint Mesmin*]. In *Catalogus codicum hagiographicorum Bibl. nat. Paris.,* vol. I. No date. 300-303.

Poncelet. *Le Saint de Micy.* In *Anal. boll.,* vol. XXIV. 1905.

Lot, F. *Caradoc et saint Patern.* In *Romania,* vol. 28. 1899.

(p. 287:)
Saint Paterne, Bishop of Vannes (April 15)

John of Tynemouth. [*Life of Saint Paterne*]. In *Acta Sanctorum,* edited by the Bollandists, vol. II. No date.

Borderie. *Saint Paterne, premier évêque de Vannes.* Vannes, 1893.

Borderie. *Histoire de Bretagne,* vol. I. No date. 331.

Duchesne. *Saint Paterne.* In *Revue Celtique.* 1893.

Duchesne. *Fastes épiscopaux de l'ancienne Gaule,* vol. II. 1900. 371.

Saint Remi, Bishop of Reims (October 1)

Bollandists, eds. [*Life of Saint Remi, Bishop of Reims*]. In *Acta Sanctorum,* vol. I. No date.

Ghesquière, ed. [*Life of Saint Remi*]. In *Acta Sanctorum Belgii*, vol. I. No date.

Krusch, ed. [*Life of Saint Remi*]. In *M.G.H., Auctore Antiquissimi*, vol. IV. No date.

(p. 288:)
Krusch. *Neues Archiv.*, vol. XX. 1895.

Flodoard. *M.G.H.*, vol. XIII. No date. 511, 512.

(p. 289:)
Krusch, ed. [*Life of Saint Remi*]. In *Scriptores Rerum Merovingicarum*, vol. III. No date.

(p. 290:)
Dubos. *Histoire critique de l'établissement de la monarchie française dans la Gaule*, book III, ch. 19. No date.

(p. 291:)
Haudecoeur. *Saint Remy, évêque de Reims, apôtre des Francs*. Reims, 1896.

Jadart, H. *Bibliographie des ouvrages concernant la vie et le culte de saint Remi. Travaux de l'Académie nationale de Reims*, vol. LXXXVII. 1891.

Jadart, H. *La Vie de saint Remi dans la poésie populaire. Travaux de l'Académie nationale de Reims*, vol. XCVII. 1895.

Cattier. *Vie de saint Remi*. Tours, Cattier, 1896.

Saint Rieul of Senlis (March 30)

Bollandists, eds. [*Life of Saint Rieul of Senlis*]. In *Acta Sanctorum*, vol. III. No date.

Jaulnay. *Le Parfait prélat*. No date.

(p. 292:)
Saint Sacerdos of Limoges (May 5)

Couderc. No title. In *Bibliothèque de l'École des Chartes*, vol. LIV. 1893. 468.

Saint Severin, Abbot of Saint-Maurice in Valais (February 11)

Bollandists, eds. [*Life of Saint Severin*]. In *Acta Sanctorum*, vol. III. No date.

Krusch, ed. [*Life of Saint Severin*]. In *Scriptores Rerum Merovingicarum*, vol. III. No date.

(p. 293:)
Krusch. *La falsification des Vies de saints burgondes*. In *Mélanges Julien Havet*. No date. 41-56.

Giry. *La Vie de saint Maur du Pseudo-Faustus*. In *Biblioth. de l'École des Chartes*, vol. 57. 1896.

Benon. *Saint Séverin a-t-il été abbé d'Agaune?* In *Rev. d'hist. eccl.*, vol. V. 1911.

Saint Solein of Chartres (September 25)

Levison, W. *Zur Geschichte des Frankenkoenigs Chlodowech*. In *Bonner Jahrbücher*, vol. CIII. No date.

(p. 294:)
Saint Vaast, Bishop of Arras (February 6)

Krusch. *Mittheilungen des Instituts für oesterreichische Geschichtsforschung*, vol. XIV. No date.

Bobbio, Jonas. [*Life of Saint Vaast*]. In *Acta Sanctorum*, edited by the Bollandists, vol. I. No date.

Bobbio, Jonas. [*Life of Saint Vaast*]. In *Scriptores Rerum Merovingicarum*, edited by Krusch, vol. III. No date.

(p. 295:)
Jubaru, P. *Clovis a-t-il été baptisé à Reims?* In Études religieuses, etc., vol. LXVII. 1896.

III. Salic Law

(p. 296:)
Kern. *Notes on the Frankish words in the Lex salica.* In *Lex salica,* Hessels and Kern. No date. 433-435.

(p. 297:)
Pardessus. *La loi salique.* Paris, 1843.

Hessels. *Lex salica, the ten texts with the glosses and the lex emendata, with notes on the frankish words in the lex salica by H. Kern.* London, 1880.

Waitz, ed. [*Lex salica*]. In *Das alte Recht der salischen Franken.* Kiel, 1846.
Merkel, ed. [*Lex salica*]. Berlin, 1850.

Behrend, J.-F. [*Lex salica*]. Berlin, 1874 and Weimar, 1897.

(p. 298:)

IV. Letters

<u>Letter from Clovis to the bishops of his kingdom</u>

Sirmond. *Concilia Galliae,* vol. I. Paris, 1629. 176.

Bouquet. No title, vol. IV. No date. 54.

Boretius. *M.G.H. Capitularia Regum francorum,* vol. I. Hanover, 1883. 1.

Maassen. *M.G.H. Concilia.* No date.

<u>Letters from Saint Remi to Clovis</u>

M.G.H. Épistolae merovingici et karolini oevi, vol. II. No date. 112, 113.

Letters from Theodoric the Great to Clovis

Mommsen, ed. *Cassiodori senatoris Variae*. In *M.G.H. Auctores Antiquissimi*, vol. XII. Berlin, 1894.

(p. 299:)
Usener. *Anecdoton Holderi*. No date. 70.

Vogel. *Historische Zeitschrift*, vol. LVI. No date.

Mommsen. Preface to *Variarum de Cassiodore*, xxxii. No date.

Letter from Saint Avitus of Vienna to Clovis

Sirmond, ed. *Sancti Aviti Viennensis archiepiscopi opera*, n. 41. Paris, 1643.

Peiper, ed. *M.G.H. Alcimi Ecdicii Aviti Viennensis episcopi opera quae supersunt*, n. 46. Berlin, 1883.

Chevalier, ed. *Oeuvres complètes de saint Avit., évêque de Vienne*, n. 38. Lyon, 1890.

(p. 300:)
Krusch. *Neues Archiv.*, vol. XII. 1887. 296.

Vogel. *Historische Zeitschrift*, vol. LVI. No date. 392.

Arnold. *Caesarius von Arelate*. No date. 203.

V. Diplomas of Clovis

(p. 301:)
Pardessus. *Diplomata, Chartae, Épistolae, Leges, etc.*, vol. I. Paris, 1843.

Pertz, K. *M.G.H. Diplomatum imperii tomus I.* Hanover, 1872.

VI. Apocryphal Documents

(p. 302:)
Havet, Julien. *Questions mérovingiennes.* In *Bibliothèque de l'École des Chartes*, vol. XLVI. 1885.

Havet, Julien. *Oeuvres de Julien Havet*, vol. I. Paris, 1896.

Appendix II

AD 538
Source Book
Bibliography

Abbott, John S. C. *The Monarchies of Continental Europe: Italy.* New York: Mason Bros., 1860.

Acton, Lord. *Essays on Church and State.* Edited by Douglas Woodruff. London: Hollis and Carter, 1952.

Acton, John E. E. Dalberg. *Essays on Freedom and Power.* Selected by Gertrude Himmelfarb. London: Thames and Hudson, 1956.

Adams, George Burton. *Civilization during the Middles Ages.* New York: Charles Scribner, 1894.

Agathius. *The Histories.* Translated by Joseph Frendo. Berlin: Walter de Gruyter, 1975.

Algermissen, Konrad. *Christian Sects.* Translated by J. R. Foster. Vol. 139 of the *Twentieth Century Encyclopedia of Catholicism;* sec. 14, *Outside the Church.* New York: Hawthorn, 1962.

Alphonsus de Liguori, St. *Dignity and Duties of the Priest, or Selva*, cent. ed. Vols. 3, 12 of *The Complete Works of Saint Alphonsus de Liguori*, Eng. trans., edited by Eugene Grimm. New York: Benziger, 1886 (3); 1888 (12).

Alphonsus de Liguori, St. *Dignity and Duties of the Priest, or Selva*, Vol. 12 of *The Complete Works of Saint Alphonsus de Liguori*. English trans., edited by Eugene Grimm. Brooklyn: Redemptorist Fathers, 1927.

Alphonsus de Liguori, St. *The Great Means of Salvation and of Perfection*, cent. ed., 3rd ed. Vol. 3 of *The Complete Works of Saint Alphonsus de Liguori*, Eng. trans., edited by Eugene Grimm. New York: Benziger, 1886.

Amiot, François. *History of the Mass.* Translated by Lancelot C. Sheppard. Vol. 110 of the *Twentieth Century Encyclopedia of Catholicism;* sec. 10, *The Worship of the Church.* New York: Hawthorn, 1959.

Amory, Patrick. *People and Identity in Ostrogothic Italy, 489–554.* Cambridge: Cambridge Univ. Press, 2003.

Anastos, Milton. *Justinian's Despotic Control over the Church as Illustrated by His Edicts on the Theopaschite Formula and His Letter to Pope John II in 533.* Recueil des travaux de l'Institut d'Études byzantines, no. 8, mélanges G. Ostrogorsky II. БЕОГРАД, 1964.

Ankerberg, John, and John Weldon. *The Facts on Roman Catholicism.* Eugene, OR: Harvest House, 1993.

Artaud de Montor, Chevalier. *The Lives and Times of the Roman Pontiffs*, vol. 1. Translated from the French. Edited by Dr. Neligan. New York: D. and J. Sadlier, 1865.

Artaud de Montor, Chevalier. *The Lives and Times of the Roman Pontiffs*, vol. 1. Retranslated, revised from *Les Vies des Papes.* New York: Catholic Publication Society of Am., 1911.

Askowith, Dora. "The Toleration of the Jews under Julius Caesar and Augustus." Part 1 of *The Toleration and Persecution of the Jews in the Roman Empire*. PhD diss., Columbia Univ., 1915. New York: 1915.

Atwater, Richard, trans. *Procopius. Secret History*. Ann Arbor, MI: Univ. of Michigan Press, n.d.

Augustine, Rev. Charles. *A Commentary of the New Code of Canon Law*, 3rd ed. 8 vols. St. Louis, MO: B. Herder, 1919.

Augustine, Rev. P. Charles. *A Commentary of the New Code of Canon Law*, 2nd ed., vol. 1. St. Louis: B. Herder, 1918.

Bagnall, Roger S., A. Cameron, S. R. Schwartz, and K. A. Worp. *Consuls of the Later Roman Empire*. Atlanta, GA: Scholars Press (for Am. Philological Asso), 1987.

Bagnani, Gilbert. *Rome and the Papacy: An Essay on the Relations between Church and State*. London: Methuen, 1929.

Barmby, Rev. James, trans. *Selected Epistles of Gregory the Great, Bishop of Rome (Books IX.–XIV.)*, pt. 2. Vol. 13 of *A Select Library of Nicene and Post-Nicene Fathers of the Christian Church*, 2nd ser., edited by Philip Schaff and Henry Wace. Grand Rapids, MI: Wm. B. Eerdmans, 1976.

Barnish, S. J. B., trans. *Cassiodorus: Selected* Variae. Vol. 12 of *Translated Texts for Historians*. Liverpool: Liverpool University Press, 2006.

Barnum, Rev. Samuel W. *Romanisn As It Is: An Exposition of the Roman Catholic System for the Use of the American People*. Hartford, CT: Connecticut Pub., 1871.

Baronio, Cæsare. *Annales Ecclesiastici* [Ecclesiastical annals], bk. 8. Lucca, It.; 1741.

Batiffol, Pierre. *Cathedra Petri: Études d'Histoire ancienne de l'Église*. Paris: Les Éditions du Cerf, 1938.

Battely, John. *The Original Institution of the Sabbath*. London, 1726.

Baudrillart, Alfred. *The Catholic Church: The Renaissance and Protestantism*. Authorized translation by Mrs. Philip Gibbs. New York: Benziger, 1908.

Baus, Karl, H-G. Beck, E. Ewig, and H. J. Vogt. *The Imperial Church from Constantine to the Early Middle Ages*. Translated by Anselm Biggs. Vol. 2 of *History of the Church*, ed. Hubert Jedin and John Dolan. New York: Seabury Press, 1980.

Baynes, Norman H. *The Byzantine Empire*. London: Oxford Univ. Press, 1952.

Becher, Matthias. *Charlemagne*. Translated by David Bachrach. New Haven, CT: Yale Univ. Press, 2003.

Bede, the Ven. *The Ecclesiastical History of the English Nation*. Translated by John Stevens. Revised by Lionel C. Jane. London: J. M. Dent, 1944.

Bede. *A History of the English Church and People*, rev. ed. Translated by Leo Sherley-Price. Revised by R. E. Latham. New York: Dorset Press, 1968.

Beecher, Rev. Edward. *Papal Conspiracy Exposed, and Protestantism Defended*. Boston: Stearns, 1855.

Beiermann, Rev. Peter. *The Convert's Catechism of Catholic Doctrine*. Rockford, IL: Tan Books, 1977.

Bemont, Charles, and G. Monod. *Medieval Europe from 395 to 1270*. New York: Henry Holt, 1902.

Bentley, Richard. *Epistola ad Joannem Millium*. Reprinted from the edition of Rev. Alexander Dyce. Toronto: University of Toronto Press, 1962.

Berenger, M., fils, trans. *Les Novelles de L'Empereur Justinien*, bk. 1. Vol. 13 of *Corps de Droit Civil Romain*. Aalen, Ger.: Scientia Verlag, 1979.

Berenger, M. fils, trans. *Les Novelles de L'Empereur Justinien*, bk. 2. Vol. 14 of *Corps de Droit Civil Romain*. Aalen, Ger.: Scientia Verlag, 1979.

Berger, Adolf. *Encyclopedia Dictionary of Roman Law*, new ser. Vol. 43, pt. 2, of *Transactions of the American Philosophical Society*. Philadelphia: Am. Philosophical Soc., 1953.

Berkhof, Hendrik. *Kirche and Kaiser: Eine Untersuchung der Entstehung der byzantinischen und der theokratischen Staatsauffassung im vierten Jahrhundert*. Zurich: Evangelischer Verlag ag. Zollikon, 1947.

Bihlmeyer, Karl. *Church History*. Revised by Hermann Tüchle, translated from the 13th Ger. ed. by Victor Mills. Westminster, MD: Newman Press, 1958.

Binius, Severinus, ed. *Concilia Generalia, et Provincialia, Quaecunque Reperiri Potuerunt, Item Epistolae Decretales, et Romanor[um]* Pontific[orum] Vitae . . . , bk. 2. Cologne, Ger.: Apud Ioannem Gymnicum, and Antonium Heirat, 1606.

Birks, Peter, and Grant McLeod, trans. *Justinian's Institutes*. Ithaca, NY: Cornell Univ. Press, 1987.

Bokenkotter, Thomas. *A Concise History of the Catholic Church*. Garden City, NY: Doubleday, 1977.

Bower, Archibald. *A History of the Popes from the Foundations of the See of Rome to the Present Time (1748–1766)*. 7 vols. Fasc. Kessinger Publishing: www.kessinger.net.

Bownde, Nicolas. *The Doctrine of the Sabbath*. . . . London, 1595.

Boyd, William K. *The Ecclesiastical Edicts of the Theodosian Code.* Vol. 14, no. 2, of *Studies in*

History, Economics and Public Law, edited by the faculty of political science of Columbia Univ. Clark, NJ: Lawbook Exchange, 2005.

Bredin, James. *Was Peter the First Pope? A Brief Account of the Roman Forgeries in the Volumes of the Councils*, pt. 1. A brief Answer to a late Treatise of the Sabbath Day. 1635.

Bromley, Thomas. *Sabbath of Rest: or the Soul's Progress in the Work of the New Birth.* Leeds, Eng.; 1744.

Brown, Peter. *The Rise of Western Christendom: Triumph and Diversity, A.D. 200–1000*, 2nd ed. Malden, MA: Blackwell, 2003.

Brown, Sydney MacGillvary. *Medieval Europe*, rev. ed. New York: Harcourt Brace, 1935.

Browning, Robert. *Justinian and Theodora*, rev. ed. London: Thames and Hudson, 1987.

Brunner, Heinrich. *Deutsche Rechtsgeschichte*, Bd. I, 2nd edition, 1906.

Burke, Redmond. "The Control of Reading by the Catholic Church." PhD diss., University of

Chicago, 1948.

Burke, Redmond. *What is the Index?* Milwaukee, WI: Bruce, 1952.

Burnet, James. *Aids to Justinian.* London: Stevens and Sons, 1936.

Burns, Thomas. *A History of the Ostrogoths.* Bloomington, IN: Indiana Univ. Press, 1984.

Bury, J. B., planner. *The Cambridge Medieval History*, 2nd ed., 8 vols. Edited by H. M. Gwatkin and J. P. Whitney. Cambridge: Cambridge Univ. Press, 1964–1967.

Bury, J. B., planner. *The Christian Roman Empire and the Foundation of the Teutonic Kingdoms*, 2nd ed. Vol. 1 of *Cambridge Medieval History*, edited by H. M. Gwatkin and J. P. Whitney. New York: MacMillan, 1936.

Bury, J. B. *History of the Later Roman Empire: From the Death of Theososius I. to the Death of Justinian*, vol. 1. New York: Dover, 1958.

Bury, J. B. *History of the Later Roman Empire: From the Death of Theososius I. to the Death of Justinian*, vol. 2. London: MacMillan, 1931.

Bury, J. B. *History of the Papacy in the 19th Century (1864–1878)*. Edited by R. H. Murray. London: MacMillan, 1930.

Bury, J. B., planner. *The Rise of the Saracens and the Foundation of the Western Empire*. Vol. 2 of *Cambridge Medieval History*, edited by H. M. Gwatkin and J. P. Whitney. New York: MacMillan, 1913.

Bury, J. B., planner. *The Rise of the Saracens and the Foundation of the Western Empire*, 1st ed., reprinted with corrections. Vol. 2 of *Cambridge Medieval History*, edited by H. M. Gwatkin and J. P. Whitney. New York: MacMillan, 1926.

Byfield, Richard. *The Doctrine of the Sabbath Vindicated*. London, 1631.

Byles, Mather. *The Christian Sabbath explained and vindicated*. New London, 1759.

Cadoux, Cecil J. *Catholicism and Christianity: A Vindication of Progressive Protestantism*. London: George Allen and Unwin, 1928.

Cadoux, Cecil J. *The Early Church and the World: A History of the Christian Attitude to Pagan Society and the State Down to the Time of Constantinus.* Edinburgh: T. and T. Clark, 1955.

Cadoux, Cecil J. *Roman Catholicism and Freedom.* London: Independent Press, 1936.

Cairns, John W., and Olivia F. Robinson, eds. *Critical Studies in Ancient Law, Comparative Law and Legal History.* Portland, OR: Hart, 2004.

The Cambridge Ancient History, vols. 1–6, 7–9. New York: MacMillan, 1923 (1); 1924 (2); 1925 (3); 1926 (4); 1927 (5); 1928 (7); 1930 (8); 1932 (9).

The Cambridge Ancient History, 5th impress., vol. 6. Cambridge: Univ. Press, 1969.

The Cambridge Ancient History, 2nd impress., vol. 10. Cambridge: Univ. Press, 1952.

The Cambridge Ancient History, vols. 11–14. Cambridge: Cambridge Univ. Press, 1999 (11); 1939 (12); 1998 (13); 2000 (14).

The Cambridge Modern History, vols. 6, 8, 12. Cambridge: Univ. Press, 1909 (6); 1907 (8); 1910 (12).

The Cambridge Modern History, vols. 8–11. New York: MacMillan, 1911 (8); 1909 (9); 1907 (10); 1909 (11).

Cameron, Averil. *The Church in the Byzantine Dark Ages.* Pamphlet. London: Dr. William's Trust, 1993.

Cameron, Averil. *Procopius and the Sixth Century.* Berkeley: Univ. of California Press, 1985.

Cameron, Averil, B. Ward-Perkins and Michael Whitby, eds. *Late Antiquity: Empire and Successors, A.D. 425–600.* Vol. 14 of *The Cambridge Ancient History.* Cambridge, UK: Cambridge Univ. Press, 2000.

Carlyle, A. J. *The Second Century to the Ninth*, 3rd ed. Vol. 1 of *A History of Mediæval Political Theory in the West*, by R. W. Carlyle and A. J. Carlyle. Edinburgh: Wm. Blackwood, 1930.

Carroll, Warren. *A History of Christendom*, vol. 2. Front Royal, VA: Christendom College Press, 1987.

Caspar, Erich. *Geschichte des Papsttums: Von den Anfängen bis zur Höhe der Weltherrschaft*, Bd. II, 1933; See 2 in yellow below. This entry we're in is Voigt's entry. Entries differ.

Caspar, Erich. *Geschichte des Papsttums*, Bd. II, 1933.

Caspar, Erich. *Die Lateransynode von 649* (Zeitschr. F. Kirchengesch. Bd. 51 [III. Folge Bd. 2] p. 75 ff.), 1932.

Caspar, Erich. *Papst Gregor II und der Bilderstreit* (ibid. Bd. 52 [III. Folge Bd. 3] p. 29 ff.), 1933;

Caspar, Erich von. *Das Papsttum Unter Byzantinischer Herrschaft*. Zweiter bd.: *Geschichte des Papsttums: Von Den Anfängen bis Zur Höhe der Weltherrschaft*. Tübingen: Verlag Von J. C. B. Mohr (Paul Siebeck), 1933.

Caspar, Erich von. *Romische Kirche und Imperium Romanum*. Erster bd.: *Geschichte des Papsttums: Von Den Anfängen bis Zur Höhe der Weltherrschaft*. Tübingen: Verlag Von J. C. B. Mohr (Paul Siebeck), 1930.

Cassiodorus, Magnus Aurelius. *The Letters of Cassiodorus*. Teddington, Eng.: Echo Lib., 2006.

Catechism of the Catholic Church. Liguori, MO: Liguori Pub., 1994.

Cathcart, William. The Papal System: Its Origin to the Present Time. Philadelphia: Am. Baptist Pub. Soc., 1872.

Catholic Encyclopedia. 15 vols. New York: Encyclopedia Press, 1913.

Chadwick, Henry. *The Church in Ancient Society: From Galilee to Gregory the Great*. In *Oxford History of the Christian Church*, edited by Henry and Owen Chadwick. Oxford: Oxford Univ. Press, 2003.

Chadwick, Henry. *East and West: The Making of a Rift in the Church: From Apostolic Times until the Council of Florence*. In *Oxford History of the Christian Church*, edited by Henry and Owen Chadwick. Oxford: Oxford Univ. Press, 2005.

Chandler, Samuel. *The History of Persecution*. London: J. Gray, 1736.

Chandler, Samuel, and Charles Atmore. *The History of Persecution from the Patriarchal Age to the Reign of George II*, new ed. 1813.

Chapman, Dom John. *Studies on the Early Papacy*. London: Sheed and Ward, 1928.

Chapman, Dom John. *Studies on the Early Papacy*. New York: Benziger Bros., n.d.

Charanis, Peter. *Church and State in the Later Roman Empire: The Religious Policy of Anastasius the First, 491–518*, 2nd ed. 1974.

Chinigo, Michael, ed. *The Teachings of Pope Pius XII*. N.p.: Methuen, 1958.

Chiniquy, Father. *Fifty Years in the Church of Rome*, 43rd ed. New York: Fleming H. Revell, 1886.

Chombaich de Colquhoun, Patrick Mac. *A Summary of the Roman Civil Law, Illustrated by*

Commentaries on and Parallels from the Mosaic, Canon, Mohammedan, English, and Foreign Law, vol. 1. Reprint of 1849 ed. Littleton, CO: Fred B. Rothman, 1988.

The Christian's Sabbath: or, a Companion for the Service and Worship of God on the Lord's Day. London, 1733.

Church, Richard W. *Miscellaneous Essays.* London: MacMillan, 1891.

Church, Richard W. *The Beginning of the Middle Ages,* rev. ed. New York: Charles Scribner, 1890.

Claudia, Sis. M. *Guide to the Documents of Pius XII (1939–1949).* Westminster, MD: Newman Press, 1951.

Clercq, Caroli de. *Concilia Galliae, A. 511–A. 695.* Vol. 148A of *Corpus Christianorum,* ser. *Latina.* Turnholti: Typographi Brepols Editores Pontificii, 1943.

Clinton, Henry Fynes. *Fasti Romani: The Civil and Literary Chronology of Rome and Constantinople from the Death of Augustus to the Death of Justin II,* 2 vols. Reprint of the 1850 Oxford ed. New York: Burt Franklin, 1960.

Cloud, David W. *Evangelicals and Rome: The Ecumenical End Times "Church."* Port Huron, MI: Way of Life Lit., 1999.

Colman, Benjamin. *The Doctrine and Law of the Holy Sabbath: in Two Sermons.* Boston, 1725.

The Confessions and Letters of St. Augustin. Vol. 1 of *A Select Library of Nicene and Post-Nicene Fathers of the Christian Church,* 1st ser. Edited by Philip Schaff. Grand Rapids, MI: Wm. B. Eerdmans, 1979.

Constable, Giles, and Robert Somerville. "The Papal Bulls for the Chapter of St. Antonin in Rouergue in the Eleventh and Twelfth Centuries." *Speculum* 67, no. 4 (October 1992): 828–864.

Cooke, Ronald. *The Death of the Pope of Rome.* Booklet. 2007.

Cotton, Paul. *From Sabbath to Sunday: A Study in Early Christianity*. Bethlehem, PA: Times Pub., 1933.

Coulombe, Charles A. *Vicars of Christ: A History of the Popes*. New York: Kensington, 2003.

Crakanthorp, Richard. *A Treatise of the Fift Generall Councel* [sic.]. London, 1637.

Croke, Brian. *Christian Chronicles and Byzantine History, 5th and 6th Centuries*. Aldershot, G.B.: Ashgate, 1992.

Croly, Rev. George. *Popery and the Popish Question*. London, 1825.

Crowley, Jeremiah J. *Romanism: A Menace to the Nation*, 2nd ed. Published in 1 vol. with author's *The Parochial School: A Curse to the Church, a Menace to the Nation*. Cincinnati, OH: Jeremiah Crowley, 1912.

Dahn, Felix. *Die Könige der Germanen*, Abt. II-IV, 1861-1866.

Dale, A. W. W. *The Synod of Elvira and Christian Life in the Fourth Century*. London: MacMillan, 1882.

Danielou, Jean, and Henri Marrou. *The First Six Hundred Years*. Vol. 1 of *The Christian Centuries*. Translated by Vincent Cronin. New York: McGraw-Hill, 1964.

Dannenbauer, Heinrich. *Grundlagen der Mittelalterlichen Welt: Skizzen und Studien*. Stuttgart: W. Kohlhammer Verlag, 1958.

Darras, L'Abbé J. E. *A General History of the Catholic Church*, vol. 2, 1st Am. ed. from last Fr. ed. New York: O'Shea, 1866 (also 1867).

D'Aubigne, J. H. Merle. *History of the Reformation in the Time of Calvin*. 4 vols. Rapidan, VA: Hartland Pub., 1999.

D'Aubigne, J. H. Merle. *The Protector: A Vindication.* Harrisonburg, VA: Sprinkle Pub., 1997.

Davis, Raymond, trans. *The Book of Pontiffs (Liber Pontificalis),* rev. 2nd ed. Vol. 6 of *Translated Texts for Historians.* Liverpool: Liverpool Univ. Press, 2000.

De Bujanda, Jesús M. *Index Librorum Prohibitorum 1600–1966.* With assistance from Marcella Richter. Vol. 11 of *Index des Livres Interdits,* directeur J. M. De Bujanda. Montreal: Médiaspaul, 2002.

De Rosa, Peter. *Vicars of Christ: The Dark Side of the Papacy.* New York: Crown, 1988.

Dewing, H. B., trans., Jeffrey Henderson, ed. *Procopius. The Anecdota, or Secret History.* In Loeb Classical Library. Cambridge, MA: Harvard Univ. Press, 2004.

Dewing, H. B., trans., in collaboration with Glanville Downey; Jeffrey Henderson, ed. *Procopius. Buildings.* In Loeb Classical Library. Cambridge, MA: Harvard Univ. Press, 2002.

Dewing, H. B., trans., Jeffrey Henderson, ed. *Procopius. History of the Wars.* Bks. 1–8. In Loeb Classical Library. Cambridge, MA: Harvard Univ. Press, 2000–2001.

Dewing, H. B., trans. *Procopius of Caesarea. History of the Wars: Books III and IV,* vol. 2. London: Wm. Heinemann, 1916.

Dictionary of Popes and the Papacy. Edited by Bruno Steimer and Michael Parker. Translated by Brian McNeil and Peter Heinigg. New York: Crossroad, 2001.

Dictionnaire de Théologie Catholique, bk. 15, pt. 2. Begun by A. Vacant and E. Mangenot; continued by É. Amann. Paris: Letouzey et Ané, 1950.

Diehl, Charles. *Byzantium: Greatness and Decline.* Translated from the French by Naomi Walford. New Brunswick, NJ: Rutgers Univ. Press, 1957.

Diehl, Charles. *Études sur L'Administration Byzantine dans L'exarchat de Ravenne (568–751).* New York: Burt Franklin, 1972.

Diehl, Charles. *History of the Byzantine Empire.* Translated from the Fr. by George Ives. New York: G. E. Stechert, 1945.

Diehl, Charles. *Justinien et la Civilization Byzantine au Vie Siècle.* Paris: Ernest Leroux, 1901.

Diehl, Charles. *L'Afrique Byzantine: Histoire de la Domination Byzantine en Afrique (538–709),* vol. 1. Reprint of 1896 ed. New York: Burt Franklin, n.d.

Diehl, Charles. *Theodora: Empress of Byzantium.* Translated by Samuel Rosenbaum. New York: Frederick Ungar, 1972.

A Discourse Concerning the Laws Ecclesiastical and Civil.... London, 1682.

Dölger, Franz. *Regesten der Kaiserurkunden des oströmischen Reichs.* 1. Teil: Regesten von 565-1025 (Corpus der griechischen Urkunden des Mittelalters und der neueren Zeit, Reihe A, Abt. I 1), 1924.

Donalson, Malcolm D. *A Translation of Jerome's* Chronicon *with Historical Commentary.* Lewiston, NY: Mellon Univ. Press, 1996.

Dow, Christopher. *A Discourse of the Sabbath and the Lords Day....* London, 1636.

Dowling, John. *The Burning of the Bibles. Defence of the Protestant Version of the Scriptures against the Attacks of the Popish Apologists.* Philadelphia: Nathan Moore, 1843.

Dowling, Rev. John. *The History of Romanism*. New York: Edward Walker, 1845.

Dowling, John. *The History of Romanism*, new ed. New York: Edward Walker, 1870.

Draper, John William. *History of the Intellectual Development of Europe*, 5th ed. New York: Harper, 1869.

Duchesne, L'Abbé. *The Beginnings of the Temporal Sovereignty of the Popes, A.D. 754–1073*. Translated from the Fr. by Arnold H. Mathew. London: Kegan Paul, Trench, Trübner, 1908.

Duchesne, L'Abbé. *Christian Worship: Its Origin and Evolution: A Study of the Latin Liturgy up to the Time of Charlemagne*. Translated from the 3rd Fr. ed. by M. L. McClure. London: Society for Promoting Christian Knowledge, 1903.

Duchesne, L'Abbe. *The Churches Separated from Rome*. Translated by Arnold Mathew. London: Kegan Paul, Trench, Trübner; 1907.

Duchesne, L'Abbé. *L'Église au VIème siècle* [The church in the 6th century]. Paris: Fontemoing (E. de Boccard), 1925.

Duchesne, L'Abbe. *Le Liber Pontificalis*, bk. 1. Paris: E. de Boccard, 1955.

Duncan-Jones, A. S. *The Struggle for Religious Freedom in Germany*. London: Victor Gollancz, 1938.

Durant, Will. *The Age of Faith: A History of Medieval Civilization—Christian, Islamic, and Judaic—from Constantine to Dante: A.D. 325–1300*. New York: Simon and Schuster, 1950.

Duruy, Victor. *The History of the Middle Ages*. Translated from the 12th ed. by E. H. and M. D. Whitney. New York: Henry Holt, 1891.

Dvornik, Francis. *Byzantium and the Roman Primacy.* New York: Fordham Univ. Press, 1966.

Dvornik, Francis. *Early Christian and Byzantine Political Philosophy,* 2 vols. Washington, DC:

Dumbarton Oaks Ctr. for Byz. Studies, 1966.

Dvornik, Francis. *The Idea of Apostolicity in Byzantium and the Legend of the Apostle Andrew.* Cambridge, MA: Harvard Univ. Press, 1958.

Dvornik, Francis. *National Churches and the Church Universal.* Westminster: Dacre Press, n.d.

Eberhardt, Newman C. *A Summary of Catholic History,* vol. 1. St. Louis, MO: B. Herder, 1961.

Edward, Henry. *The Temporal Power of the Vicar of Jesus Christ,* 3rd ed. London: Burns and Oates, 1880.

Edwardson, Christian. *Facts of Faith: Analyzing the Fundamental Doctrines of the Holy Scriptures,* rev., facs. Nashville, TN: Southern Pub., 2001.

Ehler, Sidney Z., and John B. Morrall, eds., trans. *Church and State Through the Centuries: A Collection of Historic Documents with Commentaries.* Westminster, MD: Newman Press, 1954.

Elliot, Rev. Charles. *Delineation of Roman Catholicism,* 2 vols. New York: George Lane, 1841.

Enciclopedia Universal Ilustrada: Europeo–Americana, bk. 5. Barcelona: Hijos de J. Espasa, n.d.

The Encyclopedia Britannica, 11th ed. Vols. 1–30. New York: Encyclopedia Britannica, 1910.

The Encyclopedia Britannica, 12th ed. Vols. 31–32. New York: Encyclopedia Britannica, 1922.

Eno, Robert B. *The Rise of the Papacy.* Wilmington, DE: Michael Glazier, 1990.

Evans, J. A. S. *The Age of Justinian: The Circumstances of Imperial Power.* London: Routledge, 2000.

Evans, Malcolm, and Rod Morgan. *Preventing Torture: A Study of the European Convention for the Prevention of Torture and Inhuman or Degrading Treatment or Punishment.* Oxford: Clarendon Press, 1998.

Ewald, P. *Akten zum Schisma des Jahres* 530 (N. A. 10 p. 412 ff.), 1885.

The Fallibility & Falsehood of the Church of Rome.... London, 1676.

Farrar, James A. *Books Condemned to be Burnt.* London: Elliot Stock, 1892.

Feltoe, Rev. Charles L., trans. *The Letters and Sermons of Leo the Great, Bishop of Rome.* Vol. 12 of *A Select Library of Nicene and Post-Nicene Fathers of the Christian Church,* 2nd ser., edited by Philip Schaff and Henry Wace. New York: Christian Lit. Co., 1895.

Ferguson, Everett. *Studies in Early Christianity.* In collaboration with David M. Scholer and Paul Corby Finney.
Field, John. *A Godly Exhortation....* London, 1583.

Finch, Rev. R. P. *The Christian Sabbath Vindicated....* London, 1793.

Finlay, George. *Greece under the Romans: A Historical View of the Condition of the Greek Nation.* Edinburgh: Wm. Blackwood, 1844.

Fischer, Curtius T., recog. *Diodori: Bibliotheca Historica,* 1st ed., vol. 4. Edited by Ludovicus Dinforf. Leipsic: Teubneri, 1888.

Fisher, George P. *History of the Christian Church*. New York: Chas. Scribner's Sons, 1928.

Fischer, Katherine, trans. *The Burgundian Code: Liber Constitutionum Sive Lex Gundobada, Constitutiones Extravagantes*. 3rd series, Vol. 5, of *Translations and Reprints from the Original Sources of History*, edited by John L. Lamonte and published by the Univ. of Penn. history dept. Philadelphia: Univ. of Pennsylvania Press, 1949.

Franzen, August. *A History of the Church*. Revised and edited by John P. Dolan. Translated by Peter Becker. Montreal: Palm Pub., 1968.

Freeman, Charles. *The Closing of the Western Mind: The Rise of Faith and the Fall of Reason*. New York: Alfred Knopf, 2004.

Fremantle, Anne, ed. *The Papal Encyclicals in Their Historical Context*. New York: New American Library, 1956.

Frend, W. H. C. *The Rise of Christianity*. Philadelphia: Fortress Press, 1985.

Friedberg, Emil. *De Finium inter Ecclesiam et Civitatem Regundorum Judicio: Quid medii aevi doctors et leges statuerint*. Aalen, Ger.: Scientia Verlag, 1965.

Funk, F.X. *Kirchengeschichtliche Abhandlungen und Untersuchungen*, Bd. I and III, 1897 and 1907.

Funk, F. X. *A Manual of Church History*, 2nd impression of authorized trans. from 5th German ed. by Luigi Cappadelta, vol. 1. St. Louis, MO: Herder, 1912.

Gallenga, A. *The Pope and the King: The War between Church and State in Italy*. 2 vols. London: Samuel Tinsley, 1879.

Gardner, Iain, and Samuel N. C. Lieu. *Manichaean Texts from the Roman Empire*. Cambridge: Cambridge Univ. Press, 2004.

Geanokaplos, Deno. *Byzantium: Church Society, and Civilization Seen through Contemporary Eyes*. Chicago: Univ. of Chicago Press, 1984.

Gelzer, Heingrich. *Byzantinische Kulturgeschichte*, 1909.

Gelzer, Heingrich. *Das Verhältnis von Staat und Kirche in Byzanz (Histor. Zeitschr.* Bd. 86 [N.F. Bd. 50] p. 193 ff.), 1901.

Génestal, R. *Les origines du privilège clérical (Nouvelle Revue historique de droit français et* étranger 32e Année p. 161 sqq.) ; Acta conciliorum oecumenicorum ed. Eduardus Schwartz IV 2, 1914.

Gerostergios, Asterios. *Justinian the Great the Emperor and Saint*. Belmont, MA: Institute for Byzantine and Modern Greek Studies, 1982.

Gerostergios, Asterios. "The Religious Policy of Justinian I and His Religious Beliefs." PhD diss., Boston University School of Theology, 1974.

Gibbon, Edward. *The History of the Decline and Fall of the Roman Empire*, rev. ed., 5 vols. Philadelphia: Henry T. Coates, 1845.

Gibbon, Edward. *The History of the Decline and Fall of the Roman Empire*, vols. 4–7. Edited by J. B. Bury. London: Methuen, 1909 (4); 1911 (5); 1912 (6); 1914 (7).

Gieseler, John C. L. *A Compendium of Ecclesiastical History*, 4th ed., rev. and amended, vol. 1. Translated from the German by Samuel Davidson. In vol. 4 of *Clark's Foreign Theological Library*, Edinburgh: T. and T. Clark, 1846.

Gieseler, John C. L. *A Compendium of Ecclesiastical History*, 4th ed., rev. and amended, vol. 2. Translated from the German by Samuel Davidson. In vol. 9 of *Clark's Foreign Theological Library*. Edinburgh: T. and T. Clark, 1846.

Gieseler, John C. L. *A Compendium of Ecclesiastical History*, 4th ed., rev. and amended, vol. 3. Translated from the German by John W. Hull. In vol. 30 of *Clark's Foreign Theological Library*. Edinburgh: T. and T. Clark, 1853.

Gieseler, John C. L. *A Textbook of Church History*, vol. 4, AD 1517–1648. Translated and edited by Henry Smith. New York: Harper, 1868.

Giles, E., ed. *Documents Illustrating Papal Authority A.D. 96–454*. Fasc. London: S. P. C. K., 1952.

Gillespie, George. *Aaron's Rod Blossoming: or; The Divine Ordinance of Church Government Vindicated*. Harrisonburg, VA: Sprinkle, 1985.

Gillett, Andrew. *Envoys and Political Communication in the Late Antique West, 411–533*. Cambridge, UK: Cambridge Univ. Press, 2003.

Gillett, Charles R. *Burned Books: Neglected Chapters in British History and Literature*, 2 vols. Westport, CT: Greenwood Press, 1974.

Goldberg, David, and John D. Rayner. *The Jewish People: Their History and Their Religion*. New York: Viking Penguin, 1987.

Goodenough, Erwin R. *The Church in the Roman Empire*. New York: Henry Holt, 1931.

Grant, Michael. *From Rome to Byzantium: Fifth Century AD*. London: Routledge, 1998.

Graves, Robert. *Count Belisarius*. New York: Literary Guild, 1938.

The Great Encyclical Letters of Pope Leo 13, 3rd ed. Translated from approved sources. New York: Benziger Bros., 1903.

The Greek Ecclesiastical Historians, 6 vols. London: Samuel Bagster, 1946.

Gregorovius, Ferdinand. *History of the City of Rome in the Middle Ages*, vol. 1. Translated from the 4th German ed. London: George Bell, 1900.

Gregory the 8th, Pope. *The Holy Bull*. Renewed, ratified by Sixtus, Reprinted, London, 1588.

Grier, Rev. Richard. *An Epitome of the General Councils of the Church*. Dublin: William Curry, 1828.

Grillmeier, Aloys, S.J. *From the Council of Chalcedon (451) to Gregory the Great (590–604)*, pt. 1. Vol. 2 of *Christ in Christian Tradition*. Translated by Pauline Allen and John Cawte. London: Mowbray, 1987.

Grillmeier, Aloys, S.J. *From the Council of Chalcedon to Gregory the Great (590–604)*, pt. 4. Vol. 2 of *Christ in Christian Tradition*. In collaboration with Theresia Hainthaler. Translated by O. C. Dean. London: Mowbray, 1996.

Josef Gröll, *Die Elemente des kirchlichen Freiungsrechtes mit besonderer Berücksichtigung der österreichischen Entwicklung* (Kirchenrechtl. Abhandlungen ed. By U. Stutz, Heft 75/76), 1911;

Growcock, Frederick. "Ecclesiastical Legislation in the Justinian Code." PhD diss., University of Texas, 1965.

Guerry, L'Abbé É, classés et commentés par. *L'Action Catholique: Textes Pontificaux*. Paris: Desclée de Brouwer, 1936.

Guilday, Peter, A. K. Ziegler, M. R. P. McGuire, and J. Tracy Ellis, eds. *The Catholic Historical Review* 27, no. 4, sec. 2 (April 1941–January 1942). Washington, DC: Catholic Univ. of Am. Press, 1942.

Guizot, M., and Madame Guizot de Witt. *The History of France: From Earliest Times to 1848*. 8 vols. New York: John B. Alden, 1884.

Hallam, Henry. *History of Europe during the Middle Ages*, rev. ed., vol. 1. New York: Colonial, 1899.

Hanway, Jonas. *Thoughts on the Importance of the Sabbath*. London, 1765.

Hardon, John A., S. J. *The History of Eucharistic Adoration*. Oak Lawn, IL: CMJ Marian Publishers, 1997.

Harrak, Amir, trans. from Syriac. *The Chronicle of Zuqnīn: Parts III and IV, A. D. 488–775*. Toronto: Pontifical Inst. of Mediaeval Studies, 1999.

Hartmann, Ludo Moritz. *Geschichte Italiens im Mittelalter*, Bd. I, 1897.

Hartmann, Ludo Moritz. *Geschichte Italiens im Mittelalter*, Bd. II 1 and 2, 1900/1903.

Hastings, James, ed. *Encyclopædia of Religion and Ethics*, vol. 12. Assisted by John Selbie and Louis Gray. New York: Scribner's, 1922.

Hayward, Fernand. *History of the Popes*. Translated by monks St. Augustine's Abbey, Ramsgate. New York: E. P. Dutton, 1931.

Heather, Peter. "Theodoric, king of the Goths." In *Early Medieval Europe* 4, 145–173. N.p.: Longman, 1995.

Hefele, Charles Joseph. *A History of the Christian Councils*, vol. 1 (close of Nicea–AD 325). Translated and edited by William R. Clark. Edinburgh: T. and T. Clark, 1871.

Hefele, Charles Joseph. *A History of the Councils of the Church*, vol. 2 (AD 326–429). Translated and edited by Henry Nutcombe Oxanham. Edinburgh: T. and T. Clark, 1876.

Hefele, R. Rev. Charles Joseph. *A History of the Councils f the Church*, vol. 3 (AD 431–451). Translated and edited by the editor of Hagenbach's *History of Doctrines*. Edinburgh: T. and T. Clark, 1883.

Hefele, R. Rev. Charles Joseph. *A History of the Councils of the Church*, vol. 4 (AD 451–680), and vol. 5 (AD 626– end of 2nd Nicea). Translated and edited by William R. Clark. Edinburgh: T. and T. Clark, 1895 (4); 1896 (5).

Heiks, Heidi. *508 538 1798 1843 Source Book (Preliminary)*. Knoxville, IL: Hope International, 2005, 2007.

Hergenröther, Joseph. *Catholic Church and Christian State: A Series of Essays on the Relation of the Church to the Civil Power*, vol. 1. Translated from the German. London: Burns and Oates, 1876.

Hodgkin, Thomas. *Italy and Her Invaders*. 8 vols. 1st ed. published 1880–1889. New York: Russell and Russell, 1967.

Hodgkin, Thomas, trans. *The Letters of Cassiodorus: Being a Condensed Translation of the Variae Epistolae of Magnus Aurelius Cassiodorus Senator*. London: Henry Frowde, 1886.

Hodgkin, Thomas. *Theodoris the Goth: The Barbarian Champion of Civilisation*. New York: G. P. Putnam's Sons, 1902.

Hogan, Richard M. *Dissent from the Creed: Heresies Past and Present*. Huntington, IN: Our Sunday Visitor Pub., 2001.

Holland, Joe. *Modern Catholic Social Teaching: The Popes Confront the Industrial Age 1740–1958*. New York: Paulist Press, 2003.

Honoré, Tony. *Tribonian*. London: Duckworth, 1978.

Hughes, Philip. *A History of the Church*, vol. 2. New York: Sheed and Ward, 1935.

Hutton, William Holden. *The Church of the Sixth Century: Six Chapters in Ecclesiastical History*. London: Longmans, Green, 1897.

Ihm, Claudia Carlen, comp. *The Papal Encyclicals 1878–1903*. N.p.: McGrath, 1981.

Index Titulorum Authentici in Novem Collationes Digesti. Reprint, *Seminar* (annual extraordinary number of *The Jurist*), vol. 2, 1944. Washington, DC: School of Canon Law, Catholic Univ. of Am., 1944.

Innes, A. Taylor. *Church and State: A Historical Handbook*, 2nd ed. Edinburgh: T. and T. Clark, n.d.

Ironside, Gilbert. *Seven Questions of the Sabbath*. Oxford: 1637.

Jackson, Samuel Macauley, ed. *The New Schaff-Herzog Encyclopedia of Religious Knowledge*. 13 vols. With the assistance of Charles C. Sherman and George W. Gilmore. New York: Funk and Wagnalls, 1908–12.

Jaffé, Philippus, edidit. *Einharti Vita Caroli Magni*. Berlin: Apud Wiedmannos, 1847.

Jaffé, Philippus, edidit. *Monumenta Gregoriana*. Bk. 2 in *Bibliotecha Rerum Germanicarum*. Berlin: Apud Wiedmannos, 1845.

Jaffé, Philippus, and Guilelmus Wattenbach, descripserunt. *Ecclesiae Metropolitanae Coloniensis: Codices Manuscripti*. Berlin: Apud Weidmannos, 1874.

Janus. *The Pope and the Council*. Translated from the German. Boston: Roberts Bros., 1870.

Jasper, Detlev, and Horst Fuhrmann. *Papal Letters in the Early Middle Ages*. Washington, DC: Catholic Univ. of Am. Press, 2001.

Jeffreys, Elizabeth, ed. *Studies in John Malalas*. With assistance from Brian Croke and Roger Scott. Sydney: Australian Asso. for Byzantine Studies, 1990.

John Paul II, Pope. *Dies Domini*. http://www.vatican.va/holy_father/john_paul_ii/apost_letters/documents/hf_jp-ii_apl_0507.

Johns, Warren L. *Dateline Sunday, U.S.A.: The Story of Three and a Half Centuries of Sundaylaw Battles in America*. Mountain View, CA: Pacific Press, 1967.

Johnson, Allan C., Paul R. Coleman-Norton, and Frank C. Bourne, trans. *Ancient Roman Statutes*. General editing by Clyde Pharr. Clark, NJ: Lawbook Exchange, 2004.

Johnson, Rossiter, C. Horne, and J. Rudd, eds. *The Great Events, by Famous Historians*, vol. 4. A.D. 410–842. N.p.: National Alumni, 1905.

Jolowicz, H. F. *Historical Introduction to the Study of Roman Law*. Cambridge: Cambridge Univ. Press, 1932, 1952.

Jones, Leslie Webber, ed. *Classical and Mediaeval Studies in Honor of Edward Kennard Rand*. New York: Leslie Webber Jones, 1938.

Jones, Thomas. *Mercy Triumphing over Judgement*. London, 1600s?

Jungmann, Rev. Joseph A., S.J. *The Mass of the Roman Rite: Its Origins and Development*, vol. 1. Translated by Francis Brunner. New York: Benziger, 1950.

Jurgens, William A., sel., trans. *The Faith of the Early Fathers: A Source-book of theological and historical passages . . .* , vols. 1, 3. Collegeville, MN: Liturgical Press, 1970 (1); 1979 (3).

Jurisprudentia vetus Ante-Justinianea. Lugduni Batavorum: Apud Johannem vander Linden, 1717.

Kaldellis, Anthony. *Procopius of Caesarea: Tyranny, History, and Philosophy at the End of Antiquity.* Philadelphia: Univ. of Pennsylvania Press, 2004.

Kattenbusch, Ferdinand. Lehrbuch der vergleichenden Confessionskunde, Bd. I, 1892.

Katz, Solomon. *The Jews in the Visigothic and Frankish Kingdoms of Spain and Gaul.* Cambridge, MA: Medieval Acad. of America, 1937.

Kazhdan, Alexander P., M.-A. Talbot, A. Cutler, T. Gregory, N. Ševčenko, eds. *The Oxford Dictionary of Byzantium.* 3 vols. New York: Oxford Univ. Press, 1991.

Kirsch, Johann Peter. *Kirchengeschichte.* Vol. 1 of *Die Kirche in Der Antiken Griechisch-Romischen Kulterweit.* Freiburg Im Breisgau, Ger.: Herder, 1930.

Knabe, Lotte von. *Die gelasianische Zweigewaltentheorie bis zum Ende des Investiturstreits.* Vaduz: Kraus Reprint, 1965.

Knecht, August. *Die Religions-Politik Kaiser Justinians I.,* Dissert. Würzberg, 1896.

Knecht, August. *Die Religions-Politik: Kaiser Justinians I: Eine kirchengeschichtliche Studie.* Facs. of 1896 ed. Elibron Classics, 2005. www.elibron.com.

Krueger, Paulus, recogn., retract. *Codex Iustinianus.* In vol. 2 of *Corpus Iurus Civilis.* Berlin: Apud Wiedmannos, 1959.

Krueger, Paulus, recogn. *Institutiones.* In vol. 1 of *Corpus Iuris Civilis.* Berlin: Apud Wiedmannos, 1959.

Krumbacher, Karl von. *Geschichte der Byzantinischen Litteratur,* vol. 1. New York: Burt Franklin, 1958?

Krumbacher, Karl von. *Geschichte der Byzantinischen Litteratur: Von Justinian bis zum Ende des Oströmischen Reiches (527–1453)*. Munich: C. H. Beck'sche, Oskar Beck, 1897.

Ladner, Gerhart B. "Justinian's Theory of Law and the Renewal Ideology of the 'Leges Barbarorum.'" *Proceedings of the American Philosophical Society* 119, no. 3 (June, 1975): 191–200.

Lancioni, Enrico. *The History of the Popes*. New York: Manor Books, 1978.

Landman, Isaac, ed. *The Universal Jewish Encyclopedia*. 10 vols. In asso. with Louis Rittenberg et al, board of eds. New York: Universal Jewish Encyc. Co., 1948.

Landon, Rev. Edward. *A Manual of Councils of the Holy Catholic Church*, 2 vols., new and rev. ed. London: Griffith Farran, n.d.

Lang, Andrew. *Myth, Ritual and Religion*, vol. 1. London: Senate, 1995.

Latourette, Kenneth Scott. *A History of Christianity*, vol. 1. New York: Harper and Row, 1975.

Lavington, John. *The Sanctification of the Sabbath*, 2nd ed. Exon, Eng., 1744.

Lea, Henry Charles. *The Dead Hand: A Brief Sketch of the Relations between Church and State with Regard to Ecclesiastical Property and the Religious Orders*. Philadelphia: Wm. Dornan, 1900.

Lea, Henry C. *A History of Auricular Confession and Indulgences*, vol. 1. Philadelphia: Lea Bros., 1896.

Lea, Henry C. *A History of the Inquisition of the Middle Ages*, vols. 1, 2. New York: Harper, 1888.

Lea, Henry C. *A History of the Inquisition of the Middle Ages*, vol. 3. New York: Russell and Russell, 1958.

Lea, Henry C. *Studies on Church History*. Philadelphia: Henry C. Lea's Son, 1883.

Lecky, William Edward Hartpole. *Democracy and Liberty*, new ed., vol. 2. New York: Longmans, Green, 1900.

Lecky, William Edward Hartpole. *Rationalism in Europe*, rev. ed., vol. 1. New York: D. Appleton, 1893.

Levillain, Philippe, ed. *The Papacy: An Encyclopedia*, vol. 3. New York: Routledge, n.d.

Lewis, A. H. *A Critical History of Sunday Legislation from 321 to 1888 A.D.* New York: D. Appleton, 1888.

Liebs, Detlef. *Römische Jurispredenz in Fallien (2. Bis 8. Jahrhundert)*. Berlin: Duncker and Humblot, 2002.

Lindsay, Thomas M. *The Church and the Ministry in the Early Centuries*, 2nd ed. London: Hodder and Stoughton, 1903.

Ius graeco-romanum, ed. C. E. Zachariae a Lingenthal, 1856 ff.

Loomis, Louise Ropes, trans. *Book of the Popes (Liber Pontificalis)*, vol. 1. New York: Columbia University Press, 1916.

Lortz, Joseph. *History of the Church*. Translated and adapted from the 5th and 6th German ed. by Edwin Kaiser. Milwaukee, WI: Bruce, 1947.

Lydus, Ioannes. *On Powers, or the Magistracies of the Roman State*. Translated by Anastasius Bandy. Fasc. Philadelphia: American Philosophical Society, 1983.

Maas, Michael, ed. *The Age of Justinian*. Cambridge: Cambridge Univ. Press, 2005.

MacDonald, Jeffrey L. "The Christological Works of Justinian." PhD diss., Catholic University of America, 1995.

Machiavelli, Niccolo. *The Florentine Histories*, vol. 1. Translated by C. Edward Lester. New York: Paine and Burgess, 1845.

Machiavelli, Niccolo. *The History of Florence*, new trans. London: Henry Bohn, 1847.

Magoulias, Harry J. *Byzantine Christianity: Emperor, Church and the West*. Chicago: Rand McNally, 1970.

Malalas, Ioannis. *Chronographia*. Recensuit Ioannes Thurn. Vol. 35 of *Corpus Fontium Historiae Byzantinae*, series *Berolinensis*, ediderunt H.-G. Beck, A. Kambylis, R. Keydell. Berlin: Walter de Gruyter, 2000.

Malalas, Ioannes. *Chronographia*. In *Corpus Scriptorum Historiae Byzantinae*, new ed. Bonn: Impensis Ed. Weberi, 1831.

Malalas, John. *ΧρονοιραΦia*. Athens: Heliodromion Society, 2001.

Manhattan, Avro. *The Vatican in World Politics*. New York: Gaer Asso., 1949.

Mansi, Ioannis Dominici. *Carmen elegiacum de vita sua*. Trans. Aldo Marsili. Lucca, It.: Fazzi, 1984.

Mansi, Joannes Dominicus. *Sacrorum Conciliorum: Nova, et Amplissima Collectio*, bks. 2, 3. Florence: Expensis Antonii Zatta Veneti, 1759.

Mansi, Joannes Dominicus. *Sacrorum Conciliorum: Nova, et Amplissima Collectio*, bk. 9, facs. ed. Paris: Welter, 1902.

Mansi, Joannes Dominicus. *Sacrorum Conciliorum: Nova, et Amplissima Collectio*, vol. 9, facs. reproduction. Graz: Akademische Druck-U. Verlagsanstalt, 1960.

Marcus, R. A. "Gregory the Great's Europe." *Transactions of the Royal Historical Society* 31, (1981): 21–36.

Martin, Malachi. *The Keys of This Blood: The Struggle for World Dominion between Pope John Paul II, Mikhail Gorbachev, and the Capitalist West*. New York: Simon and Schuster, 1990.

Mather, Azariah. *The Sabbath-Day's Rest Asserted*. Boston, 1725.

Mathew, Arnold Harris. *The Life and Times of Hildebrand*. London: Francis Griffiths, 1910.

Matthews, John F. *Laying Down the Law: A Study of the Theodosian Code*. New Haven, CT: Yale Univ. Press, 2000.

Maurus, Hrabanus. *De institutione clericorum libri tres: Studien und Edition von Detlev Zimpel*. Bd. 7 of *Frieburger Beiträge zur Mittelalterlichen Geschichte*. Frankfurt am Main: Peter Lang, 1996.

McBrien, Richard P. *Lives of the Popes*, 1st ed. San Francisco: Harper, 1997.

McCabe, Joseph. *Crises in the History of the Papacy: A Study of Twenty Famous Popes whose Careers and whose Influence Were Important in the Development of the Church and in the History of the World*. New York: G. P. Putnam's Sons, 1916.

McCabe, Joseph. *The Decay of the Church of Rome*. London: Methuen, 1909.

McCabe, Joseph. *The Empresses of Constantinople*. London: Methuen, 1913.

McCabe, Joseph. *The History and Meaning of the Catholic Index of Forbidden Books*. Girard, KS: Haldeman-Julius.

McCabe, Joseph. *A History of the Popes*. London: Watts, 1939.

M'Clintock, John. *The Temporal Power of the Pope*. New York: Carlton and Phillips, 1855.

M'Clintock, John, and James Strong, comp. *Cyclopædia of Biblical, Theological and Ecclesiastical Literature*, vol. 1. New York: Harper, 1895.

McCormick, Michael. *Eternal Victory: Triumphal rulership in late antiquity, Byzantium, and the early medieval West*. Cambridge, G.B.: Cambridge University Press, 1986.

McCormick, Michael. *Eternal Victory: Triumphal Rulership in Late Antiquity, Byzantium and the Early Medieval West*. Cambridge: Cambridge Univ. Press, 1987.

McGiffert, Rev. Arthur C., trans. *Eusebius: Church History, Life of Constantine the Great, and Oration in Praise of Constantine*. Vol. 1 of *A Select Library of Nicene and Post-Nicene Fathers of the Christian Church*, 2nd ser., edited by Philip Schaff and Henry Wace. Grand Rapids, MI: Wm. B. Eerdmans, 1961.

McKeon, Richard. "Canonic Books and Prohibited Books: Orthodoxy and Heresy in Religion and Culture." *Critical Inquiry* 2, no. 4 (Summer, 1976): 781–806.

McSorley, Joseph. *An Outline History of the Church by Centuries*, 2nd ed. St. Louis, MO: Herder, 1944.

Mears, T. Lambert, trans. *The Institutes of Gaius and Justinian*. Clark, NJ: Lawbook Exchange, 2004.

Meredith, Anthony. *The Cappadocians*. Crestwood, NY: St Vladmir's Seminary Press, 2000.

Metz, René. *What is Canon Law?* Translated from the French by Michael Derrick. Vol. 80 of the *Twentieth Century Encyclopedia of Catholicism*. New York: Hawthorn, n.d.

Meyendorff, John. "Justinian, the Empire and the Church." *Dumbarton Oaks Papers* 22 (1968): 43–60.

Mierow, Herbert Edward. "The Roman Provincial Governor As He Appears in the Digest and Code of Justinian." PhD diss., Princeton University, 1926. Colorado Springs: Colorado College Pub., 1926.

Migne, Jaques-Paul. *D. Eugyppii Abbatis Africani*. Bk. 2 of *Patrologiiae Latinae*. 1st ed. pub. in 1848. Réimpression anastatique par Brepols, 1994.

Migne, Jacques-Paul. *Gelasii I Papæ, Aviti, Faustini, necnon Joannis Diaconi, Juliani Pomerii*. Bk. 59 of *Patrologiiae Latinae*. 1st ed. pub. in 1848. Réimpression anastatique par Brepols, 1994.

Migne, Jacques-Paul. *Justiniani, Imperatoris Augusti, Scripta Dogmatica*. In *Patrologiæ Græcæ, Tomus LXXXVI*. In *Patrologiæ Cursus Completus*, 86:1. J.-P. Migne, 1865.

Migne, Jacques-Paul. *Magni Aurelii Cassiodori Senatoris, viri Partrich, Consularis, et Vivariensis Abbatis*. Book 70, *Patrologiae Latinae*. 1st ed. pub. in 1848. Réimpression anastatique par Brepols, 1994.

Miller, J. Michael. *The Shepherd and the Rock: Origins, Development, and Mission of the Papacy*. Huntington, IN: Our Sunday Visitor Pub., 1995.

Milman, Henry Hart. *The History of Christianity*, rev. ed., vol. 2. London: John Murray, 1863.

Milman, Henry Hart. *The History of Christianity: From the Birth of Christ to the Abolition of Paganism in the Roman Empire*, 2 vols. New York: A. C. Armstrong, 1881.

Milman, Henry Hart. *The History of Christianity; including that of the Popes to the Pontifiate of Nicolas V.*, 3rd ed. 9 vols. London: John Murray, 1872.

Mitchell, Stephen. *A History of the Later Roman Empire AD 284–64: The Transformation of the Ancient World.* Malden, MA: Blackwell, 2007.

Mohler, James A. *The Origin and Evolution of the Priesthood.* Staten Is., NY: Alba House, 1970.

Mommsen, Theodor. *Cassiodori Senatoris Variae* (Berolini, 1894).

Mommsen, Theodorus, edidit. *Chronica Minora: Saec. IV. V. VI. VII.* Vol. 3 of *Monumenta Germaniae Historica*, edidit Societas Aperiendis Fontibus. Berlin: Apud Weidmannos, 1898.

Mommsen, Theodorus, edidit. *Chronica Minora Saec. IV. V. VI. VII.*, 3 vols. In *Monumenta Germaniae Historica: Auctores Antiquissimi.* Munich: Monumenta Germaniae Historica, 1981.

Mommsen, Theodorus, recogn. *Digesta.* Retractavit, Paulus Krueger. In vol. 1 of *Corpus Iurus Civilis.* Berlin: Apud Wiedmannos, 1959.

Mommsen, Theodor, ed. Latin text. *The Digest of Justinian*, vol. 1. With assistance of Paul Krueger. English translation edited by Alan Watson. Philadelphia: Univ. of Pennsylvania Press, 1985.

Mommsen, Theodor. *The History of Rome*, new ed., vol. 1. Translated by William Dickson. London: Richard Bentley, 1872.

Mommsen, Theodor. *The History of Rome*, pop. ed., vols. 2, 3. Translated by William Dickson. London: Richard Bentley, 1888 (2); 1887 (3).

Mommsen, Theodor. *The History of Rome*, new rev. ed., vols. 4, 5. Translated by William Dickson. London: MacMillan, 1901.

Mommsen, Theodor. *A History of Rome under the Emperors*. New York: Routledge, 1996.

Mommsen, Th. *Ostgothische Studien* (N. A. 14 p. 223 ff., 451 ff.), 1889.

Mommsen, Th. Über die Akten zum Schisma des Jahres 530 (N. A. 10 p. 581 ff.), 1885.

Montesquieu. *Considerations of the Causes of The Greatness of the Romans and Their Decline*. Translated by David Lowenthal; reprinted with corrections. Indianapolis, IN: Hackett, 1999.

Moorhead, John. *Justinian*. London: Longman, 1994.

Morrison, Karl Frederick. *The Two Kingdoms: Ecclesiology in Carolingian Political Thought*. Princeton: Princeton Univ. Press, 1964.

Morse, George P. *The Mass: Its Mysteries Revealed*. N.p.: Catholics Committed to Support the Pope, 1998.

Motley, John L. *The Rise of the Dutch Republic: A History*. 3 vols. Philadelphia: David McKay, n.d.

Mourret, Rev. Fernand. *A History of the Catholic Church*, vols.1, 3. Translated by Rev. Newton Thompson. St. Louis, MO: B. Herder, 1931 (1); 1936 (3).

Mourret, Rev. Fernand. *A History of the Catholic Church*, vol. 1, 2nd impress. Translated by Rev. Newton Thompson. St. Louis, MO: B. Herder, 1944.

Mourret, Rev. Fernand. *A History of the Catholic Church*, vol. 1, 3rd impress. Translated by Rev. Newton Thompson. St. Louis, MO: B. Herder, 1946.

Muirhead, James. *Historical Introduction to the Private Law of Rome.* Third edition revised and edited by Alexander Grant. London: A. and C. Black, 1916.

Munier, C., cura et studio. *Concilia Galliae, A. 314–A. 506.* Vol. 148 of *Corpus Christianorum,* ser. *Latina.* Turnholti: Typographi Brepols Editores Pontificii, 1943.

Munro, Dana Carleton. *The Middle Ages 395–1272.* New York: Century, 1922.

Myers, Philip V. N. *Ancient History for Colleges and High Schools.* Pt. 2 of *A History of Rome.* Boston: Ginn, 1901.

Myers, Philip V. N. *The Eastern Nations and Greece,* rev. ed. Boston: Ginn, 1904.

Nessel, Rev. William. *First Amendment Freedoms, Papal Pronouncements and Concordat Practice: A comparative study in American Law and Public Ecclesiastical Law.* Doct. diss., Catholic University of America. No. 412 of *Catholic University of America Canon Law Studies.* Washington, DC: Catholic University of America Press, 1961.

New Catholic Encyclopedia, vols. 5, 9. San Francisco: n.p., 1967.

New Catholic Encyclopedia, 2nd ed. Detroit, MI: Gale, 2003.

New Catholic Encyclopedia. 15 vols. Washington, DC: Publisher's Guild, 1967 (1–15).

New Catholic Encyclopedia Dictionary. Compiled and edited under the direction of the editors of *The Catholic Encyclopedia.* New York: Gilmary Society, 1941(?).

Newton, Thomas. *Dissertations on the Prophecies,* new ed., vol. 2. Philadelphia: James Martin, 1813.

Nicol, Donald M. *The Last Centuries of Byzantium 1261–1453*. London: Rupert Hart-Davis, 1972.

Noailles, Pierre. *Les Collections de Novelles de L'Empereur Justinien*. Paris: Recueil Sirey, 1912; 1914.

Noailles, Pierre, and A. Dain, trans. *Les Novelles de Léon VI Le Sage*. Paris: Société d'Édition "Les Belles Lettres," 1944.

O., I. *The Tryal [sic.] of the Truth* .... Amsterdam, 1656.

O., J. *The Doctrine of the Fourth Commandment, Deformed by Popery*. London, 1650.

O'Brien, Rev. J. A. *The Church the Interpreter of the Bible*. Huntington, IN: Our Sunday Visitor Press, 1952.

O'Donnell, James J. *Cassiodorus*. Berkeley: Univ. of California Press, 1979.

Orientalia Christiana Periodica, vol. 33. Edited by the Pontifical Institute of Oriental Studies. N.p.: Rome, 1967.

Orr, James, J. Nuelsen, E. Mullins, M. Evans, eds. *The International Standard Bible Encyclopedia*. 5 vols. Chicago: Howard-Severance, 1915.

Ostrogorsky, George. *History of the Byzantine State*, rev. ed. Translated from the German by Joan Hussey. New Brunswick, NJ: Rutgers Univ. Press, 1969.

Oxford Dictionary of Byzantium, vol. 2. New York: Oxford Univ. Press, 1991.

Paetow, Louis J. *A Guide to the Study of Medieval History*, rev. ed. New York: F. S. Crofts, 1931.

Palanque, Jean-Rémy. *The Dawn of the Middle Ages*. Translated by Dom Finbarr Murphy. Vol. 75 of the *Twentieth Century Encyclopedia of Catholicism*, sec. 7 of *The History of the Church*. New York: Hawthorn, 1960.

Parker, T. M. *Christianity and the State in the Light of History.* London: Adam and Charles Black, 1955.

Parkes, James. *The Conflict of the Church and the Synagogue: A Study in the Origins of Antisemitism.* Cleveland: World Pub., 1961.

Ludwig, Freiherr von. *The History of the Popes,* vol. 35–40. Translated by E. F. Peeler. London: Routledge and Kegan Paul, 1949 (35); 1950 (36); 1950 (37); 1951 (38); 1952 (39); 1953 (40).

Paul the Deacon. *History of the Lombards.* Translated by William D. Foulke. Edited by Edward Peters. Originally published in 1907 as *History of the Langobords.* Philadelphia: Univ. of Pennsylvania Press, 1974.

Peitz, W. M., S. J. *Martin I und Maximus Confessor* (*Histor. Jahrbuch* Bd. 38 p. 213 ff.), 1917.

Pemble, William. *The Period of the Persian Monarchie.* London, 1631.

Percival, Henry R, ed. *The Seven Ecumenical Councils of the Undivided Church: Their Canons and Dogmatic Decrees.* Vol. 14 of *A Select Library of Nicene and Post-Nicene Fathers of the Christian Church,* 2nd ser., edited by Philip Schaff and Henry Wace. Grand Rapids, MI: Wm. B. Eerdmans, 1997.

Pfannmüller, Gustav. *Die kirchliche Gesetzgebung Justinians hauptsächlich auf Grund der Novellen,* 1903.

Pfeilschifter, Georg. *Der Ostgotenkönig Theoderich der Große und die katholische Kirche* (*Kirchengeschichtliche Studien* ed. By Knöpfler, Schrörs and Sdralek, III. Bd., 1st and 2nd Heft), 1896.

Pharr, Clyde, trans. *The Theodosian Code and Novels and the Sirmondian Constitutions.* In collaboration with Theresa S. Davidson and Mary B. Pharr. Union, NJ: Lawbook Exchange, 2001.

Phillips, J. A. *Papal Paganism.* Nashville, TN: Cokesbury Press, 1924.

Pocklington, John. *Sunday no Sabbath.* London, 1636.

Pollock, Frederick. "Anglo-Saxon Law." *The English Historical Review* 8, no. 30 (April 1893): 239–271.

Popish Cruelty Displayed. Boston: Fleet, 1753.

Porter, Edm. *Sabbatum. The Mystery of the Sabbath Discovered.* London, 1600s?

Powell, Mark E. "Papal Infallibility as Religious Epistemology: Manning, Newman, Dulles, and Küng." PhD diss., Southern Methodist University, December 2005. Ann Arbor, MI: ProQuest Information, 2005.

Prideaux. *The Doctrine of the Sabbath...*, 3rd ed. London, 1635.

Priestly, Joseph. *History of the Corruptions of Christianity*, 3rd ed., 2 vols. Boston, 1797.

Priolkar, Anant Kakba. *The Goa Inquisition.* With accounts given by Dr. Dellon and Dr. Buchanan. Bombay: A. K. Priolkar, 1961.

Procopius. *The Secret History of the Court of Justinian.* Boston: IndyPublish.com, n.d.

Pullan, Leighton. *From Justinian to Luther A.D. 518–1517.* Oxford: Clarendon, 1930.

Rabello, Alfredo M. *The Jews in the Roman Empire: Legal Problems, from Herod to Justinian.* Aldershot, G.B.: Ashgate, 2004.

Rabello, Alfredo M. *The Legal Condition of the Jews in the Roman Empire*. In Vol. 2 of *Aufstieg und Neidergang der Römischen Welt: Geshichte und Kultur Roms im Spiegel der Neueren Forschung*, edited by Hildegard Temporini and Wolfgang Haase. Principat, Dreizehnter Bd. Berlin: Walter de Druyter, 1980.

Rabello, Alfredo M. *The Legal Status of the Jews in Roman Empire and in Medieval Age*. Jerusalem: 1972.

Rahner, Hugo. *Church and State in Early Christianity*. Translated from *Kirche und Staat im Frühen Christentum: Dokumente aus acht Jahrhunderten und ihre Deutung* (1961) by Leo D. Davis. San Francisco: Ignatius Press,

Ramstein, Rev. Matthew. *A Manual of Canon Law*. Hoboken, NJ: Terminal, 1948.

Ranke, Leopold von. *The History of the Popes, Their Church and State*, rev. ed., vol. 3. Translated by E. Foster. New York: Colonial Press, 1901.

Ranke, Leopold von. *The History of the Popes: Their Church and State*, rev. ed. Translated by E. Fowler. Vol. 1, 2 in *The World's Greatest Literature*, edited by Justin McCarthy et al. New York: P. F. Collier, 1901.

Ranke, Leopold von. *The History of the Popes, Their Church and State, and Especially of Their Conflicts with Protestantism*, vol. 1. Translated by E. Foster. London: George Bell, 1887.

Renna, Thomas. *The West in the Early Middle Ages 300–1050*. N.p.: Univ. Press of America, 1977.

Rey-Mermet, Théodule. *Moral Choices*. Translated by Paul Laverdure. Liguori, MO: Liguori, 1998.

Ringgold, James T. *The Legal Sunday*. New York: Internat'l Liberty Asso., 1894.

Ripley, George, and Charles Dana, eds. *The American Cyclopedia*. Vol. 1 of *The New Werner*

Twentieth Century Edition of the Encyclopædia. New York: D. Appleton, 1905.

Rives, James B. *Religion in the Roman Empire*. Malden, MA: Blackwell, 2007.

Robertson, Archibald, ed. *Select Writings and Letters of Athanasius, Bishop of Alexandria*. Vol.

4 of *A Select Library of Nicene and Post-Nicene Fathers of the Christian Church*, 2nd ser., edited by Philip Schaff and Henry Wace. Grand Rapids, MI: Wm. B. Eerdmans, 1975.

Robinson, James T. *An Introduction to the History of Western Europe*, 2 vols. Rev., enlarged by James T. Shotwell. Boston: Ginn, 1934.

Rogers, David Morrison, comp., ed. *Theodoret: The Ecclesiastical History 1612*. Reproduced from 1st English ed., 1612. Vol. 287 of *English Recusant Literature 1558–1640*. London: Scolar Press, 1976.

Romestin, Rev. H. de., trans. *Some of the Principal Works of St. Ambrose*. With assistance of E. de Romestin and H. T. F. Duckworth. Vol. 10 of *A Select Library of Nicene and Post-Nicene Fathers of the Christian Church*, 2nd ser., edited by Philip Schaff and Henry Wace. New York: Christian Lit. Co., 1896.

Roussell, Rev. Napoleon. *Catholic and Protestant Nations Compared in Their Threefold Relations to Wealth, Knowledge, and Morality*. Boston: John P. Jewett, 1855.

Runciman, Steven. *The Medieval Manichee: A Study of the Christian Dualist Heresy*. Cambridge: Cambridge Univ. Press, 1999.

Saint Augustin: Sermon on the Mount, Harmony of the Gospels, Homilies on the Gospels. Vol. 6 of *A Select Library of Nicene and Post-Nicene Fathers of the Christian Church*, 1st ser., edited by Philip Schaff. New York: Charles Scribner, 1888.

Saint Chrysostom: Homilies on the Gospel of St. John and the Epistle to the Hebrews. Vol. 14 of *A Select Library of Nicene and Post-Nicene Fathers of the Christian Church*, 1st ser., edited by Philip Schaff. New York: Christian Lit. Co., 1890.

Schaff, Philip. *The Creeds of Christendom*, 6th ed., vol. 1. Grand Rapids, MI: Baker Book House, 1919.

Schaff, Philip. *History of the Christian Church*. 8 vols. Peabody, MA: Hendrickson, 2002.

Schiepek, Hubert. *Der Sonntag und kerchlich gebotene Feiertage nach kirchlichem und weltlichem Recht: Eine rechtshistorische Untersuchung*. In *Adnotationes in Ius Canonicum*, Bd. 27, Hrsg. von Elmar Güthoff und Karl-Heinz Seige. Frankfurt am Main: Peter Lang, Europäischer Verlag der Wissenschaften, 2003.

Schmidt, Ludwig. *Allgemeine Geschichte der germanischen Völker bis zur Mitte des sechsten Jahrhunderts*, 1909.

Schneider, G. A. *Der hlg. Theodor von Studion. Sein Leben und Wirken (Kirchengeschichtl.*

Studien ed. By Knöpfler, Schrörs and Sdralek, V. Bd. 3. Heft), 1900.

Schoell, Rudolfus, recogn. *Novellae*. Vol. 3 of *Corpus Iurus Civilis*. Berlin: Apud Wiedmannos, 1959.

Schwartz, Daniel R. "Review Article: How at Home Were the Jews of the Hellenistic Diaspora?" Review of *Heritage and Hellenism: The Reinvention of Jewish Tradition*, by Erich S. Gruen; *The Hidden Heritage of Diaspora Judaism*, by L. V. Rutgers; *Jews in the Mediterranean Diaspora: From Alexander to Trajan (323 BCE–117 CE)*, by John M. G. Barclay; and *Judaea and Mediterranean Politics, 219 to 161 B. C. E.*, by Dov Gera. Classical Philology 95, no. 3 (July 2000): 349–357.

Schwartz, Eduard. Über die Reichskonzilien von Theodosius bis Justinian (Zeitschr. Der Savigny-Stiftung f. Rechtsgeschichte Bd. 42, Kanon. Abt. XI p. 208 ff.), 1921.

Scott, S. P., trans., ed. *The Civil Law including The Twelve Tables, The Institutes of Gaius, The Rules of Ulpian, The Opinions of Paulus, The Enactments of Justinian, and The Constitutions of Leo*, vols. 1, 12–14, 17. Union, NJ: Lawbook Exchange, 2001.

Scott, S. P. trans., ed. *The Civil Law including The Twelve Tables, The Institutes of Gaius, The Rules of Ulpian, The Opinions of Paulus, The Enactments of Justinian, and The Constitutions of Leo*, vol. 15–16. Cincinnati, OH: Central Trust Co., 1932.

Scott, S. P., trans., ed. *The Enactments of Justinian: The Code, Books IX–XII*, 2nd ed. In vols. 15–16 of vols. 15–17 of *The Civil Law including The Twelve Tables, The Institutes of Gaius, The Rules of Ulpian, The Opinions of Paulus, The Enactments of Justinian, and The Constitutions of Leo*. 17 vols. Union, NJ: Lawbook Exchange, 2001.

Scott, S. P., trans., ed. *The Visigothic Code (Forum Judicum)*. Boston: Boston Book, 1910.

Sellers, Robert V. *The Council of Chalcedon*. London: S.P.C.K., 1961.

Sellery, George C., and A. C. Krey. *Medieval Foundations of Western Civilization*. New York: Harper, 1929.

Serfass, Adam. "Church Finances from Constantine to Justinian 312–565 C.E." PhD diss., Stanford Univ., 2002.

Sheppard, John George. *The Fall of Rome.* London: Routledge, 1892.

Sheppard, Lancelot C. *The Mass in the West.* Vol. 3 in the *Twentieth Century Encyclopedia of Catholicism;* sect. 10, *The Worship of the Church.* New York: Hawthorn, 1962.

Shotwell, James T. *A Study in the History of the Eucharist.* Part of PhD thesis, Columbia University. London: Eyre and Stoppiswoode, 1905.

Shotwell, James T., and Louise R. Loomis. *The See of Peter.* New York: Octagon Bks., 1965.

Martin Siebold, Das Asylrecht der römischen Kirche mit besonderer Berücksichtigung seiner Entwicklung auf germanischen Boden, dissert. Münster, 1930.

Smith, William. *The Students' Gibbon: The History of the Decline and Fall of the Roman Empire by Edward Gibbon,* abr. New York: Harper, 1889.

Smith, William, and Samuel Cheethan, eds. *A Dictionary of Christian Antiquities,* vol. 1. Hartford, CT: J. B. Burr, 1880.

Smith, William, and Henry Wace, eds. *A Dictionary of Christian Biography,* vol. 4. London: John Murray, 1887.

Snow, Charles M. *Religious Liberty in America.* Washington, DC: Review and Herald, 1914.

Spicer, William A. *The Hand That Intervenes.* Altamont, TN: Harvestime Bks., 2007. Spinka, Matthew, trans. *Chronicle of John Malalas, Books VIII–XVIII.* In collaboration with Glanville Downey. Chicago: Univ. of Chicago Press, 1940.

Sprint, John. *Propositions, Tending to Proove the necessary Use of the Christian Sabbath.* London, 1635.

Stennet, Edward. *The Insnared Taken in the Word of his Hands; or an Answer to Mr. John Covvell.* . . . London, 1679.

Stephenson, Andres. *A History of Roman Law.* Littleton, CO: Fred B. Rothman, 1992.

Stewart, Charles P. *The Roman Church and Heresy: With Special Reference to the Influence of the Vatican.* London: C. J. Thynne and Jarvis, n.d.

St. John, H. A. *Our Banquet to Nourish Pure Thought Life.* San Francisco: H. A. St. John, 1894.

Stobbe, Otto von. *Die Juden in Deutschland: wahrend des Mittelalters in politischer, socialer und rechtlicher Beziehung.* Amsterdam: Verlag B. R. Grüner, 1968.

Stroll, Mary. *The Jewish Pope: Ideology and Politics in the Papal Schism of 1130.* Leiden: E. J. Brill, 1987.

Stutz, Ulrich. *Geschichte des kirchlichen Benefizialwesens,* Bd. I, 1895; *the same, Arianismus und Germanismus (Internat. Wochenschrift Jahrg. 1909),* 1909.

The "Summa Theological" of St. Thomas Aquinas, 2nd and rev. ed. Literally translated by fathers of the English Dominican Province. London: Burns Oates and Washbourne, 1913.

Summerbell, N. *History of the Christian Church,* 3rd ed. Cincinnati: Office of the Christian Pulpit, 1873.

Summerbell, N. *A True History of the Christians and the Christian Church.* Cincinnati: Office of the Christian Pulpit, 1871.

Syzmanski, Rev. Ladislas. "The Translation Procedure of Epiphanius-Cassiodorus in the *Historia Tripartita, Books I and II*. PhD diss., Catholic University of America, 1963. In *Studies in Medieval and Renaissance Latin Language and Literature*, vol. 24. Washington, DC: Catholic Univ. Press, 1963.

Tanner, Norman P. *The Councils of the Church*. New York: Crossroad, 2001.

Tellenbach, Gerd. *Church, State and Christian Society at the Time of the Investiture Contest*. Translated by R. F. Bennett. New Jersey: Humanities Press, 1979.

Thompson, James W. *The Middle Ages, 300–1500*, 2 vols., 2nd ed. New York: Alfred Knopf, 1932.

Thompson, James W., and Edgar N. Johnson. *An Introduction to Medieval Europe 300–1500*. New York: W. W. Norton, 1937.

Thorndike, Lynn. *The History of Medieval Europe*. Boston: Houghton Mifflin, 1931?

Three Questions Answered . . . . Oxford, 1621.

Tomassi, Nino. *Scritti di Storia Giuridica*. Padova, It.: Cedam – Casa Editrice Dott, 1964.

Tomkins, Frederick. *The Institutes of the Roman Law*, pt. 1. London: Butterworths, 1867.

Tomlins, T. G., comp. *A Universal History of the Nations of Antiquity; comprising A Complete History of the Jews*. Halifax, N.S.: Wm. Milner, 1844.

Treadgold, Warren. *A History of the Byzantine State and Society*. Stanford, CA: Stanford Univ. Press, 1997.

Twiffe, William. *The Christian Sabbath Defended*. . . . London, 1652.

Ullman, Walter. *The Growth of Papal Government in the Middle Ages: A Study in the Ideological Relation of Clerical to Lay Power.* London: Methuen, 1955.

Ullman, Walter. *Law and Politics in the Middle Ages: An Introduction to the Sources of Medieval Political Ideas.* Ithaca, NY: Cornell Univ. Press, 1975.

Ure, Percy N. *Justinian and his Age.* Baltimore, MD: Penguin, 1951.

Vasiliev, Alexander A. *Justin the First: An Introduction to the Epoch of Justinian the Great.* Cambridge, MA: Harvard Univ. Press, 1950.

Verduin, Leonard. *The Anatomy of a Hybrid: A Study in Church-State Relationships.* Sarasota, FL: Christian Hymnary, 1998.

Vodola, Elisabeth. *Excommunication in the Middle Ages.* Berkeley: Univ. of California Press, 1986.

Voigt, Karl. *Staat und Kirche: Von Konstantin dem Grossen Bis Zum Ende der Karolingerzeit.* Aalen, Ger.: Scientia Verlag, 1965.

von Campenhausen, Hans. *Ecclesiastical Authority and Spiritual Power in the Church of the First Three Centuries.* Translated from *Kirchliches Amt und geistliche Vollmacht,* 1953, by J. A. Baker. Stanford, CA: Stanford Univ. Press, 1969.

von Halban, Alfred. *Das römische Recht in den germanischen Volksstaaten,* I. Teil (*Untersuchungen zur Deutschen Staats- und Rechtsgeschichte* ed by Otto Gierke 56. Heft), 1899.

von Harnack, Adolf. *Der erste deutsche Papst (Bonifatius II, 530/32) und die beiden letzten Dekrete des römischen Senats* (Sitzungberichte der Preuß. Akademie der Wissenschaften, Jahrgang 1924, philosoph.-histor. Klasse Nr. V p. 24 ff.), 1924.

von Hauck, Albert. *Kirchengeschichte Deutschlands*. 5 vols. Leipzig: J. C. Hinrichs'sche Buchhandlung, 1912–1920.

von Lingenthal, Karl E. Z., *Geschichte des griechisch-römischen Rechts*, 3rd edition, 1892.

von Schubert, Hans. *Geschichte der christlichen Kirche im Frühmittelalter*, 1917/1921.

von Schubert, Hans. *Staat und Kirche in den arianischen Königreichen und im Reiche Chlodwigs* (*Histor. Bibliothek* Bd. 26), 1912.

W., M. *The Naked Truth.* . . . 1789.

Wadsworth, Benjamin. *The Lord's Day, Proved to be the Christian Sabbath, or Reasons....* Boston, 1720.

Wainwright, Geoffrey, and Karen B. Westerfield Tucker, eds. *The Oxford History of Christian Worship*. Oxford: Oxford Univ. Press, 2006.

Walker, David M. *The Oxford Companion to Law*. Oxford: Clarendon Press, 1980.

Walker, George. *The Doctrine of the Sabbath*. Amsterdam, 163?.

Wallace-Hadrill, J. M. "The Work of Gregory of Tours in the Light of Modern Research." Lecture February 1950.

Wand, John W. C. *Doctors and Councils*. London: Faith Press, 1962.

Wand, John W. C. *A History of the Early Church to A.D. 500*. London: Methuen, 1974.

Watson, Alan. *The State, Law and Religion: Pagan Rome*. Athens, GA: Univ. of Georgia Press, 1992.

Wedewer, Hermann, and Josep McSorley. *A Short History of the Catholic Church*, 7th ed. St. Louis, MO: B. Herder, 1926.

Westbury-Jones, J. *Roman and Christian Imperialism.* Port Washington, NY: Kennikat Press, 1971.

Whitby, Daniel. *The Absurdity and Idolatry of Host Worship, Proved.* . . . London, 1679.

Whitby, Daniel. *The Fallibility of the Roman Church.* London, 1687.

Whitby, Michael, and Mary Whitby. *Chronicon Paschale 284–628 AD.* Vol. 7 of *Translated Texts for Historians.* Liverpool: Liverpool Univ. Press, 1989.

White, Fr. *An Examination and Confutation of a Lawlesse Pamphlet.* . . . London, 1637.

White, Fr. *A Treatise of the Sabbath-Day.* London, 1635.

Whitting, Philip, ed. *Byzantium: An Introduction.* New York: New York Univ. Press, 1971.

Wilberforce, W. *An Apology for the Christian Sabbath.* London, 1799.

Wilkinson, B. G. *Truth Triumphant: The Church in the Wilderness.* Mountain View, CA: Pacific Press, 1946.

Williamson, G. A., trans. *Procopius. The Secret History.* London: Folio Society, 1990.

Winter, Michael M. *Saint Peter and the Popes.* London: Darton, Longman and Todd, 1960.

Wolfram, Herwig. *History of the Goths.* Translated by Thomas J. Dunlap. New and completely revised from 2nd German ed. Berkeley: Univ. of California Press, 1988.

Woodruff, Douglas. *Church and State.* Vol. 89 of *Twentieth Century Encyclopedia of Catholicism;* sec. 9, *The Church and the Modern World.* New York: Hawthorn, 1961.

Wylie, James A. *The History of Protestantism.* 4 vols. Coldwater, MI: Remnant, 2002.

Wylie, Rev. J. A. *The Papacy: Its History, Dogmas, Genius, and Prospects.* Edinburgh: Johnstone and Hunter, 1851.

Wylie, J. Kerr. *Roman Constitutional History from Earliest Times to the Death of Justinian.* Cape Town: African Bookman, 1948.

Young, G. F. *East and West through Fifteen Centuries*, Vol. 2. London: Longmans, Green, 1916.

Zachariä von Lingenthal, Karl Eduard. *Geschichte des Griechisch-Römischen Rechts.* Aalen in Württemberg: Verlag Scientia, 1955.

Appendix III

AD 1798 1843
Source Book
Bibliography

Acomb, Evelyn M. "The French Laic Laws (1879–1889): The First Anti-Clerical Campaign of the Third French Republic." No. 486 in *Studies in History, Economics and Public Law*, edited by the faculty of Political Science at Columbia University. New York: Octagon, 1967.

Acton, Lord. *Essays in the Liberal Interpretation of History*. Edited by Wm. McNeil. Chicago: Univ. of Chicago Press, 1967.

Acton, Lord (John E. E. Dalberg-Acton). *Lectures on the French Revolution*. Edited by John Figgis and Reginald Laurence. New York: Noonday Press, 1959.

Acton, Lord (John E. E. Dalberg-Acton). *Lectures on the French Revolution*, 2nd ed. Edited by John Figgis and Reginald Laurence. New York: Noonday Press, 1962. Sec. ed., Acton, Lord (John E. E. Dalberg-Acton). *Lectures on Modern History*. Edited by John N. Figgis and Reginald Laurence. London: MacMillan, 1952.

Alzog, Rev. John. *Manual of Universal Church History*, vol. 3. Translated by F. J. Pabisch and Thos. S.Byrne. Cincinnati, OH: Robert Clarke, 1878.

Alzog, Rev. John. *Manual of Universal Church History*, vol. 3, new ed. Translated by F. J. Pabisch and Thos. S. Byrne. Dublin: M. H. Gill, [1874?].

Alzog, Rev. John. *Manual of Universal Church History*, 2nd ed., vols. 1, 2. Translated, with additions, from the 9th and last German ed., by F. J. Pabisch and Thomas S. Byrne. Dublin: M. H. Gill, 1883 (1); 1884 (2).

Alzog, Rev. John. *Manual of Universal Church History*, vols. 3, 4. Translated, with additions, from the 9th and last German ed., by F. J. Pabisch and Thomas S. Byrne. Dublin: M. H. Gill, 1880 (3); 1882 (4).

Ames, Fisher. *The Works of Fisher Ames*. Edited and enlarged by W. B. Allen. 2 vols. First published 1854. Indianapolis, IN: Liberty Fund, 1983.

Ardagh, John. *Cultural Atlas of France*. Alexandria, VA: Stonehenge Press, 1992.

Artinian, Artine. "A Reference Chronology of French History." *The Modern Language Journal* 23, no. 7 (April 1939): 522–526.

Aulard, A. *Christianity and the French Revolution*. Translated by Lady Frazer. London: Bouverie House; Ernest Benn Ltd., 1927.

Aulard, A. *The French Revolution: A Political History, 1789–1804*. Translated from the French of the 3rd ed. by Bernard Miall. 4 vols. London: Adelphi Terrace, 1910.

Baldassari, Abbé von. *Geschichte der Wegsührung und Gesangenschase Pius VI*. Translated from the French. Edited by Franz F. Steck. Tübingen: Verlag der H. Laupp'schen Buchhandlung, 1844.

Baron, Salo Wittmayer. *The Jewish Community: Its History and Structure to the American Revolution*. 3 vols. Philadelphia: Jewish Publication Soc. of America, 1942.

Beik, Paul H. *The French Revolution*. New York: Walker, 1970.

Beik, Paul H. "The French Revolution Seen from the Right: Social Theories in Motion, 1789–1799." *Transactions of the American Philological Society*, new ser., vol. 46, no. 1 (1956): 1–122.

Ben-Sasson, H. H., ed. *A History of the Jewish People*. Cambridge, MA: Harvard Univ. Press, 1976.

Ben-Yehuda, Nachman. "The European Witch Craze of the 14th to 17th Centuries: A Sociologist's Perspective." *The American Journal of Sociology* 86, no. 1 (July 1980): 1–31.

Bicheno, J. *The Signs of the Times: or the Dark Prophecies of Scripture Illustrated by the Application of Present Important Events*. Facs. of 1st Am. ed. (1796). UMI Books on Demand: www.uni.com.

Bicheno, J. *The Signs of the Times: or, the Overthrow of the Papal Tyranny in France, the Prelude to the Destruction of Popery and Despotism . . . .* Facs. of 1st Am. ed. (1794) from 2nd European ed., with additions. UMI Books on Demand: www.uni.com.

Binchy, D. A. *Church and State in Fascist Italy*. London: Oxford Univ. Press, 1941.

Blanshard, Paul. *American Freedom and Catholic Power*, 2nd ed., rev. Boston: Beacon Press, 1958.

Breckinridge, Robert J. *Papism in the Nineteenth Century, In the United States: Being Select Contributions to the Papal Controversy During, 1835–40*. Reprod. Baltimore: David Owen, 1841.

Bridier, the Abbé. *A Papal Envoy during the Reign of Terror: Being the Memoirs of Mgr. de Salamon, the Internuncio at Paris during the Revolution, 1790–1801*. Translated by Frances Jackson. London: Sands, 1911.

Burke, Edmund. *Reflections on the Revolution in France.* Published for Anchor Bks. in 1 vol. with Thomas Paine's *The Rights of Man.* New York: Doubleday, 1989.

Carlyle, Thomas. *The French Revolution.* New York: A. L. Burt, n.d.

Chadwick, Owen. *The Popes and European Revolution.* Oxford: Clarendon Press, 1981.

Channing, William E. *Memoir of William Ellery Channing,* 10th ed., vols. 1, 2. Boston: American Unitarian Asso., 1874.

Chronica Minora, vol. 1. Edidit I. Guidi. In *Corpus Scriptorum Christianorum Orientalium,* vol. 1; Scriptores Syri, bk. 1. Louvain, Belg.: Secrétariat du CorpusSCO, 1960.

Chronica Minora, vol. 2. Interprétatus I. Guidi. In *Corpus Scriptorum Christianorum Orientalium,* vol. 2; Scriptores Syri, bk. 2. Louvain, Belg.: Secrétariat du CorpusSCO, 1907.

Chronica Minora, vol. 3. Interprétati E. W. Brooks, I. Guidi, I.-B. Chabot. In *Corpus Scriptorum Christianorum Orientalium,* vol. 6; Scriptores Syri, bk. 6. Louvain, Belg.: Secrétariat du CorpusSCO, 1960.

Chronica Minora, vol. 3. Ediderunt Brooks, Guidi, Chabot. In *Corpus Scriptorum Christianorum Orientalium,* vol. 5; Scriptores Syri, bk. 5. Louvain, Belg.: Secrétariat du CorpusSCO, 1905.

Chronica Minora. Pars prior interpretatus est I. Guidi. In *Corpus Scriptorum Christianorum Orientalium*; Scriptores Syri, 3rd ser., bk. 4. Paris: E Typographeo Reipublicae, 1903.

Cobban, Alfred. *A History of Modern France.* 3 vols. London: Jonathan Cape, 1962–1965.

"The Code Napoleon." *The American Law Register* (1852–1891) 3, no. 11 (September 1855): 641–650.

Code Napoleon; or, *The French Civil Code*. Literally translated from orig. and official ed., published in Paris in 1804, by a barrister of the inner temple. New York: Halsted and Voorhies, 1841.

Collectio Brevium atque Intructionum SS. D. N. PII Papæ VI, 2 pts. Rome: 1800.

Crabb, John H, trans. *The French Civil Code* (as amended to July 1, 1976). S. Hackensack, NJ: Fred B. Rothman, 1977.

Cross, Barbara M., ed. *The Autobiography of Lyman Beecher*. 2 vols. Cambridge, MA: Belknap Press of Harvard Univ. Press, 1961.

Courtois, AbbéGaston, comp., trans. John O'Flynn. *The States of Perfection: Papal Documents from Leo XIII to Pius XII*. Westminster, MD: Newman Press, 1961.

Darst, Maury, religion ed. *The Galveston Daily News*, February 11, 1989, News section 11-A.

Dawson, Philip, ed. *The French Revolution*. Englewood Cliffs, NJ: Prentice-Hall, 1967.

D'Holbach, Baron (Paul H. T. Holbach). *Christianity Unveiled: being an Examination of the Principles and Effects of the Christian Religion*. Translated from the French by W. M. Johnson. First published 1819. New York: Gordon Press, 1974.

De Cormenin, Louis M. *The Public and Private History of the Popes of Rome*, trans. from the French, I, 232-233. Also Farrow; op. cit.

Doyle, William. *The Oxford History of the French Revolution*. Oxford: Clarendon Press, 1989.

Dunne, George H. *Religion and American Democracy. A reply to Paul Blanshard's American Freedom and Catholic Power.* Articles originally appeared in America in 1949. New York: America Press, n.d.

Duppa, Richard. *A Brief Account of the Subversion of the Papal Government.* 1798, 2nd ed. London, 1799.

Dvornik, Francis. *Early Christian and Byzantine Political Philosophy.* Washington, DC: Dumbarton Oaks Ctr. for Byz. Studies, 1966, 2:822.

Eckhardt, Carl C. *The Papacy and World Affairs: As Reflected in the Secularization of Politics.* Chicago, IL: Univ. of Chicago Press, 1937.

Eds. of *Horizon* mag. *The French Revolution*, 3rd ed. In consultation with David L. Dowd. New York: American Heritage, 1965.

Edmonds, Bill. "'Federalism' and Urban Revolt in France in 1793." *The Journal of Modern History* 55, no. 1 (March 1983): 22–53.

Encyclopedia Americana, 1941 Edition.

Englund, Steven. "Church and State in France since the Revolution." Reprint from *Journal of Church and State* 34, no. 2 (Spring 1992): 325–361.

Fitzsimmons, Michael P. *The Parisian Order of Barristers and the French Revolution.* Cambridge, MA: Harvard Univ. Press, 1987.

The French Convert: Being a True Relation of the Happy Conversation of a Noble French Lady from the Errors and Superstitions of Popery, to the Reformed Religion, by Means of a Protestant Gardener, her Servant. Amherst, NH: 1796.

Gabbert, Mark A. "The Limits of French Catholic Liberalism: Mgr Sibour and the Question of Ecclesiology." *French Historical Studies* 10, no. 4 (Autumn 1978): 641–663.

George, Henry. *The Condition of Labour: An Open Letter to Pope Leo XIII*, pop. ed. London: Henry George Found. of Gr. Britian, 1934.

Gersoy, Leo. "Three French Historians and the Revolution of 1848." *Journal of the History of Ideas* 12, no. 1 (January 1951): 131–146.

Godechot, Jacques. *The Taking of the Bastille, July 14th, 1789*. Translated by Jean Stewart. New York: Chas. Scribner's Sons, 1970.

Godwin, William. *Enquiry concerning Political Justice and its Influence on Morals and Happiness*. 2 vols. Fasc., 3rd ed. Edited with variant readings of 1st and 2nd eds. by F. E. I. Priestley. Toronto: Univ. of Toronto Press, 1946.

Gordley, James. "Myths of the French Civil Code." *The American Journal of Comparative Law* 42, no. 3 (Summer 1994): 459–505.

Gottschalk, Louis. "The Peasant in the French Revolution." *Political Science Quarterly* 48, no. 4 (December 1933): 589–599.

Gough, Austin. *Paris and Rome: The Gallican Church and the Ultramontane Compaign, 1848–1853*. Oxford: Clarendon Press, 1986.

Guenther, Otto, "Epistulae Imperatorum Pontificum Aliorum, Avellana Quae Dicitur Collectio," 2 pts. In *Corpus Scriptorum Ecclesiasticorum Latinorum*, vol. 35. Prague: F. Tempsky, 1895, (ep. 92), 348, Sept. 17, 540.

Grab, Walter. *The French Revolution: The Beginnings of Modern Democracy*. London: Bracken Bks., 1989.

Graetz, Heinrich. *History of the Jews*. 6 vols. Philadelphia: Jewish Publication Soc. of America, 1967.

Graham, Robert A. *Vatican Diplomacy: A Study of Church and State on the International Plane*. Princeton, NJ: Princeton Univ. Press, 1959.

Graham, Ruth. "The Revolutionary Bishops and the Philosophes." *Eighteenth-Century Studies* 16, no. 2 (Winter 1982–1983): 117–140.

Hagenbach, K. R. *History of the Church in the Eighteenth and Nineteenth Centuries*. Translated from the last German ed. by John F. Hurst. New York: Chas. Scribner, 1869.

Hales, E. E. Y. *Revolution and Papacy: The papacy and the revolutionary movement in Europe, 1769–1840*. Garden City, NY: Hanover House, 1960.

Halperin, S. William. *The Separation of Church and State in Italian Thought from Cavour to Mussolini*. Chicago, IL: Univ. of Chicago Press, 1937.

Hanson, R. P. C. "The Reaction of the Church to the Collapse of the Western Roman Empire in the Fifth Century." *Vigiliae Christianae* 26, no. 4 (December 1972): 272–287.

Healy, Robert M. "The Jew in Seventeenth-Century Protestant Thought." *Church History* 46, no. 1 (March 1977): 63–79.

Helmreich, Ernst C., ed. *A Free Church in a Free State?: The Catholic Church, Italy, Germany, France, 1864–1914*. Lexington, MA: D. C. Heath, 1964.

Herman, Shael. "The Uses and Abuses of Roman Law Texts." *The American Journal of Comparative Law* 29, no. 4 (Autumn 1981): 671–690.

Hesse, Carla. "The Law of the Terror." *MLN* 114, no. 4, French issue (September 1999): 702–718.

Hsia, R. Po-Chia. *The Myth of Ritual Murder: Jews and Magic in Reformation Germany*. New Haven, CT: Yale Univ. Press, 1988.

Hughes, Rev. H. L. *The Catholic Revival in Italy, 1815–1915*. London: Burns Oates and Washbourne, 1935.

Hurst, John F. *Short History of the Modern Church in Europe, A.D. 1558–1888*. New York: Chautauqua Press, 1888.

Hyslop, Beatrice. "Recent Work on the French Revolution." *The American Historical Review* 47, no. 3 (April 1942): 488–517.

Ilbert, Courtenay. "The Centenary of the French Civil Code." *Journal of the Society of Comparative Legislation*, new ser., vol. 6, no. 2 (1905): 218–231.

Jemolo, A. C. *Church and State in Italy, 1850–1950*. Translated by David Moore. Oxford: Basil Blackwell, 1960.

Kertzer, David I. *The Kidnapping of Edgardo Mortara*. New York: Alfred Knopf, 1997.

Kielland, Alexander L. *Napoleon's Men and Methods*. Translated by Joseph McCabe. London: A. Owen, early 1900s.

Kohn, Hans. "Napoleon and the Age of Nationalism." *The Journal of Modern History* 22, no. 1 (March 1950): 21–37.

Kroen, Sheryl T. "Revolutionizing Religious Politics during the Restoration." *French Historical Studies* 21, no. 1 (Winter 1998): 27–53.

Latreille, André. *L'Église Catholique et la Révolution Française: L'Ère Napoléonienne et la Crise Européenne (1800–1815)*. Paris: Librairie Hachette, 1950.

Latreille, André. *L'Église Catholique et la Révolution Française: Le Pontificat de Pie VI et la Crise Française (1775–1799)*. Paris: Librairie Hachette, 1946.

Larkin, Maurice. *Church and State after the Dreyfus Affair: The Separation Issue in France*. New York: Barnes and Noble, 1974.

Lauterpacht, H. "Revolutionary Propaganda by Governments." *Transactions of the Grotius Society* 13, Problems of Peace and War, Papers Read before the Society in the Year 1927 (1927): 143–164.

Lefebre, Georges. *The French Revolution: From 1793 to 1799*, vol. 2. Translated from the Fr. by John H. Stewart and James Friguglietti. London: Routledge, 1970.

Lefflon, Jean. [R.C.] *Historian of the Catholic Institute of Paris*, 1798.

Linder, Amnon, ed., trans. *The Jews in the Legal Solution of the Early Middle Ages*. Detroit, MI: Wayne State Univ. Press, 1997.

Linder, Amnon, ed., trans. *The Jews in Roman Imperial Legislation*. Detroit, MI: Wayne State Univ. Press, 1987.

Ludwikowski, Rett R. "The French Declaration of the Rights of Man and Citizen and the American Constitutional Development." *The American Journal of Comparative Law* 38, supplement. U. S. Law in an Era of Democratization (1990): 445–462.

Loomis, Louise Ropes. *The Book of the Popes (Liber Pontificalis)*. New York: Columbia University Press, 1916.

MacCaffrey, Rev. James. *History of the Catholic Church in the Nineteenth Century (1789–1908)*, 2nd ed., rev. 2 vols. Dublin: M. H. Gill, 1910.

Maclear, J. F., ed. *Church and State in the Modern Age: A Documentary History*. Oxford: Oxford Univ. Press, 1995.

Madelin, Louis. *The Consulate and the Empire, 1789–1809*. Translated from the Fr. by E. F. Buckley. New York: G. H. Putnam's Sons, 1934.

Madelin, Louis. *Figures of the Revolution*. Translated from the Fr. (1929) by Richard Curtis. Freeport, NY: Books for Libraries Press, 1968.

Madelin, Louis. *Fouché, 1759–1820*. Translated from the Fr. by Gerhard Heller. Societäts-Verlag, 1975.

Madelin, Louis. *The French Revolution*. Translated from the French. New York: G. P. Putnam's Sons, 1928.

Madelin, Louis. *Napoléon*. N.p.: Hachette, 1958.

Madelin, Louis. *The Revolutionaries (1789–1799)*. Translated by R. J. S. Curtis. London: Arrowsmith, 1930.

Mainardi, Patricia. "Assuring the Empire of the Future: The 1798 Fête de la Liberté." *Art Journal* 48, no. 2, Images of Rule: Issues of Interpretation (summer 1989): 155–163.

Malaussena, Katia. "The Birth of Modern Commemoration in France: The Tree and the Text." *French History* 18, no. 2 (2004): 154–172.

Mansi, Joannes Dominicus. *Sacrorum Conciliorum: Nova, et Amplissima Collectio*, facs. ed. Paris: Welter, 1902.

Marienstras, Elise, and Naomi Wulf. "French Translations and Reception of the Declaration of Independence." *The Journal of American History* 85, no. 4 (March 1999): 1299–1324.

Markoff, John. *The Abolition of Feudalism: Peasants, Lords, and Legislators in the French Revolution*. University Park, PA: Penn. St. Univ. Press, 1996.

Marques, Antonio H. R. de Oliveira. *History of Portugal*. 2 vols. in 1 bk. Columbia Univ. Press, 1972.

Martin, Malachi. *The Keys of this Blood*. New York: Simon and Schuster, 1990, dust jacket.

Mathews, Shailer. *A History of New Testament Times in Palestine*. New York: MacMillan, 1902.

Mathiez, Albert. *The French Revolution*, univ. lib. ed. Translated from the Fr. by Catherine Phillips. New York: Grosset and Dunlap, 1964.

McAvoy, Thomas T. *The Great Crisis in American Catholic History, 1895–1900*. Chicago: Henry Regnery, 1957.

McManners, John. *Church and State in France, 1870–1914*. New York: Harper and Row, 1972.

McManners, John. *The French Revolution and the Church*. A vol. in Church History Outlines, edited by V. H. Green. London: S.P.C.K., 1969.

McManners, John. *The French Revolution and the Church*. New York: Harper and Row, 1970.

Milman, Henry H. *The History of the Jews*, vol. 1. London: J.M. Dent, 1930.

Milman, Rev. Henry H. *The History of the Jews, from the Earliest Period down to Modern Times*, reprinted from the newly revised and corrected London ed., vol. 2. Boston: William Veazie, 1864.

Milman, Rev. Henry H. *The History of the Jews, from the Earliest Period to the Present Time*, vol. 3. New York: Bradley, n.d.

Milton, Joyce, Robert A. Orsi and Norman Harrison. *The Serpent and the Robe: The Pre-Columbian God-Kings; The Papal States*. 1 vol. containing 2 bks., in Empires: Their Rise and Fall, Boston Pub. Co. Boston: Boston Pub., 1986.

Morandière, Léon Julliot de La. "The Reform of the French Civil Code." *University of Pennsylvania Law Review* 97, no. 1 (November 1948): 1–21.

Morse, Anson E. *The Federalist Party in Massachusetts to the Year 1800*. Princeton, NJ: Univ. Lib., 1909.

Morse, Jedidiah. *A Sermon Delivered . . . May 9th, 1798, being the day recommended by John Adams . . . for Solemn Humiliation, Fasting and Prayer*. Fasc. Boston: 1798. UMI Books on Demand: www.umi.com.

Mourret, Rev. Fernand. *A History of the Catholic Church*, vol. 7. Translated by Newton Thompson. St. Louis, MO: B. Herder, 1955.

Nash, Gary B. "The American Clergy and the French Revolution." *The William and Mary Quarterly*, 3rd ser., vol. 22, no. 3 (July 1965): 392–412.

New Catholic Encyclopedia, s.v. "Clovis" (Thomson-Gale, 2003), 4:809-11. In asso. with Catholic University, Washington, D.C.

New York Times, 3/23/05.

Paine, Thomas. *The Age of Reason, being an Investigation of True and Fabulous Theology*, pt. 1. New York: Freethought Press, 1794.

Paine, Thomas. *The Age of Reason, being an Investigation of True and Fabulous Theology*. New York: Gramercy Bks., 1993.

Paine, Thomas. *The American Crisis*. Kessenger Publishing's Rare Reprints: www.kessinger.net.

Paine, Thomas. *Common Sense and Other Writings*. Consulting ed., George Stade. New York: Barnes and Noble, 2005.

Paine, Thomas. *The Rights of Man*. Published for Anchor Bks. in 1 vol. with Edmund Burke's *Reflections on the Revolution in France*. New York: Doubleday, 1989.

Palmer, R. R. "A Century of French History in America." *French Historical Studies* 14, no. 2 (Autumn 1985): 160–175.

Palmer, R. R. "Notes on the Use of the Word 'Democracy' 1789–1799." *Political Science Quarterly* 68, no. 2 (June 1953): 203–226.

Partner, Peter. *The Lands of St Peter: The Papal State in the Middle Ages and the Early Renaissance*. Berkeley, CA: Univ. of Cal. Press, 1972.

Phillips, Charles S. *The Church in France, 1789–1848: A Study in Revival*. New York: Russell and Russell, 1966.

Phillips, Charles S. *The Church in France, 1848–1907*. London: Society for Promoting Christian Knowledge, 1936.

Poland, Burdette C. *French Protestantism and the French Revolution: A Study in Church and State, Thought and Religion, 1685–1815*. Princeton, NJ: Princeton Univ. Press, 1957.

Pollard, John F. *Money and the Rise of the Modern Papacy: Financing the Vatican, 1850–1950*. Cambridge: Cambridge Univ. Press, 2005.

Popkin, Jeremy D. "The Provincial Newspaper Press and Revolutionary Politics." *French Historical Studies* 18, no. 2 (Autumn 1993): 434–456.

Quint, Emanuel B., and Neil S. Hecht. *Jewish Jurisprudence: Its Sources and Modern Applications*, vol. 1. Chur, Switz.: Harwood Academic Pub., 1980.

Rickaby, Joseph. S.J. *The Modern Papacy*, 1.

Rouche, Michel. *Clovis*. Fayard, France, 1996.

Rudé, George. *Revolutionary Europe, 1783–1815*. New York: Harper and Row, 1964.

Sala, G. A. *Diario Romano: degli anni 1798–99*. 3 vols. In *Miscellanea della Società Romana di Storia Patria*. Rome: presso la Società, 1882 (1, 2); 1886 (3).

Sala, G. A. *Scritti Varj*, vol. 4. In *Miscellanea della Società Romana di Storia Patria*. Rome: presso la Società, 1888.

Schapiro, J. Salwyn. *Anticlericalism: Conflict between Church and State in France, Italy, and Spain*. Princeton, NJ: Van Nostrand, 1967.

Schinz, Albert. "The Religious Awakening of France." *The Biblical World* 51, no. 2 (February 1918): 67–80.

Schmidlin, J. *Histoire des Paps de l'Epoque Contemporaire, I Pie VII*, 4.

Sharf, Andrews. *Byzantine Jewry: From Justinian to the Fourth Crusade*. New York: Schocken Bks., 1971.

Singer, C. Gregg. *The Unholy Alliance: The Definitive History of the National Council of Churches and its Leftist Policies—from 1908 to the Present*. New Rochelle, NY: Arlington House, 1975.

Slosson, Preston W. *Europe Since 1870*. Boston: Houghton Mifflin, 1935.

Smithers, William W. "The Code Napoléon." *The American Law Register* (1898–1907) 49, no. 3, vol. 40 New Series (March 1901): 127–147.

Spalding, Paul. "Toward a Modern Torah: Moses Mendelssohn's Use of a Banned Bible." *Modern Judaism* 19, no. 1 (February 1999): 67–82.

The States of Perfection. Sel., arr. by the Benedictine monks of Solesmes. Translated by Mother E. O'Gorman. N.p.: St. Paul editions, 1967.

Stauffer, Vernon. *The Bavarian Illuminati in America: The New England Conspiracy Scare, 1798*. First published in 1918. Mineola, NY: Dover, 2006.

Stein, Robert. "The Abolition of Slavery in the North, West, and South of Saint Domingue." *The American* 41, no. 3 (January 1985): 47–55.

Stowell, Wm. Henry H. *The Separation of the Churches and the State of France*. Amherst, MA: Stanhope Press, 1917.

Sydenham, M. J. "The Republican Revolt of 1793: A Plea for Less Localized Local Studies." *French Historical Studies* 12, no. 1 (Spring 1981): 120–138.

Szajkowski, Zosa. "The Comtadin Jews and the Annexation of the Papal Province by France, 1789–1791." *The Jewish Quarterly Review*, n.s., vol. 46, no. 2 (October 1955): 181–193.

Szajkowski, Zosa. "The Sephardic Jews of France during the Revolution of 1789." *Proceedings of the American Academy for Jewish Research* 24 (1955): 137–164.

Tellenbach, G. *Church and State and Christian Society at the Time of the Investiture Contest*. Translated by R. F. Bennett. Oxford, Eng.: Basil Blackwell, 1966.

The European Magazine and London Review, March 1798.

The Times, London, March 12, 1798.

Trevor, Rev. George. *Rome: From the Fall of the Western Empire*. London: Religious Tract Society, n.d.

Van Kley, Dale K. *The Religious Origins of the French Revolution: From Calvin to the Civil Constitution, 1560–1791*. New Haven, CT: Yale University Press, 1996.

Volney, C. F. *The Ruins, or, Mediations of the Revolutions of Empires: and the Law of Nature*. New York: Truth Seeker, 1913.

"Voltaire." *Dictionnaire Philosophique*. Paris: Garnier-Flammarion, 1964.

Wallace-Hadrill, J. M, and John McManners, eds. *France: Government and Society*. London: Methuen, 1957.

Walsh, James J. *The Popes and Science: The History of the Papal Relations to Science During the Middle Ages and Down to Our Own Times*, Knights of Columbus ed. New York: Fordham Univ. Press, 1911.

Watson, R. *An Apology for the Bible: In a Series of Letters Addressed to Thomas Paine....* New York: Phillips and Hunt, [1700s?].

White, Ellen G. *Evangelism*. Hagerstown, MD: Review and Herald, 1973.

White, Ellen G. *The Great Controversy*. Nampa, ID: Pacific Press, 1911.

White, Ellen G. *Testimonies for the Church*. Mt. View, CA: Pacific Press, 1948.

Witte, John, Jr. "That Serpentine Wall of Separation." Review of *Thomas Jefferson and the Wall of Separation between Church and State*, by Daniel L. Dreisbach, and *Separation of Church and State*, by Philip Hamburger. *Michigan Law Review* 10, no. 6, 2003. Survey of Books Relating to the Law (May 2003): 1869–1905.

Woloch, Isser. "In the Aftermath of the French Revolution." *The History Teacher* 28, no. 1 November 1994, 7–11.

Yates, Gerard F., ed. *Papal Thought on the State: Excerpts from Encyclicals and Other Writings of Recent Popes.* New York: Appleton-Century-Crofts, 1958.

We invite you to view the complete
selection of titles we publish at:

www.TEACHServices.com

Scan with your mobile
device to go directly
to our website.

Please write or email us your praises, reactions, or
thoughts about this or any other book we publish at:

P.O. Box 954
Ringgold, GA 30736

info@TEACHServices.com

TEACH Services, Inc., titles may be purchased
in bulk for educational, business, fund-raising,
or sales promotional use.
For information, please e-mail:

BulkSales@TEACHServices.com

Finally, if you are interested in seeing
your own book in print, please contact us at

publishing@TEACHServices.com

We would be happy to review your manuscript for free.

www.ingramcontent.com/pod-product-compliance
Lightning Source LLC
Chambersburg PA
CBHW070548160426
43199CB00014B/2417